SOCIAL WORK
CASE
MANAGEMENT

MODERN APPLICATIONS OF SOCIAL WORK

An Aldine de Gruyter Series of Texts and Monographs

SERIES EDITOR

James K. Whittaker

Ralph E. Anderson and Irl Carter, **Human Behavior in the Social Environment: A Social Systems Approach** (fourth edition)

Richard P. Barth and Marianne Berry, **Adoption and Disruption: Rates, Risks, and Responses**

Larry K. Brendtro and Arlin E. Ness, **Re-Educating Troubled Youth: Environments for Teaching and Treatment**

Kathleen Ell and Helen Northen, **Families and Health Care: Psychosocial Practice**

Marian Fatout, **Models for Change in Social Group Work**

Mark W. Fraser, Peter J. Pecora, and David A. Haapala (eds.), **Families in Crisis: The Impact of Intensive Family Preservation Services**

James Garbarino, **Children and Families in the Social Environment** (second edition)

James Garbarino, Patrick E. Brookhouser, Karen J. Authier, and Associates, **Special Children—Special Risks: The Maltreatment of Children with Disabilities**

James Garbarino, Cynthia J. Schellenbach, Janet Sebes, and Associates, **Troubled Youth, Troubled Families: Understanding Families At-Risk for Adolescent Maltreatment**

Roberta R. Greene, **Social Work with the Aged and Their Families**

Roberta R. Greene and Paul H. Ephross, **Human Behavior Theory and Social Work Practice**

Jill Kinney, David Haapala, and Charlotte Booth, **Keeping Families Together: The Homebuilders Model**

Paul K. H. Kim (ed.), **Serving the Elderly: Skills for Practice**

Robert M. Moroney, **Shared Responsibility: Families and Social Policy**

Robert M. Moroney, **Social Policy and Social Work: Critical Essays on the Welfare State**

Peter J. Pecora and Mark Fraser, **A Practical Guide to Evaluating Family Preservation Services**

Peter J. Pecora, James K. Whittaker, Anthony N. Maluccio, Richard P. Barth, and Robert D. Plotnick, **The Child Welfare Challenge: Policy, Practice, and Research**

Norman A. Polansky, **Integrated Ego Psychology** (second edition)

Albert E. Trieschman, James K. Whittaker, and Larry K. Brendtro, **The Other 23 Hours**

Harry H. Vorrath and Larry K. Brendtro, **Positive Peer Culture** (second edition)

Betsy S. Vourlekis and Roberta R. Greene (eds). **Social Work Case Management**

Heather B. Weiss and Francine H. Jacobs (eds.), **Evaluating Family Programs**

James K. Whittaker and James Garbarino, **Social Support Networks: Informal Helping in the Human Services**

James K. Whittaker, Jill Kinney, Elizabeth M. Tracy, and Charlotte Booth (eds.), **Reaching High-Risk Families: Intensive Family Preservation in Human Services**

James K. Whittaker and Elizabeth M. Tracy, **Social Treatment, 2nd Edition: An Introduction to Interpersonal Helping in Social Work Practice**

SOCIAL WORK
CASE
MANAGEMENT

Betsy S. Vourlekis and Roberta R. Greene
Editors

ALDINE DE GRUYTER
New York

About the Editors

Betsy S. Vourlekis is assistant professor in the department of social work, University of Maryland, Baltimore County.

Roberta R. Greene is Associate Dean, University of Georgia School of Social Work. She has authored numerous journal articles. Dr. Greene co-authored with Paul Ephross *Human Behavior Theory and Social Work Practice* (Aldine de Gruyter, 1991).

ALDINE DE GRUYTER
A division of Walter de Gruyter, Inc.
200 Saw Mill River Road
Hawthorne, New York 10532

The paper used in this publication meets the minimum requirements of American National Standard for Information Sciences—Permanence of Paper for Printed Library Materials, ANSI Z39.48-1984. ⊗

Library of Congress Cataloging-in-Publication Data

Social work case management / Betsy S. Vourlekis and Roberta R.
   Greene, editors.
      p.   cm. — (Modern applications of social work)
   Includes bibliographical references and index.
      ISBN 0-202-36075-X (alk. paper). — ISBN 0-202-36076-8 (pbk. :
   alk. paper)
      1. Social case work—United States—Management.   2. Social work
   administration—United States.   I. Vourlekis, Betsy S.   II. Greene,
   Roberta R. (Roberta Rubin), 1940– .   III. Series.
   HV43.S576   1991
   361.3'2'0973—dc20   91-14802
                                                                        CIP

Manufactured in the United States of America
10 9 8 7 6 5 4 3 2 1

This book is dedicated
to our social work colleagues who are practicing
case management

Contents

Acknowledgments

The idea for this book evolved during the time we were both on the staff at the National Association of Social Workers, fielding on a daily basis multiple demands for information about case management and opportunities to shape policy makers' ideas about it. Many colleagues at NASW worked along with us, and their thinking contributed immeasurably to our understanding. Norma Taylor, Isadora Hare, Verne Lyons and Joan Zlotnik helped distinguish issues in different fields of practice and identify case manager practitioners. Susan Hoechstetter, Sandra Harding, and Sunny Harris kept us abreast of legislative initiatives at the federal level, as we all labored to interpret social work case management. The excitement and gratification of working with this able group of professional associates on an issue of such pervasive public interest was the real motivating force behind the book.

To our contributors we gave the delicate task of writing chapters as we wanted them written, in order to conform to the structure of the book we had in mind. That they did so, while bringing their own perspective and thought, and with enthusiasm and respect for the necessary deadlines of such an endeavor, we gratefully acknowledge. It is their efforts that illuminate the case management practice reality.

We owe special thanks to Laurel Rumpl who provided invaluable editing assistance, and to Nancy Smith who gave administrative support above and beyond the call of duty.

Betsy S. Vourlekis
Roberta R. Greene

Preface

This is a book about the practice of case management. It is based on the assumption that when key elements are in place, the direct practice of case management belongs within the spectrum of methods for and approaches to helping clients which constitute generic social work practice. That is to say, it is a form of practice that is professional, is compatible with basic social work views of problem formulation and intervention, and makes use of critical social work practice skills.

Case management is a core component of service delivery in every sector of human services today. Both private and public programs are turning to case management to meet the needs of vulnerable people who require complex arrays of services and multiple helpers on an ongoing basis. The need for case management is generated by a powerful combination of forces. Fragmentation, conflicting eligibility requirements or coverage provisions, and discontinuities in care abound in our human service system, whether the presenting problem is health or homelessness. When more than one organization or provider is involved, each with its own program or service boundary, coordination of resources and helping efforts for a specific individual is problematic. Many communities do have a rich assortment of resources to meet diverse needs. However, up-to-date knowledge of the appropriate resource to meet a specific need from among a bewildering array of alternatives is difficult for the consumer/client as well as the primary helper or helping organization. Case management addresses these as well as other realities of human service provision.

Professional social workers are in the front lines in designing, managing, and providing case management. Social workers in training will enter job markets that are clamoring for case management expertise. Administrators and policymakers are examining case management as a program component in constantly widening arenas. This book is designed to provide an in-depth examination of the functions and skills of social work case management as it is practiced in a variety of settings and with different client populations. Our intent is to portray the richness and diversity of practice while at the same time presenting a core generic framework that is applicable in all instances.

We do not claim that case management is "nothing different than traditional casework." The political and policy reality surrounding the present-day use of case management makes such a statement irrelevant, whether one believes it or not. Case management models abound. Some have very little relationship to what social work practice is all about. Nor are we proposing that only social workers can and should do case management. That, too, is beyond the possible no matter whether desirable or not. On the one hand, other professionals such as physicians and nurses have claimed case management roles. And on the other hand, paraprofessional, volunteer, and family member case managers are widely used.

We recognize that questions have been raised within the profession of social work about whether social workers are properly prepared to do case management, and whether case management is an appropriate activity for social workers. Given the diversity of models, turf/role confusion, and multiple professions involved in case management practice, our professional uncertainty about case management is understandable.

This is all the more reason to be clear about our model of social work case management. In the real world of human services, professional social workers are vitally involved in the direct practice of case management. All major human service delivery systems are implementing or are considering implementing case management components, with major repercussions on job definition and availability. To a considerable extent, our continuing ability to shape and influence case management programs will depend upon our skillful and professionally defined practice within them. Furthermore, for the profession of social work to be influential in shaping and further refining case management at the policy, program planning, or direct practice level it must have a well-articulated and agreed-upon view of the practice of case management that is supported by significant numbers of social work practitioners actually doing it, and doing it well.

For both current and future practitioners, an understanding of case management practice that is systematically connected to their social work knowledge, skills, and values will provide greater clarity to their role and functions. It will provide reinforcement and incentive to carry out valued activities and tasks. And it will enhance a sense of acceptance and validation within their chosen profession. In the organizational setting, or in any setting for that matter, practitioners have always struggled to maintain for social work practice a core self-definition, autonomously derived, in the face of bureaucratic needs, financial realities, professional role overlap, and efforts at deprofessionalization.

In this respect, case management practice is no different and requires the same buttressing and shaping from professional education and acculturation.

We also believe that the public policy debate and decision-making about case management can benefit from the infusion of a systematic exposition of what social work case management has to offer. The combination of intense public interest in case management and the similarity and overlap of its targets, concerns, and methods with those of traditional social work calls for a clear delineation and demonstration of our expertise. Key elements of our professional practice can be matched with known realities and specific objectives, which different case management programs may be designed to achieve. Such elements as relationship building, sensitivity to psychological needs and processes that accompany physical and social problems, a dynamic understanding of the systems with which clients and case managers negotiate, flexibility to intervene skillfully with both client and the resource system or network—these skills and knowledge, and their use in the hands of trained personnel—can be crucial to the success of case management objectives.

With neither full ownership nor control over the domain of case management, we nevertheless can do two things: (1) systematically educate and train our practitioners to maximum competency, which is clearly a part of their social work preparation, and (2) influence policymakers and program administrators to consider the specific benefits of our approach to and competency in case management practice. This book tries to contribute to these tasks.

Chapters 1 and 2 provide the general framework for a consideration of social work case management direct practice. Chapter 1 presents the current environmental context for case management practice. This includes background and the scope of its use in both the public and private service delivery systems, the prevalence of social work practitioners, and a discussion of some of the problematic aspects of case management within the social work profession itself. Chapter 2 develops a working definition of social work case management. Key features are presented and discussed. Eight generic direct practice functions are described:

- client identification and outreach
- individual and family assessment and diagnosis
- service planning and resource identification
- linking clients to needed services
- service implementation and coordination

- monitoring of service delivery
- advocacy to obtain services
- evaluation.

Parallels to social work method as well as differences in emphases between case management and social casework are examined. These functions and the skills, activities, and tasks that support them are more fully developed in Chapters 3 through 12.

The reader will find it helpful to begin with Chapters 1 and 2 for an overview of the practice environment and understanding of the full range of practice functions and settings before proceeding to a chapter dealing with a specific function within a specific case management program.

Chapters 3 through 10 offer a detailed discussion and illustration of the case manager's direct practice functions. A function is presented in the context of a specific setting or field and with a particular client population. Each chapter identifies key skills, and special issues, constraints, and opportunities. Case examples illustrate tasks and activities typically carried out by the case manager. An overview of the case management program, including funding sources, goals, and client-system characteristics, gives the reader an appreciation of the interplay of context and practice. The primary focus is on the "how to's" of matching effectively the functions of case management with the realities of clients and service delivery systems.

Lorraine Davis's chapter on client identification and outreach looks at case management with teenage parents. She discusses the process of weaving together a network of services and resources that is sufficiently broad and diverse to give the case manager an attractive menu of options with which to attract and involve this client group.

Two chapters deal with the assessment function. Grace Lebow and Barbara Kane discuss assessment in the private practice of case management with elderly clients. They emphasize that the goal of assessment is to obtain as accurate a picture of the client in his or her own world as is possible, leading to a care plan that encourages and supports the client's continued functioning in the least restrictive circumstances. Isadora Hare and James Clark examine client assessment in school settings and educational programs. They present an ecological framework for assessment, and identify reliable standardized assessment instruments that can be used to complement traditional in-depth interviewing and home studies.

Marcy Kaplan addresses care planning in case management with children who are HIV positive or have AIDS. She illustrates and discusses the emotional ramifications for children and their families of the different decisions that must be made, and the skill of the case manager in eliciting and working through these issues as a critical aspect of creating a viable care plan. She examines the boundary questions and related concerns that emerge from the social work case manager's efforts to promote a family-centered approach and family involvement in care planning.

Chapter 7 looks at the linking function. Kenneth Kaplan explores the many facets of resource acquisition, a critical activity that ensures that there is something to which the case manager can link the client. He reminds us that case management often occurs on an emergency or crisis basis, and considers some of the implications of this. He also provides a helpful discussion of "delinking," when resources no longer are needed, or may not be working in the best interest of the client.

Chapters 8 and 9 deal with the function of service implementation and coordination, looking at this from the vantage point of two very different client populations. John Belcher examines research findings on case management efficacy, and argues for a clinical model of case management in work with individuals who have chronic mental illness. He stresses that challenges to sustaining a viable relationship, understanding client thinking and behavior, and structuring and pacing of treatment objectives require a clinician's special expertise. Naomi Miller creatively illustrates case management at work in an employee assistance program. Although the term *case management* is not widely used in this arena (except in certain specialized programs or, in the case of "managed care," as a component of health and mental health benefit management), Miller suggests that case management's dual intervention focus on the client and the wider resource/service environment serves both employee and employer well.

Rebecca Hegar discusses the monitoring function as it is carried out in child welfare services. She considers the key matters of role boundaries, legal accountability, and the worker's use of authority, which are particularly salient in this setting, but germane to case management in many different circumstances as well. Chapter 11 examines the advocacy function in the context of the military. Robert Gemmill and his colleagues represent all of the service branches. Their discussion of advocacy—the deliberate application of a strategy of power—in a setting where power differential is pronounced and institutionalized provides a frank look at the case manager's need to take risks.

Monika White and Lynn Goldis offer a comprehensive view of the evaluation function in case management. They provide a model of quality assurance that pervades the organization within which case management services exist, and illustrate the role and participation of each member of the program, including the case manager direct practitioner.

Chapter 13 considers the role requirements of case management as boundary-spanning practice. We highlight and summarize the skills utilized by the case manager as that practitioner seeks to implement case management's dual focus on client-system and service-system. We suggest that mastery of the case manager role demands acceptance of a "political" aspect to the professional use of self as well.

The settings and/or client groups discussed in this book were chosen to be representative of areas of significant social work involvement currently. We have included examples of private and entrepreneurial case management as well. However, important groups and settings have been left out: head trauma patients or other medical rehabilitation clients, and insurance-connected managed mental health care, to cite just two examples. The book is not intended to provide comprehensive coverage of the total range of fields, settings, and groups within which and to whom case management is currently offered. Rather we have tried to develop a cohesive view of social work case management direct practice and to illustrate the range and flexibility of its applications. We hope that the principles and important distinguishing features of social work case management are clearly reflected, regardless of the setting or client population to which they may be applied. We believe that this approach will allow students, educators, practitioners, and policymakers better to recognize and understand what social work case management direct practice is and who may benefit from it.

Betsy S. Vourlekis
Roberta R. Greene

Chapter 1

The Policy and Professional Context of Case Management Practice

Betsy S. Vourlekis

As society has grown more diverse and the U.S. health and social services systems more complex, ensuring at-risk populations appropriate, timely, coordinated, and cost-effective care has become an ever greater concern. Increasingly, policymakers, agency administrators, and direct-services practitioners are turning to case management as the method of choice for delivering services to clients and their families with complex, multiple problems or disabilities.

The explosive interest in case management as a component of system design and delivery for the human services confronts the profession of social work with a challenge. The attention to and concern with access, fragmentation, service gaps, and need for individualized care and planning resonate deeply with social work practice values and certainly with the social worker's day-to-day practice experience. It is exciting and gratifying to witness widespread policy and program recognition of what have been social work's traditional focus and functions.

However, this same public policy interest in case management, leading to rapid deployment of case-managed service systems, has resulted in multiple models of case management—including some that appear remote from traditional social work. This interest has occasioned professional turf fighting over ownership of the role as well as widespread use of paraprofessionals and volunteers. It has raised inflated expectations with respect to what case management can achieve.

For social work practitioners embarking on practice careers, the excitement, opportunities, and professional challenges case management offers are readily apparent. Effective social work case management practice requires a comprehensive view of the scope, purposes, and extent of case management today, and a realistic understanding of the important concerns about case management that have been raised

1

within the social work profession. With such a view and understanding, social workers will be in a position to recognize and shape important new avenues for practice—opportunities to link valued functions and roles to major human services delivery initiatives—and to carry out their case management practice with enhanced professional identification.

Scope of Case Management

Case management has been defined as:

> a set of logical steps and a process of interaction within a service network which assure that a client receives needed services in a supportive, effective, efficient, and cost effective manner. (Weil et al. 1985, p. 2)

Although definitions abound, and case management is widely described and thought of as both a system and a service, it is, as in the preceding definition, typically defined in terms of the outcomes it is expected to achieve. These outcomes include improving access to services, fixing responsibility for coordinating and monitoring care, ensuring optimal care and care outcomes, and, increasingly, cost-effectiveness and cost control. Policymakers are often far clearer about the desired outcomes than they are about the mechanism to achieve them. Thus, case management is often an ambiguous and poorly understood process that is hitched to an ambitious set of expectations. This is a good recipe for popularity, but also for eventual disillusionment.

The interest in case management as a component of the delivery of human services is pervasive. It cuts across the public and private sectors and all fields of practice. Settings utilizing case management have expanded to include schools, health and mental health clinics, hospitals, businesses, major insurance companies, and trust departments of banks, which are setting up case management as an additional component to their financial services. Case management is being used extensively with the frail elderly and the deinstitutionalized mentally ill, developmentally disabled children and adults, pregnant teenagers, and homeless people. It is now being implemented widely with acquired immunodeficiency syndrome (AIDS) patients and their families. No longer only a feature of programs serving "special populations," case management has become a component of major health insurance benefit administration, affecting millions of beneficiaries. Because of this widespread interest, there is a compelling practical demand for case management (sometimes called "care coordination") services.

Federally Funded Programs

The 1970s gave rise to major program initiatives using case management systems. Beginning in 1972, Medicare waivers (Section 222 of the Social Security Amendments, P.L. 92-603) authorized research and demonstration projects in the provision of community-based care for the frail elderly as an alternative to costly institutional care. Similar demonstrations were authorized by Medicaid (Section 1115, P.L. 92-603). Case management was a required component of demonstration projects to facilitate client access to appropriate services in what had come to be acknowledged as a fragmented and bewildering health and social services delivery system (Austin et al. 1985).

Deinstitutionalization litigation and increasing attention directed to the deficiencies of community mental health centers in meeting the needs of chronically mentally ill people were part of the impetus leading to the National Institute of Mental Health (NIMH) community support programs in the late 1970s. These programs introduced case management as a component of service delivery to the mentally ill for the purpose of accessing services, coordinating treatment efforts, and providing continuity of care to a patient population with long-term needs. More recently, NIMH studied case management with the chronically mentally ill and the homeless in an effort to identify special attributes of effective practice and to disseminate these models widely to the field. Social workers are frequently providers and supervisors of what is being called "intensive case management" (Rog, Andranovich, & Rosenblum 1987, p. 8).

Similar needs for individualized, coordinated care with case accountability lodged in one place gave rise to mandated case management service components in serving the developmentally disabled (Developmental Disabilities Act of 1970, P.L. 91-517), the elderly (Older Americans Act, revisions of 1978, P.L. 95-478), and children with special needs (Education for All Handicapped Children Act of 1975, P.L. 94-142). In the child welfare system, federal legislation in 1980 emphasizing family reunification and mandating permanency planning for children in foster care (Federal Adoption Assistance and Child Welfare Act of 1980, P.L. 96-272) included requirements for case planning and case review.

Medicaid amendments in the 1980s have continued to expand the utilization of case management in state programs. In 1981, case management systems were permitted as part of the Community and Home Based Waiver provision (Section 2176, Omnibus Budget Reconciliation Act of 1981, P.L. 96-499). This waiver was intended to allow more flexibility in providing community-based care in lieu of costly institutionalization. Faced with escalating nursing home costs, states were eager to find lower cost alternatives. States were further encouraged to use case management in Medicaid in 1985 when case management was authorized as a new optional service. States may now incorporate case management into their state Medicaid plans, designating which populations will be offered the service (Consolidated Omnibus Budget Reconciliation Act, P.L. 99-272). Under Medicaid, case management is defined as "services which will assist individuals eligible under the plan in gaining access to needed medical, social, educational and other services" [Section 1915(g)(2), Social Security Act].

By 1988, 19 states had approved Medicaid state plan amendments for case management to targeted groups. Six additional states had submitted plan amendments that were awaiting approval. States reported that social workers and nurses were the most frequently used providers of case management services (National Governors' Association 1988).

Other important federal legislation of the 1980s included case management provisions. Revisions to the Older Americans Act of 1984 (P.L. 98-459) added new responsibilities for case management to Area Agencies on Aging. Case management as part of community-based care for the chronically mentally ill now is mandated for anyone receiving public funds or services in Title V, State Comprehensive Mental Health Services Plan, of the Omnibus Health Act of 1986 (P.L. 99-660; National Association of State Mental Health Program Directors 1986). Comprehensive legislation to meet the needs of homeless people (Stuart B. McKinney Homeless Assistance Act of 1987, P.L. 100-79) passed in 1987 designates block grant funds to states to provide services, including case management, to homeless people who are chronically mentally ill. Funding for health care grant programs in the same legislation provides for reimbursement to states for case management as an optional component. The nation's new welfare law, the Family Support Act of 1988 (P.L. 100-485), recognizes case management as an important tool in the coordination and monitoring of education and training services for welfare recipients. State agencies have the option of requiring that a case manager be assigned to each family participating in the job opportunities and basic skills training programs (Harris 1989).

Legislation in 1990 continued to incorporate case management opportunities. Medicaid provisions authorized 100 million dollars for community-based services for the developmentally disabled. AIDS legislation (Ryan White Comprehensive AIDS Resources Emergency Act of 1990, P.L. 100-381) included three major service initiatives, each capable of funding case management services, among others. Over 200 million dollars was authorized for (1) emergency funds to cities with the highest AIDS and HIV incidence, (2) block grants to states for comprehensive planning and service delivery, and (3) early intervention services for persons who are HIV-positive.

Case-Managed Health and Mental Health Care

In addition to the use of case management in publicly funded programs, the 1980s have witnessed its adoption as an anticipated tool of cost containment in private health and mental health benefit plans. Managed health and mental health care is now the norm, whether provided through traditional managed-care settings such as health maintenance organizations (HMOs), or through employer self-insured or third-party payer indemnity plans. The skyrocketing costs of health benefits paid by employers have provided the impetus to intercede between consumer and provider to manage access and utilization of services. Private, for-profit companies now offer case management services to employers and insurers, and most major insurance companies have built-in case management components.

Currently, social workers have not been involved extensively in these case management systems, although increasingly they are being employed as mental health benefit managers. However, the model of case management and the exuberant claims for cost savings attached to it, are having a powerful impact on both the public's and policymakers' understanding of case management.

Case management in the managed health care context has been defined as

> a systematic approach to identifying high-cost patients, assessing potential opportunities to coordinate their care, developing treatment plans that improve quality and control costs, and managing patients' total care to ensure optimum outcomes. (Fisher 1987, p. 287)

The extent to which this model of case management is or will be compatible with generic social work practice remains to be seen. However, the importance of advocacy is acknowledged, education of patient and family is stressed, and interpersonal skills to motivate clients are viewed as necessary (Fisher 1987).

Private Case Management

The private practice of case management, or case management provided on a fee-for-service basis to privately paying clients, is a small but growing arena. The client's wish for access to and coordination of services is the primary goal, although presumably a cost-conscious consumer is interested in the value received. Cost accountability, to the extent any exists, is between the client and the provider. According to one recent survey, social workers are the most frequently employed professional in privately delivered case management (Secord 1987). Although private case management services are most often provided to and on behalf of the elderly and their families, there is a growing interest among families with severely mentally disabled offspring as well. Parents who expect their disabled children to outlive them are interested in setting up trustee arrangements that include specified services, activities, and resources with a case manager to oversee and coordinate them.

The Profession's Response and Concerns

Social work's involvement in case management direct practice is clearly established. Social work and social workers have been in the forefront of designing case management systems and delivering case management services for some time. They have been influencing policy deliberations at the state and national levels with model projects. Professional social workers fill great numbers of staff positions in which they directly provide and supervise case management practice in arenas as diverse as services to the homeless and private fee-for-service case management for the elderly.

In many fields and settings where social workers were already practicing, the emergence of case management as a "new approach" was greeted with the response, "But we have been doing case management for years. We called it casework." The historical roots and precursors of key concepts of case management can be found in the early writings and thinking of the social work profession (Weil et al. 1985). Nevertheless, regardless of the perceived or actual similarities between traditional casework and case management, it is important to recognize that from a public policy perspective case management is being treated as something new.

Just as with other key aspects of social work practice—the psychosocial perspective, for example—case management has been "discovered" and has moved to the larger playing field of policy deliberation and innovation. This is a field with multiple players representing many professions in addition to social work, and covering programs and services that traditionally have been characterized by high levels of social work involvement and leadership as well as those which have not.

Realistically social workers cannot "own" case management or claim it as their exclusive domain. Models and practice of case management are and will continue to be shaped by many different views of clients, services, and priorities. Role and turf overlap and differing models and primary expectations in case management practice have prevented and will continue to prevent a straightforward meshing of case management and social work practice.

Despite the prevalence of social work practitioners in case manager roles and the apparent similarity in the central mission of coordination and continuity of care between case management and social work direct practice, many social workers have questioned the appropriateness or usefulness of the profession's identification with case management for several reasons. The very term *case manager* is sufficient to activate the powerful professional duality of purpose. This duality is expressed in social work's two approaches—often, unfortunately, viewed as contradictory—to helping. These approaches are efforts directed at social action and remediation of faulty environmental conditions "versus" individual assistance, which emphasizes coping and adjustment. Case management, to some, represents the very worst aspect of individualized approaches to helping: managing people and their cases.

Case management has been identified as a return to conservative helping strategies and a lowering of professional sights from large-scale system improvement (Schilling, Schinke, & Weatherly 1988). Such professional misgivings are heightened as case management systems are being put in place at a time of constrained resources and absence of political will for substantial reform, which must also be a part of system change. Powerful and convincing arguments have been and can be made for the need for both social action and reform and individual, case-by-case assistance. The issue for case management is that the same professional dialectic is being raised as has been raised so often before. Working it through, finding space and energy and commitment within the profession for both action arms, indeed, supporting the efforts of one with the efforts of the other, is needed for social workers to deal effectively with case management.

The expectations for case management systems to meet the critical objectives of cost containment, service access, coordination, and continuity of care have not yet been carefully researched and reviewed. As expectations, they justifiably make social workers nervous. Social workers have had a professional flirtation with a too-close and unrealistic linking of their practice method and a global societal desired outcome—they learned this the hard way in the instance of casework and the eradication of poverty in the 1960s. Certainly there is a professional challenge to formulate an understanding and approach to case management that incorporates key components of social work practice and carefully links these to realistic outcome expectations.

The implementation of case management has generated two other factors that contribute to social work's professional discomfort. Just as with so many previous social work roles, the combination of functions in many models of case management has not been viewed uniformly as requiring professional skill. In actual practice, case managers are frequently poorly paid paraprofessionals, increasing the tendency for social workers to distance themselves from the role. What it is that makes this a professional role and skilled practice and when and for whom it is called for must be carefully distinguished if social work is to encourage and support students and practitioners. In addition, the emphasis in case management practice on the indirect service functions of resource locating, coordinating, and monitoring threatens the social work direct practitioner's hard-won identification as a skilled clinician. The relationship-based, clinical components of social work case management need to be understood and validated, and their influence on the successful completion of other service functions appreciated.

To the extent that case management systems and services have cost containment and cost control features, and increasingly more of them do, both the overt goal and many of the cost analysis skills to go with it are not ones that traditionally have been emphasized in social work education and practice. The identification of case management with saving money, important as that factor is in accounting for the popularity of the role, is far from the traditional client-centered value stance of social work. However, as Kane (1988) pointed out, case management in the context of overall budget allocations for a group of clients is a realistic and social work value–congruent approach. Given that resources are always finite, maximizing the services and well-being for an identified group of clients within existing resource limits can be viewed as an important aspect of social justice. An exclusive emphasis on case-by-case advocacy, no matter how well intentioned, can obscure or even undermine such an effort.

Conclusion

Case management has become an important component of this nation's efforts to provide human services. The proliferation of programs using this approach will dictate personnel needs and requirements in every major field of practice. Social workers are major contributors to frontline case management practice, program formulation, and management in many arenas. Although the social work response has been ambivalent, for understandable and important reasons, social work case management is prevalent and is badly needed. A clear understanding of critical elements that characterize this professional role will allow the profession to promote, on a selective basis, its use to policymakers, teach it to students, and reinforce and validate "good practice" guidelines for practicing social work case managers.

References

Austin, C.D., J. Low, E.A. Roberts, and K. O'Connor. 1985. "Case Management: A Critical Review." Mimeo, Pacific Northwest Long Term Care Gerontology Center, University of Washington, Seattle.

Fisher, K. 1987. "Case Management." *QRB* 13(8):287–90.

Harris, S. 1989. *A Social Worker's Guide to the Family Support Act of 1988.* Washington, D.C.: National Association of Social Workers.

Kane, R.A. 1988. "Case Management: Ethical Pitfalls on the Road to High-Quality Managed Care." *QRB* 14(5):161–66.

National Association of State Mental Health Program Directors. 1986. *NASMHPD Report: The U.S. Congress.* Alexandria, VA: NASMHPD.

National Governors' Association. 1988. "Targeted Case Management as an Optional Service." Mimeo.

Rog, D.J., G.D. Andranovich, and S. Rosenblum. 1987. *Intensive Case Management for Persons Who Are Homeless and Mentally Ill.* Washington, D.C.: Cosmos Corp.

Schilling, R.F., S.P. Schinke, and R.A. Weatherly. 1987. "Service Trends in a Conservative Era: Social Workers Rediscover the Past." *Social Work* 33(1): 5–9.

Secord, L.J. 1987. *Private Case Management for Older Persons and Their Families.* Excelsior, MN: Interstudy.

Weil, M., and J.M. Karls, and Associates. 1985. *Case Management in Human Service Practice.* San Francisco: Jossey-Bass.

Chapter 2

Case Management: An Arena for Social Work Practice

Roberta R. Greene

Despite its growing popularity as a strategy for helping people, case management is not without controversy. There is considerable debate, among other issues, about professional ownership and status and concern about the breadth and ethics of the case manager's role. To confuse the matter further, a number of models of case management exist and the role of case manager is often not filled by a social worker.

However, social workers and case managers share a surprising amount of common ground, especially in terms of the functions of the social work case managers. This chapter outlines the key features that make case management a natural and exciting part of social work practice. It also discusses the direct practice components as delineated by Weil, Karls, and Associates (1985). Those components serve as the organizational framework for Chapters 3 through 12, which discuss practice functions in specific settings.

Defining Social Work Case Management

Case management has been a traditional part of social work since the days of Mary Richmond (Johnson & Rubin 1983; O'Connor 1988). Although the term *case management* is relatively new, the roots of social work case management go back to the early settlement houses and the charity organization societies (Rubin 1987; Weil et al. 1985). The systematic approach to information collection and assessment, the value of equity in resource allocation, and the interest in case coordination are among the key objectives handed down to social workers today. Inherent in case management practice are several key features (see Table 2.1). These features are addressed in this section.

Considerable evidence in the social work literature suggests that "as a general form of social casework, case management can legitimately be

Table 2.1. Key Features of Social Work Case Management Practice

Social work case management practice
- is a process based on a trusting and enabling client–social worker relationship
- utilizes the social work dual focus of understanding the person in the environment in working with populations at risk
- aims to ensure a continuum of care to clients with complex, multiple problems and disabilities
- attempts to intervene clinically to ameliorate the emotional problems accompanying illness or loss of function
- utilizes the social work skills of brokering and advocacy as a boundary-spanning approach to service delivery
- targets clients who require a range of community-based or long-term care services, encompassing economic, health/medical, social, and personal care needs
- aims to provide services in the least restrictive environment
- requires the use of assessment of the client's functional capacity and support network in determining the level of care
- affirms the traditional social work values of self-determination and the worth and dignity of the individual and the concept of mutual responsibility in decision-making.

claimed as one of social work's core technologies" (O'Connor 1988, p. 97). The notion that case management should be considered part of the social work domain is reflected in the *NASW Standards and Guidelines for Social Work Case Management for the Functionally Impaired* (1984). The standards state that case management is a process based on the recognition of a trusting and enabling relationship within generic social work practice and "like all aspects of social work practice, case management rests on a foundation of professional values, knowledge, and skills" (ibid. 1984, p. 3). This key feature makes case management a natural part of social work practice.

The historic social work struggle to best enhance the well-being of individuals, families, and groups—by effecting change in the person, the environment, or both—is reflected in case management. The person-in-the environment focus, in which the social worker assesses the client within the context of the external world and provides both direct and indirect service, is the major unifying factor. This feature of case management "combines the best ideas of direct-service practice with the best ideas of community practice on behalf of a particular at-risk population" (Roberts-DeGennaro 1987, p. 466).

Social work case management integrates aspects of all the traditional methods of social work practice, and provides a conceptual unity to problem-solving with systems theory as the underlying theoretical base (Roberts-DeGennaro 1987; Rubin 1987). For example, the *Encyclopedia of Social Work* (Minahan et al. 1987) referred to social work case management as a boundary-spanning approach to service that attempts to ensure that clients with complex, multiple problems and disabilities receive all the services they need in a timely and appropriate fashion. These are additional key features of case management practice. In addition, Roberts-DeGennaro stated that "the case manager's role is to assist clients by helping them deal with any or all systems problems" (1987, p. 468).

Social worker case managers are not only familiar with this as a practice focus, but find it a compatible framework for service delivery. They call upon their social work skills to carry out their case management activities at all levels of service: the direct-service level dealing with individuals and families, the program-planning level having to do with organizational structure and support, and the policy development level dealing with the rationale and financial and political implications of a communitywide program.

> For the clinician, case management may be one of the intervention options in psychosocial or medical treatment. For the administrator, case management may be a central component in a program seeking to provide a continuum of care for a target population. For the program developer and legislator, case management may be the rationale controlling a community-wide long-term care system. (Steinberg & Carter 1983, p. 1)

Case management is a process of service coordination and accountability and a method of ensuring the client's right to service. Its hallmark is to hold one person responsible for overcoming fragmentation in the service delivery system (Austin 1987; Rubin 1987; Weil et al. 1985). Another feature of social work case management is that it is a clinical social work approach for dealing with the emotional problems accompanying illness and loss of function (Amerman, Eisenberg, & Weisman, 1985; Grisham, White & Miller, 1983; Tolliver et al. 1986).

Amerman et al., in a discussion of the findings from the National Long-Term Care Channeling Demonstration, indicate that their experience during the project showed that a large number of clients needed a "purposeful counseling relationship as a necessary part of the intervention . . . [to deal with the] emotional problems associated with the stress of loss of function" (1985, p. 169). However, the case management function, as it was carried out in the demonstration, "precluded the simultaneous provision of social casework, or counseling services" (ibid.). Amerman et al. insisted that case management "must incorporate intrapsychic, interpersonal and environmental interventions . . . [and that] therapeutic relationships must be well defined" (ibid., p. 174).

Coming to terms with whether case managers are therapists is important to the profession (Austin 1987; Hepworth 1986). It is recognized that the extent to which case managers act as brokers or therapists may vary from program to program. At the same time, it is difficult to imagine that case managers can meet their objectives without utilizing an interactive process that incorporates clinical skills, such as relationship formation, ego support, assessment, and diagnosis. In addition, it is difficult to imagine a case management program that will adequately meet the client's service needs without advocating and planning for a sound delivery system.

Many researchers agree that case management requires an astute blend of both the broker and therapist roles, a key feature of case management practice that makes it an exciting part of social work practice (Adelson & Leader 1980; Johnson & Rubin 1983; Lamb 1980; Tolliver et al. 1986). Lamb (1980), who argued that good therapists are good managers, is among those researchers who believe that it is virtually impossible to separate the provision of resources from the psychotherapeutic aspects of service. In a discussion of whether case management is "to be restricted to coordinating and expediting care delivered by others or will also include therapeutic functions delivered by the case manager," Johnson and Rubin (1983, p. 49) suggested that it is more constructive to look at combining the boundary-spanning and clinical tasks of case management.

Another feature of *social work* case management is that it targets clients in need of an array of community-based services or individuals in long-term care. In such situations, it is often necessary to match client needs with community resources over a prolonged period. Whether the client is a developmentally disabled child or an individual who is chronically mentally ill, he or she will require a range of services that encompass economic, health/medical, social, and personal care needs. These needs may include assistance in finding suitable housing and help with shopping, meal preparation, and household tasks. Social workers are particularly adept at this form of "resource consultation" (Northen 1982).

Community-based or long-term care services have been utilized in all fields of social work practice, including child welfare, aging, and mental health, and are increasingly being used in employee assistance programs and to serve teenage parents and their families. Although the presenting problems of clients receiving such services may vary and meet such diverse needs as finding foster care for children, assuring the frail elderly personal or medical care, and securing people with acquired immunodeficiency syndrome (AIDS) home health care, there are three unifying factors: (1) the purpose is to provide a continuum of care for an individual who is a member of an at-risk target population, (2) the responsibility assumed by the case manager is aimed at coordinating and linking the components of the service delivery system, and (3) the goal is to ensure a comprehensive program that will meet an individual's need for care to maximize and enhance independence.

Social work case managers have long advocated for long-term or community-based systems of care that provide service options along a well-planned continuum of care. The concept of continuum of care suggests a comprehensive range of services, spanning the gamut from preventive and support services such as health screenings and transportation to nursing home or hospice care. A case in point is the provision of services to persons with AIDS. According to Rowe and Ryan (1987) of the George Washington University Intergovernmental Health Policy Project, dramatic increases in the number of cases of people with AIDS are expected within five years. This increased caseload will require an extraordinary case management system—a system that, in most instances, is not yet designed. The chronic, debilitating nature of the disease calls for the development of intermediate-care facilities, skilled-nursing facilities, and community care facilities. Additional support services to ensure continuity of care will also be required to meet patients' essential needs and to reduce hospital costs. Social workers have been in the forefront of planning services for people with AIDS, particularly support services, that supplement basic medical care. Most of these are psychosocial in nature, provided outside the hospital, and are designed to maintain the individual in the community. This approach is essential for all target populations in any system of care, and social work case management is the key to effective utilization (Greene 1988; Rowe & Ryan, 1987).

The social work principle of basing the level of care upon the individual's functional capacity—from those who are most independent to those who are least independent—is another key feature of case management systems. Programs that are guided by this philosophy provide services in the least restrictive environment, yet another key feature (Hooyman, Hooyman, & Kethley, 1981). The focus is assessing the person who has a functional (social, physical, or mental) disability and accessing services to assist that person with activities of daily living. As part of the assessment, social workers are adept at considering the family and other support networks. They bring to that process an understanding of the effect that illness or loss of function can have on the entire family system and an appreciation for what a facilitative environment can do for functional capacity.

Without a case management program that provides the proper assessment and community-based system of care, many individuals with disabilities would be in danger of institutionalization. It is the social work case manager who has the responsibility for matching the level of care to the level of service either through direct action or by service planning and design.

Social workers make positive contributions to the practice of case management by bringing to it their professional value base. A key feature of case management is that it affirms the traditional values of self-determination and the worth and dignity of the individual as well as the concept of mutual responsibility in decision-making. Enhancing the right to self-determination, protecting the right to confidentiality and privacy, ensuring the primacy of the client's interests, and striving for interprofessional cooperation on behalf of the client are among the principles found in the NASW Standards and Guidelines for Social Work Case Management for the Functionally Impaired (NASW 1984) that support quality practice. The standards also state that social work case managers must abide by the practice principles developed for long-term care facilities (NASW 1981), health care settings (NASW 1987), and clinical social work (NASW 1984). An example is hospital discharge planning. With powerful financial incentives existing for hospitals to release patients as quickly as possible, the existence of a professionally coordinated, highly skilled discharge planning process is crucial to ensure that planning occurs on behalf of the patient and not as a mere convenience to the institution (Vourlekis 1985).

Weil et al. pointed out that case management needs to be accompanied by a service philosophy. Without such a philosophy, they believed it would be "extremely difficult for the system to focus on the clients' needs and to solve service integration and resource problems" (1985, pp. 13–14). They emphasized that the traditional social work values of the worth and dignity of the individual as well as the concept of mutual responsibility in decision-making must underpin case management practice. Treating the client as unique, promoting independence and client involvement, and ensuring treatment over time when necessary also are seen as essential.

Every case manager knows that there are situations in which these values will be tested. Case managers struggle with the ethics of resource allocation and professional authority. They also face conflicts related to caseload size and program goals vis-à-vis the client's right to individuated assessment and treatment. Conflicts about gaps in services, gatekeeping mechanisms, authorization power, caps on expenditures, and fiscal authority may all contribute to the ethical dilemmas case managers face. Such dilemmas make many case management systems highly fluid and politicized arenas in which to work. Nonetheless, these dilemmas must be resolved within the framework of social work ethics for the case manager to function effectively. In addition, professionally trained case managers must be employed in these settings. Case management with the chronically mentally ill and with children infected with human immunodeficiency virus (HIV) are among the examples discussed in later chapters of the book.

There is a growing consensus about the key elements that might be said to constitute social work case management practice. In that spirit, the following definition is put forward:

> Social work case management is an *interpersonal process* based upon a *relationship* between case manager and client (system). Mutually developed care plans are intended to enhance/maximize the *functional capacity* of those in need of long-term assistance and their support networks and facilitate and ensure the effective delivery of a range of services along a continuum of care. Interventions reflect social work *values* and are aimed at improving the match between the client's capacity and the demands of the environment. This includes ameliorating problems accompanying loss of function or illness, building support networks, effecting *client level* service coordination, and producing *systems level* effectiveness.

The following section, which deals with the eight direct service functions of case management, attempts to operationalize this view of social work case management.

The Major Components/Functions of Case Management

A review of case management functions suggests that the range of services may be affected by such factors as the target population, the type of agency employing the case manager, caseload size, environmental constraints, and the nature of the service delivery system. The extent to which a full continuum of services is available in a community and whether the case manager's role is seen as solely administrative or service focused also shapes case management functions (Intagliata 1982; Intagliata & Baker 1983). Despite this variation in implementation, there does appear to be general agreement about the core functions of case management.

This section of the chapter discusses the eight direct-practice functions delineated by Weil et al., which they suggest are progressive and "present in some form in all case management programs" (1985, p. 29). Parallels to social work method as well as differences in emphases between case management and social casework also are examined.

Client Identification and Outreach

The first objective of any case management program is to identify and enroll the most appropriate clients. This involves delineating the target population and identifying individual clients within that population for whom the particular services are especially suited (Steinberg & Carter, 1983; Weil et al. 1985). Steinberg and Carter (1983) point out that because most programs have limited resources, taking the necessary steps in case finding will prevent the inappropriate use of resources. An example might be targeting people who are at risk of entering a nursing home (or could be discharged from one) instead of utilizing community services if available.

In selecting case-finding strategies, case managers must consider how to involve individuals who are difficult to reach. The existing patterns of service utilization of people with AIDS and HIV provide a striking example. Because of the stigma society has attached to people with AIDS, client identification and outreach is particularly difficult. Fears of disclosure, abandonment, and helplessness are not uncommon among individuals seeking service. Many are reluctant to seek help, often delaying much-needed treatment and support. For this reason, social work case managers are seeking innovative methods of outreach. In communities such as San Francisco, New York, Houston, and Baltimore, programs increasingly utilize multidisciplinary teams of health care providers "with a case manager assigned to each patient, to maximize use of home care and community support services" (American Psychiatric Association 1984).

Individual and Family Assessment and Diagnosis

Case management follows a problem definition and intervention format similar to the social casework method (Hamilton 1951; Hollis 1977; Perlman 1957). In that approach to solving human problems, assessment is a procedure used to examine the client's problem or situation for purposes of selecting interventions or treatment modalities. It is a process that involves getting to know the whole person—his or her motivations, strengths, weaknesses, and capacity. Assessment for case management services includes appraisals of the client's needs and the resources available through the client's informal supports, including family members, friends, and organizational membership; the impact of the disability on the client and the family; the client's preexisting health or mental health problems; the cultural implications of age-specific behaviors and family functioning, and the client's religious practices and values; the system of formal community resources; and the family's ability to assist the client, as well as to perform case management tasks on the client's behalf (NASW 1984).

An assessment for the purposes of delivering case management services focuses on ascertaining the biopsychosocial functioning of the individual in need of services. It examines the structure of daily living to determine the individual's capacity (with the aid of social supports) for meeting environmental demands. Assessment of the activities of daily living may encompass such specific items as the capacity to use the telephone, shop, prepare meals, do housekeeping, use a car or public transportation, handle one's own finances, or dress and feed oneself (Greene 1986).

It should be emphasized that when assessing an individual client's suitability for case management services, it is critical to know not only the client's current level of functional capacity but his or her "probable highest level of functioning" (Levine & Fleming 1984, p. 10). This allows for planning for services in the least restrictive manner. In short, the emphasis on functional assessment in case management is related to the client's well-being, the ability to live as independently as possible, and the appropriate use of community resources.

The contribution of social workers as case managers is particularly evident during assessment. It is at that time, according to Weil et al. (1985), that the course of case management for the individual is determined, the relationship between worker and client is established, and the database for subsequent service planning is established. Steinberg and Carter (1983) underscored the importance of having the most highly trained clinician in the program carry out assessments. They pointed out that an assessment, marked by high-quality interviewing and diagnostic skills, allows for individualization of the client's situation, the establishment of a working relationship, and the best use of community resources.

Service Planning and Resource Identification

In social work method, assessment is the information-gathering stage when order is given to the data collected about the client system. The service planning and resource identification process, which is akin to the written psychosocial study, then establishes a blueprint for those services to be mobilized on behalf of the client. This stage of case management is characterized by the setting of clear priorities and explicit goals with specific statements about how objectives are to be achieved. This specificity has brought a new dimension to viewing the needs of clients and has improved many social service programs.

Social work process dictates that the case manager involve the client (system) in determining his or her service needs and how goals will be met. For the chronically mentally ill, for example, this means engaging people in problem-solving. Simply identifying resources for individuals who may be "suspicious," "withdrawn," and "defeated" by many unsuccessful encounters with the system is not enough. The social work case manager must develop and maintain a trusting relationship with the client, be able to use empathy to promote communication, and understand the complexities of choosing and implementing step-by-step solutions.

Linking of Clients to Needed Services

Linking involves referring or transferring clients to the services and entitlements that are determined to be necessary and available in the care plan. This is similar to the caseworker acting as "resource consultant." From this perspective, "case management is essentially a problem-solving function designed to ensure continuity of service and to overcome systems rigidity, fragmented service, misutilization of certain facilities, and inaccessibility" (Joint Commission on Accreditation of Hospitals 1976, pp. 20–21).

Working towards removing potential barriers to service utilization and delivery is a clear case management priority (Intagliata 1982; Levine & Fleming 1984). Levine and Fleming stated that referral "requires doing whatever is necessary to get the client to the service" (1984, p. 13). At the same time, the case manager is doing whatever is necessary to obtain services (for example, networking, making phone calls, visiting other agencies). Social work philosophy suggests that the case manager also must "help build capacities in and around the client" so that independence can be maximized and, wherever possible, prolonged services will not be needed (Steinberg & Carter 1983, p. 23).

Service Implementation and Coordination

Service implementation and coordination or seeing that the work is done in a harmonious fashion is what determines the relative success of case management practice. So much so, that Weil et al. suggest that "getting all the pieces of the service plan in place so that they are carried out in a logical sequence is the heart of service coordination" (1985, p. 35). This may mean that assertive follow-up activities and troubleshooting fill much of the case manager day (Steinberg & Carter 1983).

When services are provided by many agencies, particular "efforts should be made to coordinate care to ensure the continuity and complementarity of the interventions" (NASW 1984, p. 9). These coordinating activities, as many others, can often be shared by the social worker, the client, and the client's family or informal support system. The NASW standards advise that the client's, family's, and social worker's involvement in the tasks of case management need not be mutually exclusive. . . . Families can be excellent monitors and supervisors of service. Armed with information and knowledge, the client and his or her family may be able to contact service agencies and to coordinate the efforts of two or more service providers. (ibid., p. 11)

Monitoring of Service Delivery

Monitoring or overseeing services provided to clients is carried out at both the client and agency level, and requires ongoing contact with the client and service providers. Steinberg and Carter (1983) suggested that mediating conflicts between service providers or between the client and service provider falls within the realm of the case manager's activities and can serve to cement service contracts and to ensure that appropriate and effective services are provided with minimum delay.

Weil et al. (1985) viewed overseeing the work of staff at other agencies as one of the more difficult aspects of the case manager's responsibilities in that it often involves supervision without administrative sanctions. The staff in contracted agencies may see the case manager's goals as "extraneous to their own" and the case manager as an "intruder." Rubin (1987) suggested that firsthand contact, including visits to clients while the service is being provided, is an excellent means of facilitating feedback and improving relationships.

Advocacy to Obtain Services

Advocacy is a social work intervention strategy that is concerned with the poor or inequitable distribution of resources. Data collected during the implementation and monitoring phases can be used not only to ensure quality of care, but also to augment the advocacy effort (Greene 1988). Advocacy efforts center around obtaining equitable and suitable services *with* and *for* the client. Because many of the clients in need of case management services are, in varying degrees, frail, vulnerable, or dependent, advocacy becomes a skillful blend of speaking on behalf of the client and encouraging the client to speak for himself or herself. The goal of advocacy, although perhaps ideal, is to empower clients to speak on their own behalf.

Advocacy may involve struggling to get an individual client a particular resource such as housing or may be focused on convincing decision-makers to alter agency regulations for a group of clients; policy level advocacy and legislative action may be aimed at influencing legislators to change regulations and laws. "To negate advocacy on any level is to dismiss a basic tenet of social work practice" (Sosin & Caulum 1982, p. 15).

Advocacy on behalf of one or more person implies that the condition or problem has ramifications of a broader nature (Harbert & Ginsberg 1979). For example, for many young schizophrenics in skid row urban areas, services are being given by programs originally designed to assist vagrant alcoholics. These programs do not meet the needs of such a mixed client population. Advocacy to secure targeted projects designed to consider the wide range of services needed by the chronically mentally ill and their street subculture is needed (Segal & Baumohl 1980).

The rationale for using advocacy to secure goods and services or other resources is best expressed by Pinderhughes:

> Sound functioning in an individual or community requires, among other things, the ability to master the environment and to influence positively the forces affecting the ability to cope. In simple language, this may be conceptualized as power. Lack of power or powerlessness and helplessness are the root causes of poor social functioning and of the disorganization in people and in the systems that surround them. . . . If our institutional response and problem-solving endeavors are directed to the elimination of that powerlessness, then we are truly "starting where the client is". (1976, pp. 1–2)

Evaluation

Evaluation of services and service delivery systems is an integral component of social work case management. It is necessary for accountability to the consumer, to the funding source, and to policymakers. Measures of quality of service are needed to determine whether providers are offering acceptable types and levels of service, and to ensure that service conforms to generally acceptable standards of good practice, that a commitment of resources results in a reasonable level of service, that the service provided has the intended effect, and that the limited supply of services is channeled to those clients who are most at risk.

Steinberg and Carter (1983) underscored the importance of good information collection to evaluating case management service systems. They pointed out that each program must determine the questions case managers will ask at the client-worker level, the agency or program level, and the service system level to have the information necessary to determine effectiveness.

In a study of consumers of acute-care psychiatric services at San Francisco General Hospital, for example, Ball and Havassy found that the homeless mentally ill often saw their inability to avoid readmission as arising from "their lack of basic resources for survival" (1984, p. 918). Heretofore, repeated admissions of psychiatrically impaired homeless persons often have been attributed to the intrinsically recurrent nature of their disorders, their "excessive dependency needs," and their "poor compliance" with community aftercare plans. The San Francisco study, in which 86 percent of the 112 respsondents cited a need for affordable housing and 74 percent for sufficient financial support, suggests the importance of program evaluation in case management practice.

Social work's future in the case management arena is less than certain: several professions are vying for leadership, social workers are reluctant to take case management jobs, and current educational programs do not address the traditional social work practice that embodies case management. These are among the issues that have led some to say that social work's "claim" to case management is only theoretical, or that the profession may not "lay sole claim" to this territory despite the conceptual similarities between social casework and case management (Austin 1987; Johnson & Rubin 1983).

Debate will and should continue about social work's place in case management systems. It is suggested here that all case management programs should not be considered social work, nor should every person hired to be a case manager be seen as engaged in social work practice. Rather, it is best to think of a range of programs and a variety of job descriptions. Some programs will reflect the characteristics generally associated with social work case management more than others. The profession can take pride in these and work to make other systems more responsive.

References

Adelson, G. and M.A. Leader. 1980. "The Social Worker's Role: A Study of Private and Voluntary Hospitals." *Hospital and Community Psychiatry* 31: 776–80.

American Psychiatric Association. 1984. *Task Force Report on the Homeless Mentally Ill*. Washington, D.C.: American Psychiatric Association.

Amerman, E., D. Eisenberg, and R. Weisman. 1985. "Case Management and Counseling: A Service Dilemma." Pp. 169–77 in *Experience from the National Long-Term Care Channeling Demonstration*, C. Austin et al., editors. Seattle, WA: Institute on Aging, University of Washington.

Austin, C.D. 1987. "Case Management: Reinventing Social Work?" Paper presented at the NASW Professional Symposium, New Orleans, September 9.

Ball, J. and B. Havassy. 1984. "A Survey of the Problems and Needs of Homeless Consumers of Acute Psychiatric Services. *Hospital and Community Report* 35(9):917–21.

Greene, R. 1988. *Continuing Education for Gerontological Careers.* Washington, D.C.: Council on Social Work Education.

Greene, R.R. 1986. *Social Work with the Aged and Their Families.* New York: Aldine de Gruyter.

Grisham, M., M. White, and L.S. Miller. 1983. "Case Management as a Problem-solving Strategy." *Pride Institute Journal of Long Term Health Care* 2(4):22–27.

Hamilton, G. 1951. *Theory and Practice of Social Casework.* New York: Columbia University Press.

Harbert, A. and L.O. Ginsberg. 1979. *Human Services for Older Adults: Concepts and Skills.* Belmont, CA: Wadsworth.

Hepworth, D. 1986. *Direct Social Work Practice: Theory and Skills.* Chicago: Dorsey.

Hollis, F. 1977. *Casework: A Psychosocial Therapy.* Rev. ed. New York: Random House.

Hooyman, E., N. Hooyman, and A. Kethley. 1981. "An Interdisciplinary Curriculum Model for Training Gerontological Social Workers." Paper presented at Council on Social Work Education Annual Program Meeting, March.

Intagliatia, J. 1982. "Improving the Quality of Community Care for the Chronically Mentally Disabled: The Role of Case Management." *Schizophrenia Bulletin* 8(4):655–74.

Intagliata, J. and F. Baker. 1983. "Factors Affecting Case Management Services for the Chronically Mentally Ill." *Administration in Mental Health* 11(2):75–91.

Johnson, P.J. and A. Rubin. 1983. "Case Management in Mental Health: A Social Work Domain?" *Social Work* 28:49–55.

Joint Commission on Accreditation of Hospitals. 1976. *Principles for Accreditation of Community Mental Health Service Programs.* Chicago: IL Accreditation Council for Psychiatric Facilities.

Lamb, H.R. 1980. "Therapist–Case Managers: More Than Brokers of Services." *Hospital and Community Psychiatry* 31(11):1–13.

Levine, I.S. and M. Fleming. 1984. *Human Resource Development: Issues in Case Management.* Baltimore: Center of Rehabilitation and Manpower Services, University of Maryland.

Minahan, A. et al., eds. 1987. *Encyclopedia of Social Work.* Silver Spring, MD: NASW.

NASW. 1981. *Standards for Social Work Services in Long-Term Care Facilities.* Professional Standards, Policy Statement 9. Silver Spring, MD: NASW.

———. 1984. *Standards and Guidelines for Social Work Case Management for the Functionally Impaired.* Professional Standards, No. 12. Silver Spring, MD: NASW.

———. 1987a. *Standards for Social Work in Health Care Settings.* Addendum. Silver Spring, MD: NASW.

Northen, H. 1982. *Clinical Social Work.* New York: Columbia University Press.

O'Connor, G. 1988. "Case Management: System and Practice." *Social Casework* 69:97–106.

Perlman, H.H. 1957. *Social Casework. A Problem Solving Process*. Chicago, IL: University of Chicago Press.

Pinderhughes, E.B. 1976. "Power, Powerlessness and Empowerment in Community Mental Health." Paper presented at Annual Convocation of Commonwealth Fellows. Chestnut Hill, MA, October.

Roberts-DeGennaro, M. 1987. "Developing Case Management as a Practice Model." *Social Casework* 69:466–69.

Rowe, M. and C. Ryan. 1987. *AIDS as Public Health Challenge*. Washington, D.C.: Intergovernmental Health Policy Project, George Washington University.

Rubin, A. 1987. "Case Management." Pp. 212–22 in *Encyclopedia of Social Work*, A. Minahan et al., editors. Silver Spring, MD: National Association of Social Workers.

Segal, S. and J. Baumohl. 1980. "Engaging the Disengaged: Proposals on Madness and Vagrancy." *Social Work* 25:358–65.

Sosin, M. and S. Caulum. 1982. "Advocacy: A Conceptualization for Social Work Practice." *Social Work* 27(4):347.

Steinberg, R.M. and G.W. Carter. 1983. *Case Management and the Elderly*. Lexington, MA: D.C. Heath.

Tolliver, L.M., C. Austin, R.R. Greene, B. Soniat, and M. White. 1986. "A Differentiation between Casework and Case Management." Paper presented at the 39th Annual Scientific Meeting of the Gerontological Society of America, Chicago.

Vourlekis, B.S. 1985. Statement of the Coalition on Medicare and Medicaid Regulations. Submitted to the United States Senate Special Committee on Aging Hearing Medicare DRG's: Challenges for Post-Hospital Care. Silver Spring, MD: National Association of Social Workers.

Weil, M., and J.M. Karls, and Associates. 1985. *Case Management in Human Service Practice*. San Francisco: Jossey-Bass.

Chapter 3

Client Identification and Outreach: Case Management in School-Based Services for Teenage Parents

I. Lorraine Davis

Reaching teenage parents to offer services and support requires a systematic effort and a broad view. Individual case managers use all of their clinical expertise and professional creativity to identify and reach out successfully to their clients. However, more outreach is needed. Case management and its functions must be embedded in a comprehensive program approach designed to change policies and influence resource allocation to create options for teenage parents. It is the availability of options—options that address real, felt needs of a diverse group of young people—that leads to successful identification and outreach.

This chapter discusses the broad view and multiple efforts and strategies utilized to create options for teenage parents in the state of Wisconsin. Case managers play a key role: they simultaneously work with individual clients and with the multiple systems that must be influenced so that clients and their needs are "seen" and acknowledged (identification) and successfully connected to case management services (outreach).

Description and History of Teenage Pregnancy Programs

The history of teenage pregnancy programs in Wisconsin schools dates back to 1973, when the state legislature passed a bill that created a funding source from state special education monies (ch. 115, subch. IV, Education for School Age Parents, Wis. Stat.). The programs evolved from 10 or 15 school district programs that offered only remedial academic subjects with some prenatal offerings just to females, to more than 60 centers (districts with a teacher and a defined program) today,

27

which provide instruction in basic skills for academic subjects; social services to facilitate accessibility to needed resources; information on available counseling services in the school district and in the community; vocational guidance, career development, and education for employment activities; information on related maternal and child health support systems, and resources in addition to instruction in prenatal and neonatal care, child development, infant and child care, nutrition, and family planning. These centers serve both males and females.

Some of the development was providence; however, coupled with a *case management approach* and utilizing a *systems background*, much of it was no accident. Even though the outcomes could not have been precisely predicted, some foresight was exercised. Sensing that the community was ready for a significant change in terms of teenage pregnancy programs, the case manager for school-age parent programs (SAPAR) identified and attempted to connect with as many forces in the community that were grappling with the issue as possible. Case management in this instance meant developing in-service programs and state conferences with a comprehensive approach and including a wide assortment of people and agencies as presenters. Interagency relationships and caring relationships with district teenage pregnancy staff were established. These changes led to the inclusion and involvement of all segments of the community who were even remotely interested in or already were working on matters that affected teenage pregnancy from the viewpoint of prevention, intervention, and beyond.

To begin building a comprehensive teenage pregnancy program, the case manager

- increased the numbers of visitations to school districts to discuss their views regarding the change in the statutes governing "school-age mothers"
- made significant efforts to determine what the district teenage pregnancy staff considered as the positives and negatives with respect to statute changes and what significant inclusions/exclusions they desired
- increased outreach to the organization that had exhibited the greatest effort and concern (up to that point) for school-age parent services
- increased contacts with the Department of Public Instruction (DPI) legislative liaison and with committee chairs in the legislature who might, at some later date, be considering bills introduced on teen pregnancy

• critically examined and scrutinized closely each draft of the bill being readied for introduction to the legislature for the aforementioned changes to the statute.

The rationale behind this broad approach was to develop a coalition of people (no matter how loosely woven) who would emerge at a certain point to seize the moment. As providence would have it, a series of these opportunities arose beginning in 1982 with the initiation of steps to change the school-age mother statute to 1986, when the department's equity statute (sec. 118.13 Wis. Stat.) expanded and the legislative council's pregnancy prevention committee was developed.

In 1983, Wisconsin Act 374 changed the state statutes to remove school-age mother programs from the category of exceptional educational needs. Wisconsin Act 56 (1985) expanded school-age mother services to include school-age fathers. It also extended a school-age parent's eligibility for program participation from a period of only four months to any time before graduation from high school or age 21. New rules and regulations governing SAPAR were promulgated in 1986.

Strategies for Successful Case Management

Quiet, behind-the-scenes building of relationships is a necessity for successful case management. Weaving together people in agencies and programs dealing with adoption, dropouts, genetic counseling, job training, health, day care, equity, women's issues, fathers, family planning, child abuse issues, human growth and development, nutrition, parenting, and career planning is essential to the success of SAPAR.

The case manager must look at the overall picture and his or her philosophy must be that of molding a comprehensive service delivery. The case manager must appear to be a person who can be everywhere all the time. Although this is impossible, the relationships built help create this image. The person has touched base in a significant way with others who care as deeply about the present and future clients as he or she does. The outreach aspect depends heavily on these components.

Within the school setting and its structure and bureaucratic needs, case management is different from and reaches far beyond the role of a coordinator. A coordinator takes care of the mechanics of everyday functioning and runs interference for program staff. The case manager can be likened to a compact disk: attention is given simultaneously to all systems as they interact upon one another and advance on their own.

Applying the case management definition provided in Chapter 2 to the situation discussed in this chapter, the case manager was the supervisor for both the SAPAR and school social work services at the state level; the client system was the school districts. Program managers in individual districts expressed to the case manager their fear that those students who had been identified for program participation would not be able to avail themselves of the services because school board action would be required before program modifications could be made. Under the aegis of special education, board action was unnecessary. Under regular education, however, no program modifications could be made for any student without board approval. The case manager, who spirited the law through its many changes in the legislature, ensured that a specific section was included in the school-age parent law that stated, "Each school board shall make available . . . program modifications."

Throughout the entire process, the case manager consulted with students, parents, and district teachers in teenage parent programs about specific needs so that criteria set down in the rules would actually facilitate the day-to-day service delivery rather than pose barriers to service. Such consultation set the tone for a case management approach with individual school district programs. In those districts where there was a social work case manager, programs were likely to take on a more comprehensive nature.

The case manager also made conscious attempts to establish a solid base for a continuum of services through coalition building. The case manager exchanged ideas and engaged in problem-solving activities with the Adolescent Pregnancy Prevention Board (created by Act 56); the coordinator of the Carl D. Perkins Vocational Education Act (homemaker set-aside); personnel responsible for Maternal and Child Health Grants; the sex equity coordinator for the Department of Public Instruction; and people associated with Wisconsin Women's Council Choices Initiative, the Department of Health and Social Service (DHSS) Pregnancy Prevention Grants, the DPI Human Growth and Development, the Job Training Partnership Act, the DHSS Economic Self-Sufficiency Grants, the Wisconsin Employment Opportunity Program, the Wisconsin Day Care Improvement Project (sec. 46.99, Wis Stat.), and nutrition programs (Women, Infant, and Children/DHSS and DPI "Nutrition in Teenage Pregnancy").

The purposes behind these strategies were to increase the availability of funding for expansion of services to individual districts' programs through the grants process, to make school districts aware of viable resources for building comprehensive programs, and to help districts expand offerings, thereby making the programs more relevant and realistic to the actual everyday needs of pregnant teenagers, thus encouraging identification with the program.

Specifically, the coordinator of the Carl D. Perkins Vocational Education Act (homemaker set-aside) and the case manager for SAPAR, who both realized that a need existed to determine the continuum of services to teenage parents, convened a meeting of key community members to discuss the issue and to begin establishing a clear-cut goal. In addition, the case manager set into motion planning for one of the most comprehensive teen pregnancy conferences at that time.

The case manager also became an active member of a coalition spearheaded by the Wisconsin Women's Council. As a member, the case manager intended to develop services for young women to show them that they did have options other than becoming teenage mothers. The case manager addressed the issue of the responsibility of teenage fathers by providing testimony (along with other key teenage pregnancy people) to the Legislative Council on Teen Pregnancy Prevention regarding the responsibilities and inclusion of fathers in the school-age parent statutes and extending service beyond four months. Finally, the case manager became intricately involved with child care issues (Early Childhood Day Care Committee; sec. 46.99, Day Care Provisions) and health issues (Healthy Birth Task Force).

Case managers who have successfully established a firm base for a continuum of services through a coalition must next identify clients who need those services.

Identification of Clients

The primary purpose of services to teenagers in school-based settings is to ensure that these students are provided with an atmosphere in which they will be motivated to complete their high school education. In school-based settings, case managers are not dealing with a client who, by law, would be forced to report pregnancy—neither are the case managers dealing with a long-term case. Rather, contact with the client may occur only during the last trimester of the pregnancy simply because case managers are not always able to engage in early identification.

Identification often is difficult because students sometimes are able to hide their pregnancy until the last trimester and few other students are likely to bring peer pressure for services. Identification is not just a matter of screening students to see which ones the schools will serve. Annually, students give birth to nearly 7000 babies; yet the school only reaches 7 percent of these students. From a case management point of view, an increase in the types and degrees of service does influence increased identification. Intense interaction with other state agencies also feeds into identification in that schools encompass a wide range of ages and therefore have the potential for serving the same clients as community agencies.

However, several barriers to identification exist:

- Pregnant teenagers who are aware of the stigma that is attached to being singled out for "special service" may decide to hide their pregnancy—they do not want to seem "weird" or to be compared unfavorably with other students.
- Many pregnant students and parents do not want to be labeled "special ed" or "disabled" to receive services. However, the eventual change in the wording of the statute resulted in an increase in the willingness to utilize services.
- Pregnant students often are reticent to come forward because of attitudes regarding morality by school staff: "They got themselves into this mess, so they don't deserve special treatment."
- Attitudes that the program is "promoting" or somehow encouraging teenage pregnancy because it serves those who have erred and do not deserve to be treated with dignity can impede efforts of early identification.
- Means for identifying students needing services must not appear to be accusatory regarding teenage sexual activities and the resulting consequences.

Means for overcoming these barriers include increasing, enhancing, and improving services. For example, services could be expanded to offer Lamaze training, instruction in child care, programs to strengthen employment skills, courses in career development and child growth and development, and transportation to and from the programs offered. In addition, services could be offered until graduation or age 21. To promote early identification, services could be provided on a continuum from prevention (sexuality classes for those teenagers who are sexually active) to intervention (prenatal classes) to postintervention (postnatal instruction in child care, jobs, and job training). Such services could be made more convenient to teenagers if they were provided directly in the high schools rather than in an alien setting outside the school. This effort would also reduce the number of students who are placed on homebound status (that is, services in the home). In addition, school programs that promote job training could be provided.

Another means for encouraging early identification is through referrals. Identification and referral are closely tied together. For example, a counselor who, through individual counseling, suspects pregnancy may refer the teenager to a particular program. Community doctors, nurses, agencies, and clinics also may identify and refer. Other referrals come from parents who suspect pregnancy, school staff through their work with teenagers, the pregnant teenager herself, and students who have used the service and found it to be good. In addition, the reputation of a program may encourage a self-referral. Pregnant teenagers must have the option of being served whether they elect to receive the service or not.

The more options made available to pregnant teenagers and the more flexible those options, the more likely the increase in self-identification. Program variations must allow for the inclusion of those people with complex and different sets of circumstances and the exclusion of those students who do not wish to participate directly in a program but would like to take advantage of specific services.

Outreach

Some of the aforementioned problems of identification are lessened if students are made aware of a program through specific outreach. Outreach, an essential component in identification, may take many forms: pamphlets, the grapevine consisting of other students who have received services, visibility of the program because it is housed in the students' own high school, and students talking to other students.

School districts may engage in the following:

- encouraging recruitment of and actual recruiting of pregnant teenagers who have graduated to serve on boards of teenage parent organizations and to become involved in planning for services
- inviting pregnant teenagers to be presenters at conferences and in-service programs concerning, for example, child abuse issues surrounding teenage parenting
- awarding substantial scholarships to teenage parents so they may continue their education beyond high school
- providing time slots for teenagers who have already given birth to return and serve as mentors
- securing grants to provide "real" on-the-job training during summer sessions—job training that results in actual jobs for those teenagers who complete the program.

However, such outreach efforts may be fraught with difficulties. Case managers may need to consider that many of the fathers may not be school aged. They may be older boyfriends who are out of school and thus are not easily accessible and do not fall under anyone's jurisdiction. In addition, in some cases the father may be related to the teenager who is pregnant or has given birth. This is an added dimension that complicates the issue, because it may involve sexual abuse and a great reluctance on the part of the girl to discuss the issue. Another difficulty is that teenage pregnancy services to some teenagers may be short-term. Such services will affect the teenager's ability to make long-range plans for her and her baby. However, once the student has given birth, the system may no longer have control over what happens to the student and her baby.

To help overcome these outreach difficulties, it is necessary to meld services with the "quirks" of the system or meld service resources despite them. Case management of teenage parent programs in a school-based setting means managing those components that affect the client and manipulating and orchestrating those resources to provide the greatest benefits for the teenager on both an immediate and long-range basis. Case management in such a setting also calls for a great deal of flexibility and creativity. Case managers must be flexible enough to rework services to fit needs if necessary. They must have the creativity to seek different funding sources to provide child care, transportation, job training, and other services if required. Finally, it is important that case managers be familiar with the legal trappings of the agency and be willing to put into action any changes needed in the statutes to enhance services.

Suggested Readings

Brindis, C., R. Barth, and A. Loomis. 1987. "Continuous Counseling: Case Management with Teenage Parents." *Social Casework* 68:164–72.

Furstenberg, F.F. Jr., R. Lincoln, and J. Menken (Eds.). 1981. *Teenage Sexuality, Pregnancy and Childbearing*. Philadelphia: University of Pennsylvania Press.

Lindsay, J.W. and S. Rodine. 1989. *Teenage Pregnancy Challenge: Strategies for Change* (Book One) and *Programs for Kids* (Book Two). Buena Park, CA: Morning Glory Press.

Loomis, A. 1987. *A Public-Private Partnership for School Drop-out Prevention of Pregnant and Parenting Teens*. San Francisco: Teenage Pregnancy and Parenting Program of San Francisco.

Chapter 4

Assessment: Private Case Management with the Elderly

Grace Lebow and Barbara Kane

The assessment function in social work case management is akin to an anthropologist's exploration of people in their habitat but with the trained eye and ear and experience of the social work clinician. It is a data-gathering process that leads to a specific plan of care and to a practical means of implementing that care. By analogy with the methodology of the anthropologist, the observations of the case manager, when combined with those of informants, frame a picture of the client's functioning in his or her world. The outcome of the assessment should lead to a plan that encourages the most appropriate choice of resources under the least restrictive circumstances.

In this chapter, the discussion of the assessment function in case management focuses on the clinicians' experience with older people and their families. However, the characteristics of this assessment function can apply to other segments of the population as well. For example, this model also has been used to assess and carry out case management functions in contexts such as with a quadriplegic young man attending college, with a retarded young woman needing relocation, and with a middle-aged disabled polio victim of the 1950s needing more care.

This chapter also describes key strategies and attempts to address the basic questions, What is assessment? Who is the client the clinician is assessing? What are the goals of case management and of assessment? How does this fit as a function of case management? What are some basic premises that guide the clinician's work? The conclusions drawn in this chapter are based on the experiences in the setting of private geriatric case management. This setting is a recent one, spanning only the past ten years, and it is interesting and useful to trace the reasons for its emergence.

Foundation of the Assessment Function

The need for individually tailored services for elders and their families has arisen out of demographic and social changes in American society. Increased numbers of older people are living longer, have more chronic ailments, and have fewer children to take care of them. Moreover, more of these older people are living independently than ever before, with family members spread across the United States. In addition, more women are in the work force and thus, are unavailable for traditional caregiving. These changes have led to a swelling demand, beyond what most established agencies are prepared to handle, for professional home-based services that can provide the kind and extent of personal attention needed.

In addition to this growing need for case management services throughout the population, other factors applying specifically to those in middle- and upper-income groups have created the demand for services in the private-practice sector. For instance, people in these groups often do not fit the guidelines that would make them eligible for the public- and private-agency services. In other cases, people who are eligible are unwilling to accept such services. In still other cases, families with the means seek a level of individualized service that the traditional agency sectors can rarely provide because of their generally large caseloads. For these reasons, family members turn to the case manager in private practice to fill this gap in the service delivery system.

Private-sector case managers act as a single point of entry into the complex array of agencies and services. Families can rely on one professional to locate and arrange, coordinate, and monitor an entire package of services, or any portion of these services. Along with these services, the older person looks to this professional for a sense of security knowing, this is someone knowledgeable about the older person's life condition who will be available and responsive to that person. As one client so aptly observed, "This is my good friend. This is the one person I can count on anytime, no matter what comes up."

Private-care managers have a great degree of latitude in their work with older adults. Generally not tied to any one agency, they have no conflict of interest in their use of the entire community and its resources, both public and private agencies, and in their choice of professionals and specialists. Therefore, the best possible referral selections can be made for their clients. A small number of case managers have some services under their auspices, typically homemakers and nursing assistants. These agencies usually are responsible for the training and monitoring of their personnel and believe that they can offer a higher quality of service in this way. In the program discussed later in this chapter, social workers with a bachelor of social work degree—BSW assistants—help carry out task-oriented services for older clients.

Assessment, as the foundation for all other case management functions requires a high level of training and clinical skills. Clinical expertise is called forth in diagnosing the current situation and the level of physical, psychological, and social functional capacity. Because of the prevalence of depression, dementia, and other multiple physical, psychiatric, and mental status difficulties, the professional must be experienced and knowledgeable medically, psychiatrically, and clinically. At the same time, the skilled clinician will recognize the need for evaluations by other specialists such as neurologists, psychiatrists, and rehabilitation therapists. Both the care plan and interventions develop directly from this biopsychosocial assessment. If, for example, an 80-year-old man were to be evaluated incorrectly as functioning at too high a level, then an inappropriate residential choice could result, adding undue stress to his already fragile state. At assessment, most often the first encounter with the client, the skilled clinician has an opportunity to set the therapeutic tone for the interaction. The personal entry by this clinician into a private life requires skill at engagement, sensitivity, and diplomacy.

Much of the challenge to the case manager is that often the older person does not seek any change. The older person may not want to be studied or managed in any way. This person has invested his or her energy in trying to keep things the same, often denying that change may be needed either within himself or herself or with the environment. Indeed, use of the terms *case manager* and *case management* make the role and process more palatable to the reluctant client.

The Assessment Function in Private Practice

This section elaborates on the assessment function by examining how it is carried out in a particular private-practice setting.

Counseling and consultation with family members often is not enough to address the specific nature of their problems. Rather families ask for professional help to determine what services and resources are available and suitable and how to go about selecting and obtaining them. Often, they ask for assistance in introducing these services to their parents. In response to this need, the authors founded one of the nation's first geriatric private practices, Aging Network Services (ANS) in Bethesda, Maryland. In 1982, the first clients of ANS were family members who presented the following problems:

Son: I'm bringing mother home to live with me in Washington. I
                  want a program of activities for her and guidance in helping
                  with her adjustment to this change.
Observation: The mother's dementia has progressed so that the son believes
                  it is too risky for her to remain in her own home so far away.
                  The mother seems agreeable to the move although the son is
                  uncertain about how well she understands this.

Sibling: My retarded sister was evicted. Can you help with relocation?
Observation: The sister wants to find an appropriate and affordable living
                  arrangement near her for her 63-year-old retarded younger
                  sister. She is concerned about her own health and wants to
                  explore the possibilities of future care management for her
                  sister.

Daughter: I want to avert crisis by advance preparation.
Mother: Maybe at a later time. I'm okay for now.
Observation: A 93-year-old woman in the Washington, D.C., area has an
                  only daughter living out of town. The mother lives alone in
                  her own home with only minimal help from friends and
                  neighbors. The mother suffered a series of falls lately that the
                  doctor ascribes to ministrokes. The daughter would like to
                  know how to introduce the idea of our care management
                  services to her mother.

For many of these families, the usual strains of meeting the needs of
the elderly family member were exacerbated by geographic separation.
A typical case ANS clinicians encountered involved a request for
professional assessment of a parent living in the Washington, D.C.,
metropolitan area by an adult child living elsewhere:

> I am a 45-year-old, hardworking computer programmer living in Atlanta
> with my husband and two young children. I have an 80-year-old mother
> living in Washington who is getting much more forgetful. She also has a
> heart condition and diabetes. I love her deeply and want to move her here
> but she wants to stay where she is. I don't known how far I should push. I
> just want what's best for her and for us. I need an objective look at the
> situation. I am staying up nights worrying about whether or not she will
> remember to unplug the coffee pot.

The profile in this example of a worried daughter out of town with a
mother living alone with memory problems and several other medical
conditions is common in private practice. Most of the clients ANS
clinicians see are parents or older relatives who have some degree of
mental status impairment. The children are willing to pay for private

and personalized services to be provided for their parents with a care manager who also will be available to them for communication about their parents.

Of course, the geographical problem can be reversed. ANS often is the recipient of similar requests from children living in the local area with an elderly relative living elsewhere. For this reason, ANS established a network of colleagues throughout the United States, including most metropolitan areas and some outlying areas. These private-practice social workers, screened rigorously by ANS after meeting the formal standards of the master of social work degree and state licensing or other certifications, are on call to receive referrals from ANS. Every referral made to an ANS member comes with a detailed family assessment that is compiled from interviews with all adult children in the family or with significant others.

This process has been extended to geographically separated families in which no family members reside in the local area. In these cases, ANS performs the assessment using a family questionnaire and telephone interviews before referring the case to a network member.

Care management in a private setting either by ANS or its network members is marked by a stability not usually seen in other settings when sufficient staff resources may not be available. Because of the intensive nature of private work, caseloads are small: approximately 20 families per care manager. At ANS, staff serve as therapists and brokers of service and supervise BSW assistants.

The Assessment Process

Whether in a private practice or agency setting with elders or with other client populations, assessment for the purpose of care management is a continuous dynamic process with four overlapping phases:

1. assessing the fit between the client and the service
2. assessing the family or significant others
3. assessing the (older) person and his or her environment
4. assessing the situation over the course of service.

Phase 1: Assessing the Fit between Client and Service

At the time that a family member makes the first telephone call to ANS and asks about its services, the initial phase of assessment begins. A rapid determination of the suitability of the case as presented by the caller for the private-practice setting is a difficult task, requiring an experienced clinician. Typically this determination is made during the initial phone call or introductory meeting before the service is started.

However, some situations call for immediate referral elsewhere or are otherwise deemed inappropriate. For example, callers who talk about their relative being abused or at risk of abuse, being seriously neglected, and refusing all help are referred to protective services. Family members who present a situation in which their parents are gesturing suicide or other aggressive behavior and need immediate psychiatric attention to stabilize are immediately referred to a psychiatrist or hospital with the possibility of later service. In addition, callers who hold onto an unrealistic expectation of service such as "wanting mom to be told that moving in with her oldest child is best for her" are considered to be in a situation that is inappropriate for ANS service. When it is apparent that the fee-for-service arrangement would strain the family, the family is referred to a public nonprofit agency. In each of these situations, the clinician explains to the caller the reason the ANS service does not meet the family's needs and how the referral to another agency, resource, or professional is better suited to the caller's problem at the current time. The clinician also gives them information about ANS services for possible use at a later time when there may be a better fit between client and service.

After this initial assessment of probable fit, the care manager needs to clarify some important points before agreeing to work with a client. It is most important that the care manager clarify the expectation of service because, in most situations, the family member is asking for assistance after prior attempts to solve the problem have failed. The family knows that private help is more expensive but may feel that the higher cost will guarantee a successful outcome. It is wise to have the family state its hopes about what will be gained so that these issues can be addressed properly. For example, a son wants ANS services to help him convince his dad to move out of the family home and relocate in a retirement community nearby to the son and family. Dad has made it clear that he has no intention of moving. In situations such as this one, the care manager helps the family to appreciate the parent's right to self-determination and that the older person needs to pace any change within the relationship with the care manager.

At the same time, the care manager is careful to acknowledge and explore family members' hopes. Usually families are intellectually aware that their agenda for help may conflict with the parent's agenda. Still, they feel confused about their responsibility as sons or daughters in the use of authority with their parents to get them to accept assistance. Adult children often feel negligent when they have reason to believe that their parents are vulnerable and yet will not accept their suggestions and attempts for help. Every effort should be made to give preventive help in the older person's own setting until the physical risks become a serious reality. Unfortunately, however, matters sometimes have to get worse before they get better. A hospitalization because of an accident usually spells out the reality for after-care assistance. These kinds of situations in which some degree of risk is involved are painful and delicate to handle. There are no right or wrong answers and each situation needs careful consideration.

Phase 2: Assessing the Family or Significant Other

After making the determination to proceed with service and clarifying expectations, the second phase, the family assessment, begins. Who to see first? In what order? In the home or in the office? These are difficult questions but they can be addressed in terms of a few workable principles. Most clear-cut is the situation in which the family, including the older member, is in agreement about what is needed and about using the services of outside professionals. If the physical locations permit, an office or home appointment involving the older person and his or her family might be set up as a first meeting.

However, most families requesting ongoing private-care management services involve an older member who is cognitively impaired or resistant, to some degree, to outside intervention. In these situations, it is sometimes more often constructive for the care manager to meet first with the family members alone for several reasons. First, this initial meeting gives an opportunity for the care manager and other family members to form, in a sense, a cooperative partnership in evaluating the needs and strengths of the family and especially of the older person. Second, this comanager team makes it possible to plan together the most effective and sensitive approach in introducing this change agent. Third, in this setting, the people seeking assistance (almost always the adult children) need time alone with the care manager to try to articulate what they want from the service, because their request for service drives the whole process in relating to the client system.

Telling one's story to a professional can feel overwhelming, particularly when families or significant others are unclear about what is needed to remedy the situation. To help with this process, ANS devised a detailed family questionnaire to be filled out before the first interview. From the outset, the questionnaire involves families as partners in an ongoing process by educating them in assessing their own family situation. For example, it contains a checklist of activities of daily living for evaluating the older person's functioning abilities. It asks families to list friends, neighbors, and relatives who help the parent, leading to the question, "How would you rate the present support system?" This helps both the family member and care manager assess the gaps in the overall support network. The final question on the form is, "Now that you have had time to outline this information, tell us what your major concerns are and specifically what type of assistance you are looking for." Many families have commented that this case management tool helped them to think through their family needs, thereby corroborating ANS's emphasis on involving the family in the assessment.

A review of the completed questionnaire before meeting the family provides the care manager with basic data. It thus serves as a guide for the interview process, allowing the family to use the interview time most productively by elaborating on these basic data. This elaboration invariably introduces pertinent historical data that are valuable in determining the appropriate course of action. In circumstances in which the family members are not in the same geographical area, this meeting is held by way of individual telephone consultations or sometimes in a conference call with family members in several locations. Experience has shown that these consultations not only add significant information, but most important help to involve the family as a more unified support system for their parents. The following case example illustrates the kinds of data collected in a family assessment interview as well as significant service-focused issues raised for discussion:

> An only son, Mr. Ott, Jr., who resides out of town, is worried that his father's memory has been getting worse over the past three months, as evidenced by his getting lost driving around his neighborhood. He is also concerned that his father is losing weight and may be forgetting to eat. Mr. Ott, Sr., has been widowed for a year and has continued to live in his own home alone, with a professional housecleaner coming once every two weeks. The son wants the father to move to an assisted-living retirement home soon; however, the father sees no problems and wants to remain at home.

Mr. Ott, Jr., is requesting ongoing care management services. He is told that the first step will be to get as much information as possible about his father's functioning in his setting before a care plan can be developed. Part of the assessment will include consultation with his father's doctors. In the office meeting with Mr. Ott, Jr., the care manager expounds on the following information from the questionnaire:

Referral and Background Information

- presenting problem
- detailed exploration of circumstances leading to present situation

- why help sought now and not before
- early history, significant ethnic and cultural background

Psychological and Mental Status Functioning

- first notice of memory failing (date, event)
- traumatic events/losses around this period
- how the father coped with wife's death one year ago
- general personality traits and coping mechanisms

Activities of Daily Living Functioning

- description of a typical day
- driving record
- ability to handle banking and household management
- shopping and food preparation

Support System

- who the father counts on and for what
- who, if anyone, checks on the father daily
- relationships with friends, neighbors, others
- participation in organized activities such as church

Family Relationships

- description of past and present primary family relationships
- frequency and nature of visits and calls with family
- family reactions to their father's diagnosis of Alzheimer's disease and to his attitude about outside help

In the family meeting with Mr. Ott, Jr., it was agreed that the care manager would introduce a BSW assistant to the father. The assistant would develop a relationship with the father, take him to the doctor, do errands with him, and continue to observe his functioning. Based on this relationship, the care manager hoped that the father would accept the short-range goal of a homemaker four hours a day. The relationship also will facilitate the longer range goal of introducing the idea of a move to a place with built-in assistance and monitoring.

Another issue is how Mr. Ott, Jr., will tell his father about the social worker's visit and how the social worker will introduce herself at the time of the home visit. At the point of initial inquiry, the son and father were engaged heavily in an ongoing six-month battle over the issue of the father's moving. The son took the father to see two retirement homes in Atlanta, 10 minutes away from the son's home. The father did not like the idea, leaving both feeling defeated and angry. Mr. Ott, Sr., commented that he did not want to go to "either of those nursing home places." With this background information, the care manager knew that her presence might frighten the father into associating her visit with placement in a nursing home. So she suggested to the son that she be introduced as a consultant who helps older people remain at home.

The next question for discussion was who was going to pay for the service and what this meant in terms of client alliances and confidentiality. Mr. Ott, Jr., decided that he would pay for the assessment visits to avoid adding obstacles to his father's acceptance of help. The son's paying for service, however, does not mean that he directs the outcome. He understands that he is paying for an objective appraisal and that the intervention process has to be guided by the father's readiness. The care manager explains that general findings from the assessment will be shared with the son, and confidences between the father and the care manager and BSW assistant will be respected.

ANS care managers have learned that some words may trigger negative connotations for the older population. Thus, once there is sufficient background understanding of the client, adult children can be guided toward choosing more acceptable words such as "consultant" or "resource specialist" when talking about the professional coming to the home. A considerable amount of time is taken in this family assessment interview to understand the particular nature of the elder's resistance to arrive at a mutual agreement about a sensitive introduction that does not turn the person away and that respects his or her dignity.

The first family assessment interview typically ends with a discussion of what role the family wants to play during this initial phase. In this case, the son realizes that his pushing has created an emotional stalemate with his father and he agrees to back off in this regard. He will continue to handle his father's financial affairs with power of attorney. His hopes are that his father will accept the care manager and BSW assistant as other significant people in his life. The son was direct in his request for an objective evaluation "that will help me be clearer on my roles and responsibilities toward my father."

Phase 3:   Assessing the Older Person

Once the issues of payment for service and introduction of the care manager have been resolved, the third phase of the assessment function begins: assessing the biopsychosocial functioning of the older person. Continuing with the example of the Ott family, the care manager made a home visit to meet with the father. Mr. Ott, Jr., also was present in a supportive capacity. During the course of the interview, the care manager tried to put the father at ease several times, because his suspicions and fears were obvious. She did this by reassuring him that although his son wanted him to move, she wanted to hear his point of view on the subject. He then was able to relax and expound on how much his home meant to him.

Home visits offer an enriched assessment opportunity for the care manager, but different skills are required for these home assessments than for those conducted in an office setting. Though well-versed in the various assessment tools and scales, care managers do not use these in a paper and pencil fashion with the client. Instead, the observing eye is the tool used to focus on the richness of material that evidences itself in the home visit. How a person keeps house, how he or she tells about the people in the pictures on the coffee table, how the person explains the medication that is lying on the counter and describes his or her system for remembering nine different pills, and how the person walks around the house all tell a living story. The care manager learns about the physical and psychological functioning of the client by opening up opportunities in this real laboratory of life.

For example, the care manager observed that all around Mr. Ott's apartment were piles of mail, old newspapers, and scraps of paper with telephone numbers and names on them. When the care manager referred to them, "My, you have a lot of business to attend to," Mr. Ott, Sr., responded, "Yes, I used to be able to keep things organized but now I'm losing things more." She commented on a family portrait hanging on the wall and noted that Mr. Ott was only able to name three out of six family members. She noticed an opened novel on the coffee table and that sparked a conversation about his reading material. A telephone call interrupted the session but also gave the care manager an opportunity to witness how he handled the call.

By the end of the interview, Mr. Ott, Sr., was in a more congenial mood, showing the care manager his prized collection of stamps and coins. The care manager said she would be back the following week with her assistant, who might be helpful for running errands and taking him to upcoming doctor appointments, because he recently had to give up driving. He agreed, but later on indicated some apprehension to his son about another visit.

Though this first home visit added to the richness of the data regarding this man's overall functioning and his initial receptivity to an outsider, it is only the beginning. That one point in time occurred when Mr. Ott's resistance and suspicions were probably strongest. The actual extent of his capacities and limitations still were unknown. This is where the use of BSW assistant is invaluable. With frequent visits and at a more financially manageable cost to the family, the BSW assistant is able to make further observations, form a consistent ongoing relationship, and offer practical assistance such as taking the client to the doctor and to other specialists. As rapport develops between the two, the client's apprehension usually lessens and the chances for introducing future services improve.

The BSW assistant's degree is in social work or in a behavioral or therapeutic science. In addition, the assistant has experience working with older adults. Like the care manager, the BSW assistant needs to have knowledge of normal aging as well as about the disabilities and illnesses of older people. The assistant has a unique role with older clients that requires special skills. Unlike the care manager, the assistant spends much of the time performing various activities of daily living with the client such as grocery shopping, going to the bank, and organizing mail and papers. In the relationship with the client, the assistant straddles the fine line between a counselor and a friend—that involves sensitivity and some awareness of transference and counter-transference issues. For example, with transference issues with Mr. Ott, Sr., there were indications that he looked to the case assistant for some romantic intimacy that he had had with his wife. So the case assistant was careful to address him by his last name and in other ways to maintain a friendly yet professional stance. With regard to countertrans-ference, the case assistant found herself feeling angry at the son for not taking a more responsive role. This reflected her own personal family situation, in which her two brothers had slackened off in their involve-ment with their own invalid father. For this reason, supervisory sessions are held frequently. The assistant reports his or her observations and activities to the care manager at these sessions so that transference and other clinical issues can be understood. Together, they discuss the next steps in the assessment phase.

In terms of the example with Mr. Ott, Sr., the assistant accompanied the care manager on her second visit. She engaged Mr. Ott, Sr., in conversation about topics of interest to him. She offered to take him to his doctor's appointment scheduled for the following week and left her business card with her home number and her picture on the back. Before coming to pick him up for the medical appointment, she phoned to make sure he remembered her and the appointment, reminding him to look at her picture. On the way back from the doctor's office, Mr. Ott, Sr., expressed his gratitude for her being there to remember what the doctor was saying. He said, "I like borrowing your memory for these kinds of things."

Here, an initial connection between Mr. Ott, Sr., and the BSW assistant was established. During the course of the next couple of weeks, she was able to add to the repertoire of assessment information about the needs and strengths of this older person. For example, she observed Mr. Ott standing on a high stool to get pots from the cabinet. Based on this observation, it was easy for her to help him reorganize the kitchen to make it safer. She noticed that the food in the refrigerator consisted mainly of sweet things and reported this to the care manager. In a sense, the assistant was able to help the care manager capture Mr. Ott's world through the eyes of a moving lens rather than a series of snapshots.

As with any assessment, the care manager serves as the axle on the wheel in terms of calling on other specialties for evaluation. However, evaluation by others may seem like an invasive examination by too many outsiders. This is especially true for older people who, having experienced many losses or disabilities, wish to protect themselves from others discovering their frailties. With this in mind, it is important that care managers pinpoint the most significant areas that require additional specialists to avoid overwhelming and alienating the older person and to continue to support their strengths.

In this case example, the presenting problem as stated by Mr. Ott, Jr., was his father's weight loss and his worsening memory problem. In the past, Mr. Ott, Sr., had let his son know that he could handle his own medical affairs. Before his request for ANS services, Mr. Ott, Jr., felt that his involvement with the doctor was now necessary. He described how, on his last trip to Washington, he was more firm and persuasive with his balking father about the need for a good work-up by his internist. They both went to see the doctor and were told that the father needed neurological and other tests to assess his memory. The father did not want to go and his son returned home frustrated and worn down. This was the point at which he called on ANS for assistance.

After the BSW assistant and Mr. Ott, Sr., achieved sufficiently good rapport, he agreed to have her set up an appointment and take him to the neurologist. However, this posed a typical ethical dilemma for the care manager. Under what circumstances and to what degree is it acceptable to try to convince a client to do something while still respecting his right to self-direction? Care managers constantly grapple with this and other similar issues related to the issue of autonomy, particularly when the older person has some degree of mental status impairment but is not at the point of needing guardianship. Because so much of the private-practice caseload consists of this particular subgroup of older people, it is a major issue for discussion and must be thought through with each client situation.

In the Ott family example, Mr. Ott, Sr., was observed to show poor judgment with regard to his health needs. Intervention was seen as preventative in nature and aimed at developing a solid and practical home care plan that would allow him to remain at home in accordance with his desires. This approach is based on the philosophy that it is generally preferable to support a person's wishes to remain independent in his or her own setting and to introduce the least amount of change possible in a person's life.

The private geriatric social worker has a great deal of latitude in his or her work with older people. In the assessment phase of care management, this is evidenced by the way in which the social worker puts together the multidisciplinary team. The staff at ANS have developed good working relationships with other specialists who can be brought in as needed for assessment. When the client already has a primary-care physician, any intervention is always in collaboration with that doctor. There is little restriction on how the private team is formed and who plays on the team. The players understand that the system works best when the private social worker acts as the coordinator and clearinghouse for information.

As illustrated by the case example, the solo practitioner also has latitude in the amount of time and attention given to a client in appraising the client's functioning and in implementing a care plan. Although the care manager and family have agreed on an arrangement in terms of time spent, the care manager is not restricted by heavy caseloads and paperwork. This allows the care manager to use his or her energies to work in creative ways in behalf of the client. Accountability is to the client and to the ethics and values of the profession. At ANS, care managers consult with one another and with outside consultants on clinical and other issues that pose difficult ethical and confidentiality issues.

Phase 4:   Reassessing the Situation

Because the client picture is constantly changing, the care manager must continually review the individual in his or her environment. The origin and nature of this changing scene is interesting. The source can be the environment. For instance, home health aids quit or are fired, family members move in or out of town, other support people become less available, neighborhoods become unsafe, or financial resources become more limited. However, the most common changes are in the physical or mental status of the older person. The change may be precipitous, for example, the result of a sudden illness or fall, necessitating review of the entire situation; or the change can be slower, such as the gradual deterioration that accompanies Alzheimer's disease or Parkinson's disease. Regardless of the nature of the change, the care manager must be aware of the dynamic and complicated picture that the older, frail person presents.

In our case example, based on the medical report showing that Mr. Ott, Sr., probably has Alzheimer's disease and the care manager's observations that he was sometimes forgetting to eat meals or not eating properly or adequately, homemaker services were introduced, at first for only a few hours a day. This acceptance was based on the positive rapport that had developed with the BSW assistant over a period of months. The time that she spent in preparing the homemaker to understand Mr. Ott's idiosyncrasies and then in ongoing supervision and support of the homemaker helped to make this alliance work. Six months into the service period, however, Mr. Ott fell on the ice. A reassessment of home care needs was essential and a revised care plan set, which included visits from a physical therapist.

Reassessment is a vital component throughout the life of a case and requires the ongoing attention of the skilled clinician. It is often not until well into the process with the whole family that patterns of both family interaction and the family's interaction with the care manager are observable. For example, Mr. Ott, Jr., initially was relieved to have service initiated. However, during the third month, he began to distance himself from both his father and the assistant. It appeared to be a factor of jealousy. When these reactions came to the fore in the monthly conversations with the care manager, an office consultation was arranged to resolve the problem.

Reassessment keeps care managers alert as the original goals change in response to the ever-changing needs of the person and his or her situation. It is important that the care manager, as orchestrator of the team, discuss these changing objectives with other team members and with the family.

Conclusion

The case example chosen for study in this chapter involved an only son. In families with siblings or other caregivers such as grandchildren, spouses, nieces and nephews, stepchildren, and friends, the care manager's clinical skills are tapped in different ways. A common problem is that family members may have different expectations for that relative. The care manager's task is to understand each person's perception of the problem and guide that person toward a realistic understanding of the level of functioning of the older person. The care manager and family members can then set goals that meet the needs of the relative and are agreeable to everyone concerned. The professional assessment itself often helps to soften these conflicts so that the family then can work as a more cooperative unit.

The assessment function is the foundation on which all other care management functions emanate. It is a unique function in that it can also stand alone, offering a diagnostic appraisal of the person in his or her environment. For this foundation to be strong, the assessment function demands the highest level of expertise and skill on the part of the clinician, both in the diagnosis of the client and in the engagement of the client unit into the process.

Bibliography

American Society on Aging. 1988. *Generations, Special Issue on Case Management.*

Butler, Robert H., M.I. Lewis, and T. Sunderland (1991) *Aging and Mental Health: Positive Psychosocial and Biomedical Approaches.* Columbus, OH: Merrill.

Melamed, Brina. 1985. "Issues Related to Private Practice Geriatric Care Management." Paper presented New York: October 5–6, 1985.

NASW. 1984. *NASW Standards and Guidelines for Social Work Case Management for the Functionally Impaired.* Prepared by the NASW Case Management Task Force. Silver Spring, MD: NASW.

NCOA. 1988. *Case Management Standards.* Guidelines for Practice by National Institute on Community-Based Long Term Care. Washington, D.C.: NCOA.

Office of Technology Assessment. 1990. *Confused Minds, Burdened Families: Finding Help for People with A.D. and Other Dementias.* Washington, D.C.: USGPO.

Ragan, Pauline K. 1979. *Aging Parents.* Los Angeles: University of Southern California Press.

Silverstone, Barbara and Helen K. Hyman. 1976. *You and Your Aging Parent.* New York: Pantheon.

Wasser, Edna. 1966. *Creative Approaches in Casework with the Aging.* New York Family Services Association of America.

Chapter 5

Case Management Assessment in School Social Work and Early Intervention Programs for Disabled Infants and Toddlers

Isadora Hare and James P. Clark

The Policy Context of Case Management in Schools

In reviewing the historical development and public-policy context of case management, writers often refer to the Education for All Handicapped Children Act (P.L. 94-142) enacted in 1975 (Weil, Karls, & Associates 1985, p. 10; Vourlekis, this volume). This significant piece of legislation was one of a series of federal laws that formalized case management services for a number of different vulnerable population groups, in this case, children and young adults with disabilities as students in public schools. While this law does not specifically refer to case management, its provisions regarding the obligation of public schools to provide a free, appropriate public education in the least restrictive environment, and its prescriptive procedural due process requirements resulted in schools appointing case managers to oversee and monitor its principles and provisions.

These provisions include child find services, nondiscriminatory testing and assessment, the determination of eligibility by a multidisciplinary team, the development of an individualized education program (IEP), parent participation, and placement in the least restrictive environment selected from a continuum or "cascade" (Allen-Meares, Washington, & Welsh 1986, p. 141) of various types or levels of instructional settings ranging from those most integrated with "regular education" students to those most segregated from them. The IEP must be reviewed annually and every three years the student must have a full re-evaluation. If the direct-practice functions of case management delineated by Weil et al. (1985, p. 29) and utilized as a framework for this

51

book are superimposed upon these provisions in P.L. 94-142, the similarities are apparent. The chart below lists key provisions of P.L. 94-142 and identifies the corresponding case management function for each:

P.L. 94-142 provisions	Case management functions
Child find	Client identification and outreach
Multidisciplinary evaluation and nondiscriminatory testing	Individual assessment and diagnosis
Individualized education program (IEP)	Service planning and resource identification
Placement in the least restrictive environment	Linking clients to needed services
Providing special education and related services: free appropriate public education	Service implementation and coordination
Annual review of IEP	Monitoring service delivery
Procedural due process and parental participation	Advocacy
Triennial reevaluation	Evaluation

The case manager positions created by local school districts to implement P.L. 94-142 have been filled by persons of varying professional backgrounds including social workers. However, in addition, school social workers were profoundly affected by the law in other ways.

Public Law 94-142 provided for "special education" and "related services" for children with disabilities.[1] The term *special education* is defined as "specially designed instruction, at no cost to the parent, to meet the unique needs of a handicapped child." What was significant for social workers was the provision that "related services" be provided in tandem with special education. *Related services* are defined as "transportation and such developmental, corrective, and other supportive services as are required to assist a handicapped child to benefit from special education." Thirteen such services were defined in the 1977 regulations to the act. "Social work services in schools" were included as one of these related services, and were defined as including:

(i)   Preparing a social or developmental history on a handicapped child;
(ii) Group and individual counseling with the child and family;
(iii) Working with those problems in a child's living situation (home, school, and community) that affect the child's adjustment in school; and

(iv) Mobilizing school and community resources to enable the child to receive maximum benefit from his or her educational program.

For the first time, social workers received legal sanction for their services in schools as well as the possibility of federal funding to supplement the costs of creating school social work positions. Consequently, the number of school social workers employed by school districts has increased dramatically since 1975. The legal definition of social work services in schools referred to direct-service provision and also contained elements of what is now regarded as case management: assessment through the preparation of a social or developmental history, service planning and resource identification, linking clients to needed services, and service implementation and coordination.

When the Education of the Handicapped Act (EHA) was reauthorized and amended in 1986 through P.L. 99-457, case management received specific and focused attention. This law added a new Part H to the EHA, a discretionary grant program relating to handicapped infants and toddlers. Early intervention services are provided for children from birth through two years who are developmentally delayed in the cognitive, physical, speech and language, psychosocial, and self-help areas. At the state's discretion, the term may also include those who are at risk of substantial developmental delay. Ten types of early intervention services were named in the law, including case management services [sec. 672(2)E(vii)]. An individualized family service plan (IFSP) is mandated, which must contain an assessment of the child's level of development and the family's strengths and needs relating to enhancing that development. The IFSP must also specify the name of the case manager, who must be from the profession "most immediately relevant" to the child's and family's needs, and "who will be responsible for the implementation of the plan and coordination with other agencies and persons" (sec. 677[d]6). In commenting on the dual concepts of the IFSP and case manager, Bishop (1990) points out that the family-centered philosophy of P.L. 99-457 recognizes that the family is the constant in the child's life, while service systems and personnel fluctuate.

The regulations on P.L. 99-457 define case management as a coordinating function that includes activities designed to assist and enable an eligible child and family to obtain appropriate early intervention services. It is described as an active, ongoing process that involves assisting parents to gain access to the early intervention services and other services identified in the IFSP; coordinating the provision of all relevant services; facilitating the timely delivery of services; and continuously seeking the appropriate services and situations necessary to benefit the development of the child (Title 34 CFR sec. 303.6[a][2]). Specific case management activities include (Title 34 CFR sec. 303.6[b]):

(1) Coordinating the performance of evaluations and assessments;
(2) Facilitating and participating in the development, review, and evaluation of individualized family service plans;
(3) Assisting families in identifying available service providers;
(4) Coordinating and monitoring the delivery of available services;
(5) Informing families of the availability of advocacy services;
(6) Coordinating with medical and health providers; and
(7) Facilitating the development of a transition plan to pre-school services, if appropriate.

These activities are consistent with traditional school social work practice and with roles and competencies that have been proposed for social workers working with infants and toddlers and their families (Clark 1989). They are also consistent with the federal regulatory definition of social work services for implementing P.L. 99-457, which includes (Title 34 CFR sec. 303.12[d][11]):

(i)   Making home visits to evaluate a child's living conditions and patterns of parent-child interaction;
(ii)   Preparing a psychosocial developmental assessment of the child within the family context;
(iii) Providing individual and family-group counseling with parents and other family members, and appropriate social skillbuilding activities with the child and parents;
(iv)   Working with these problems in a child's and family's living situation (home, community, and any center where early intervention services are provided) that affect the child's maximum utilization of early intervention services; and
(v)   Identifying, mobilizing, and coordinating community resources and services to enable the child and family to receive maximum benefit from early intervention services.

Each eligible child and family must be assigned one case manager, who is responsible for coordinating all services across agency lines and for serving as the single point of contact in helping parents to obtain the services they need. Persons qualified to be case managers (Title 34 CFR sec. 303.6[d]) include those who meet the specifications of the IFSP, and who have demonstrated knowledge and understanding about eligible children, the law and its regulations, and the system of payment for early intervention services in their state.

Practice Applications

Case management has therefore become an integral part of services to disabled children. Under P.L. 94-142 it consists both of those case managers who oversee the entire process of assessment, eligibility, and placement, and that member of the case management team who provides (1) an assessment of psychosocial, family, cultural, economic, health, and school-related factors that affect the child's academic performance and learning style; (2) direct services to implement the IEP; and (3) the mobilization and coordination of appropriate resources in the home, school, and community. While social workers are listed among the qualified personnel who are to provide early intervention services, they have no special claim on case management functions according to Part H of the EHA. The various professionals named in the law are all currently working to develop training and materials on the subject (Bailey 1989; Garland, Woodruff, & Buck 1988; Zipper & Nash 1990). School social workers have a long tradition of home-school-community linkage, which involves services now conceptualized as case management activities. School social workers thus have much to contribute to the evolution and elaboration of case management, but have been slow to publish on the topic.

In addition to case management services in the education of children with disabilities, this process is also being increasingly employed in school programs serving so-called children at risk of educational failure, particularly those who are potential dropouts. These students became the focus of educational reform efforts in the mid-80s after educators, business people, and policymakers came to realize that raising academic standards alone would not solve America's educational problems given the demographic economic realities of contemporary America. Two examples of such programs utilizing social workers as well as other professionals are of interest.

The Stay in School Partnership program operated jointly by Fordham University's graduate schools of education and social service focuses on addressing the needs of New York City students in the elementary grades who have a high absentee rate and who are at risk of academic failure or of dropping out. A critical goal of the project is to intervene in both school and home to create a positive environment conducive to academic achievement and regular school attendance. The role of the social worker/case manager involves initiating collaborative relationships between family, school, peers, and community when psychosocial or educational problems interfere with the quality of a child's learning and social functioning. "Associated with this function is the responsibility to facilitate student and family advocacy when necessary, and to assist in planned change and development of resources in the school and the community to aid the school to carry out its teaching and learning function" (Anon. n.d., p. 2). The assessment function in this model is directed to problems the child has in school, family problems, the level of care or neglect in the home, and client strengths and weaknesses in utilizing external supportive problem-solving means (J. Wagner, personal communications, 1990).

The federally funded Center for the Study and Teaching of At Risk Students (C-STARS) at the University of Washington's Institute for the Study of Educational Policy has also developed a case management model program for dropout prevention from kindergarten through high school. The target population includes students who have been truant or exhibit signs of physical or sexual abuse, children who come to school hungry, those with poor grades, and those who are disruptive in the classroom. C-STARS describes interprofessional case management as "a series of logical and appropriate interactions within a comprehensive service delivery network of schools, health, and social service agencies designed to maximize opportunities for at-risk students and their families to receive needed services in a supportive, efficient and coordinated manner; it is school-based and community-supported" (Smith & Stowitschek 1989, p. 2).

Assessment receives major focus in the model. C-STARS stresses "development of an efficient, systematic process for assessment . . . since this is the base for future decisions and planning" (ibid., p. 19). Recommended components include a comprehensive referral form, specific measures to help determine a student's risk level including self-reporting measures, behavioral questionnaires for teachers to complete, parent interviews, and a review of academic records. Once this is completed, the other phases of case management follow.

In summary, over the last fifteen years policy changes have occurred relating to the education of children with disabilities, early intervention services for infants and toddlers with disabilities, and education reform efforts targeted at children at risk of school failure because of numerous psychosocial, cultural, and economic factors. These new policies have resulted in the development of educational models based on case management concepts. School social workers are active in many of these programs in collaboration with teachers and other school professionals. From their experience as well as the historical roots of the profession, they have much to offer as this form of service delivery evolves.

The Assessment Function in Case Management

Assessment is a critically important case management function, so important that the success of case management practice is often determined by the case manager's ability to conduct an accurate and meaningful assessment (Roberts-DeGennaro 1987). A thorough and accurate assessment provides data that are essential in planning and individualizing the case management process. The case management plan and subsequent case management functions are carried out based on this assessment information. Thus, these assessment data determine the course of case management for the client (Weil 1985).

Case management assessment can be defined as a process in which the client and case manager collaboratively and systematically collect and analyze data that address these key questions:

1. What is the *current social functioning* of the client, including individual strengths and needs?
2. What *features of the client's social environment* facilitate or inhibit improved social functioning?
3. What *goals and objectives* for improved client functioning (in order of priority) should be identified and included in the case management plan?
4. What *resources and services* are necessary to accomplish these goals and objectives?
5. What procedure(s) and schedule will be utilized for *monitoring progress* toward these goals and objectives?
6. What *outcome criteria* will be used to evaluate results?

Data that answer these questions are used to formulate the written case management plan.

Client needs identified in the initial assessment will inevitably change over time. Thus, it is critical to view the assessment process as cyclical, i.e., ongoing and sensitive to the changing needs of clients as the case management process proceeds. In establishing a procedure and schedule for monitoring progress (question 6 above) it is important to consider that best results are obtained when progress is monitored directly and frequently by the case manager.

The case manager draws upon a variety of assessment procedures that match the particular situation of the client and the specific purpose for conducting the assessment. Data collection procedures might include interviews with the client and relevant others, the development of a social case history, direct observation of the client, and standardized norm-referenced or criterion-referenced assessment instruments. In addition to assessment conducted directly by the case manager, assessments conducted previously by other service providers might also be reviewed and considered in planning and decision-making.

In this definition the client is viewed not as a passive recipient of service but rather as an active participant in the assessment process. The underlying principles of social work—including respect for persons, individualization, a focus on strengths and coping skills, client self-determination—apply in case management assessment as in other aspects of practice as it has developed over time (McDermott 1975). Ruth Smalley, defining diagnosis in social work practice, wrote:

That diagnosis, or understanding of the phenomenon served, is most effective . . . which is developed, in part, in the course of giving the service, with the engagement and participation of the clientele served; which is recognized as being subject to continuous modification as the phenomenon changes; and which is put out by the worker for the clientele to use, as appropriate, in the course of the service. (1967, p. 134)

Writing of case management, Moxley stresses that "the case manager does not assume a unilateral role in the assessment process but shares responsibility, involvement, and decision-making with the client" (1989, p. 30). From a social work perspective, this aspect of assessment in case management cannot be emphasized strongly enough.

The Assessment Function in School Social Work Practice

Assessment is a critically important function in case management practice in schools. Data gathered in the school social work assessment shape the direction of the case management process for the individual student. Assessment data help further to clarify and define the referring problem, form the basis for developing clearly stated goals and objectives for behavior change, and assist in making decisions regarding appropriate intervention strategies and needed services. Data gathered in the assessment also provide a reference point that can be used to monitor progress or changes in the student's functioning, and to evaluate the effects of interventions and services that are provided. Ultimately, the assessment must provide information that will assist in improving the student's academic or behavioral performance in the educational setting.

The focus of the school social work assessment is on the social functioning of the student in the home, school, and community systems. Generally, the purpose of the assessment is to "identify legitimate difficulties, establish working relationships, and plan appropriate strategies for educational programming and support service provision." (National Council of State Consultants for School Social Work Services 1981, p. 51). More specifically, activities undertaken as a part of the assessment process are directed at problem definition and analysis, the establishment of working relationships with key school personnel, parents, and community service providers, and acquiring information that will assist in determining what resources and interventions are likely to be effective in solving the presenting problem and need to be included in the intervention plan. Thus, subsequent case management functions such as service planning and resource identification, linking clients to needed services, service implementation and coordination, monitoring, advocacy, and evaluation (Weil 1985) are based on these assessment data and activities.

The theoretical framework most often underlying the school social work assessment is an ecological-systems approach, which focuses on the interactions of the individual student in the school, family, and community systems. With an emphasis on the interactions of the student in these systems, consideration can be given to characteristics of the individual student, as well as characteristics of the systems that may be interacting to cause and maintain the problem in school. This manner of approaching assessment facilitates the consideration of "pupil-changing as well as environment-changing interventions" (Allen-Meares 1987, p. 25). This is particularly useful in school social work practice in that academic performance problems, or behavioral and social problems exhibited by students, may well be caused, or least exacerbated, by certain school policies and procedures, or by inappropriate expectations on the part of school personnel. In such cases intervention may need to be directed at these system variables rather than solely at the behavior of the individual student.

School social work assessment data will often be used to determine students' eligibility for certain programs or services such as special education. When this is the case, data describing the social functioning of students in interaction with school, family, and community systems are extremely useful not only in the determination of eligibility process but also in the development of IEPs in the event a student is determined to be educationally handicapped and in need of special education.

The ecological-systems approach to the school social work assessment provides data that go beyond the description of particular individual characteristics of the student such as intelligence, academic performance, and fine and gross motor skills, which traditionally has tended to be the assessment orientation of special education professionals. The assessment is not limited to describing and substantiating these individual characteristics but rather examines the student-system interactions. This type of assessment generates a broader base of information that can be used to establish goals and objectives for behavior change, to design intervention strategies, to monitor progress, and to evaluate intervention effects. This is the kind of information needed to facilitate the case management process.

Assessment Domains and Procedures

The school social work practitioner must carefully select assessment procedures that have congruity with the purpose for conducting the assessment and that yield data that will guide the case management process. This means the assessment data must provide specific and meaningful information regarding the current social functioning of the student as well as what resources and services are needed to address the referral concern and to resolve the presenting problem. This includes the consideration of resources and services in the school system such as school social work services, school counseling services, remedial academic programs, and truancy prevention programs, as well as services in the community, e.g., mental health services, family services, and public social services. The school social worker is the educational specialist most likely to be familiar with this array of community services and is in the most advantageous position to help students, school personnel, and families to access and utilize these services in an appropriate manner. Working to link the efforts of school, families, and the community, the school social worker can also assist in the coordination of the school program with these community services in a meaningful and productive way.

As Weil points out, "the format and emphasis of an assessment depend on the general needs of the target population, the specific needs of the client, and the client's present and possible functioning" (1985, p. 32). The school social work assessment is broad based and problem-solving in orientation. It embraces a number of domains and utilizes a variety of assessment procedures and instruments.

A comprehensive list of major domains that should be assessed for their relevance to the child's performance in the educational setting includes the following:

1. family structure and demographic characteristics;
2. major events or crises in the family's history such as divorce, death, unemployment, migration, and natural disasters;
3. the cultural and socioeconomic status of the family;
4. family functioning and coping mechanisms;
5. significant features surrounding the child's birth and developmental milestones;
6. crises in the health of the child such as surgery or hospitalizations;
7. the sequence and details of the child's educational experiences;
8. the child's current educational environment;
9. the child's adaptive behavior and social interactions; and
10. resources available to the family.

Depending on various factors in the child's profile, the school social work assessment might be differently structured, or might concentrate on one domain or another. For example, in the case of an infant or toddler with disabilities, an assessment of family functioning would be essential to the formulation of the IFSP required by P.L. 99-457. In the case of a mentally retarded child who is being assessed for special education, adaptive behavior would be a major component.

Traditionally, much of this information was obtained by a social worker engaging in an interview with the parent or parents. The data obtained were then compiled into a social history.

Over time various domains received particular focus and standardized instruments have been developed to acquire quantified measures of behavior, e.g., adaptive behavior. These can also be used to analyze and specify particular aspects of the child's behavior requiring intervention.

Ideally, both the social history interview and standardized instruments should be utilized in the school social work assessment. The social history interview is important because it affords an opportunity for the school social worker, on behalf of the school system, to build an alliance with the parents and to bridge the concerns of the parents and the policies of the school. Data obtained from the interview, observations of the child, a review of the child's school record, and the results of standardized testing should be combined. This provides a comprehensive psychosocial profile of child and family that will ensure nondiscriminatory interventions and will facilitate the child's learning and development with positive parental participation.

The following discussion will first review the social history as an overarching traditional approach to school social work assessment. It will then focus on specific domains of assessment such as adaptive behavior, social skills, and family assessment. Within each of these domains reference will be made to specific tools or instruments that can be used for measurement. Finally, a description will be provided of a comprehensive assessment instrument developed recently by school social workers in Iowa. The Assessing Successful Interactions Problem-Solving Assessment and Intervention System (Bryce, Piechowski, & Wilson 1990) focuses on social functioning in a broad sense, incorporating assessment of the behaviors of the child and the various systems with which the child interacts.

The Social History

The social history has long been a part of school social work practice. Mary Richmond, describing a pioneering survey conducted by the National Association of Visiting Teachers and Home and School Visitors stated that changes in a child's environment, in or out of school, are "based on study and information brought back to the teachers after a study of the individual child in his neighborhood environment and in that of his home" (1922, p. 199). It continues to be an important aspect of any psychosocial assessment of a child's needs in the school situation.

Some authorities prefer the term *social developmental study* to indicate that the assessment is more comprehensive than the review of past factors. It should be based on interviews with parents and/or other caregivers, teachers, and the student. The school social worker should also gather relevant data from the student's cumulative folder, in-school observations both inside and outside the classroom, out-of-school observation in the home and neighborhood, review of significant information from other agencies, and the administration of assessment instruments (Illinois State Board of Education 1983, p. 21).

Dane (1990, p. 63) emphasizes the importance of documenting behavior both at school and at home, particularly for learning-disabled children. Assessing a child's functioning at home provides the opportunity to view developmental variations in a cultural context. Indicators of social adjustment may be more observable in the home where the child feels more comfortable than in the tension-filled setting of the school, and "may provide clues to strengths that can be transferred to the classroom" (ibid.). The social history therefore protects the student's right to a bias-free assessment, vital both to placement in the least restrictive environment and appropriate educational programming.

The social assessment "can be utilized to evaluate a student for school social work services, or as one component in a multidisciplinary evaluation for potentially providing special education programming" (National Council of State Consultants for School Social Work Services 1981, p. 51). The practitioner should adapt the format of the social developmental study to meet the requirements of the local school district and the purposes of the document. Sections of the social history should include identifying data about the parents and family, such as age, education, and occupation; the presenting problem and reason for referral; developmental history; health history; school history and current educational environment; social-emotional functioning of the student; and relevant social and family data including socioeconomic and cultural factors. The final component should be a listing of recommendations for program and planning decisions based upon the preceding data and evaluation (National Association of Social Workers 1984, pp. 3–4; Byrne, Hare, et al. 1977, pp. 49–50; Florida Association of Visiting Teachers/School Social Workers 1988, p. 13).

The style and content of the social history in school social work is heavily influenced by its purpose and setting, namely, facilitating the educational progress of the child in the school. The school's "need to know" must be balanced with the family's "right to privacy" (Florida Association of Visiting Teachers/School Social Workers 1988, p. 15). For example, in a situation when a student appears suddenly depressed and not motivated to perform school work it may be helpful for school personnel to know that there are interpersonal stresses or conflicts occurring in the family. Respecting the family's right to privacy, however, might mean that school personnel need not know the specific details of these stressful situations in order to assist the student effectively. A parent's substance abuse problem or a sibling's serious illness are very private matters that families may want to keep confidential and that may not be critical to addressing the student's school performance difficulty. Consequently, the social history document should be succinct, and more factual than evaluative in style (Byrne, Hare, et al. 1977, p. 48). Any written diagnostic assessments or recommendations should relate to the educational performance or needs of the child.

Data relating to sensitive intrapersonal and intrafamilial dynamics, such as marital conflicts, child abuse, or substance abuse, should preferably be attributed to the person providing this information. For example, "Mrs. X reported that her husband had a serious drinking problem and often hit the children when he was intoxicated." Families' and adult students' rights of access to school records is protected by the Family Educational Rights and Privacy Act of 1974 (P.L. 93-380, known as the Buckley Amendment). According to this law any item in the records may be subject to a validity challenge. Style and content must be selected accordingly.

While the development of various standardized tests, checklists, and instruments has contributed to the measurement of psychosocial factors contributing to a child's development and educational performance, these should not be used as a substitute for the social history and particularly the interviews with parents/caretakers. The process of conducting the social history is as important as the product. Through the process, the school social worker is able to establish rapport with the parents, convey empathy regarding the parents' concerns and anxieties about their child, and answer the parents' questions about due process procedures for special education placement, disciplinary procedures, or alternative programs within the school. Because the social worker is a school employee, the good working relationship established in this way can be generalized to the school as a whole.

Conducting the social history interview involves a two-way process: the school social worker elicits information from the parents, but also provides the parents with an experience that is both therapeutic and empowering (Fiene & Taylor 1989, pp. 4–5). Therapeutic aspects of the interview might include the opportunity for parents to feel accepted and safe enough to express frustration and anger resulting from unsuccessful attempts to obtain what they would consider to be appropriate assistance for their child in school. The interview might also be therapeutic by providing parents an opportunity to deal with their own denial of problems their child may have been experiencing in school. The interview becomes an empowering experience when the school social worker provides information to parents regarding their legal rights or regarding services the school has available, or supports the parents in actively working with school personnel to develop a plan for addressing the presenting problem. This is particularly important for families who are "less comfortable negotiating assistance systems, whether because of language, class, or sociocultural differences" (Dane 1990, p. 79) or because of their own negative experiences with school, as is the case with some parents who performed poorly in school and did not receive appropriate assistance or who may have experienced social rejection as a result of inappropriate placement in a segregated special education program. It also positions the social worker to act as the child and family's "in-system advocate" at the time of assessment and throughout the educational case management process (ibid.); and it equips parents to acquire the skills to collaborate as partners with professionals and/or to become their own effective case manager (Garland, Woodruff, & Buck 1988, p. 6; Bishop 1990, p. 14; Dane 1990, p. 80).

Adaptive Behavior Assessment

Adaptive behavior is a domain that has received particular attention in assessment in school settings. Adaptive behavior assessment is an essential component of special education assessments, particularly those which are directed at identifying students who may be mentally handicapped and in need of a special education program or services. The American Association on Mental Deficiency (AAMD) has defined mental retardation as follows: "Mental retardation refers to significantly subaverage general intellectual functioning existing concurrently with deficits in adaptive behavior and manifested during the developmental period" (Grossman 1983, p. 1). This definition is very similar to most states' criteria for identifying students as mentally handicapped and in need of special education. It requires assessment of both general intellectual functioning and adaptive behavior because as Reschly has stated, "Adaptive behavior along with general intellectual functioning, defines the essential domains of mental retardation. Deficits in adaptive behavior must be documented in order to justify the classification of mental retardation" (1987, p. 7).

AAMD has defined adaptive behavior as "the effectiveness or degree with which the individual meets the standards of personal independence and social responsibility" (Grossman 1983, p. 1). While there is a great deal of similarity in the type of behaviors that are assessed, adaptive behavior assessment instruments vary considerably with respect to how items are conceptualized and organized into categories and subcategories. Based on extensive review of empirical studies, standardized adaptive behavior instruments, recent versions of the AAMD classification scheme, and various other considerations, Reschly (1987) has proposed that four broad adaptive behavior categories can be identified: (1) independent functioning, (2) social functioning, (3) functional academic competencies, and (4) vocational and occupational competencies. The categories of independent functioning and social functioning are typically the primary focus of adaptive behavior assessment conducted by school social workers. Adaptive behavior assessment in these categories yields data that are useful in planning the course of case management for students and families.

Allen-Meares and Lane (1983) and Reschly (1987) concur in identifying two primary purposes for conducting adaptive behavior assessments. The first purpose is the identification and placement of students who are eligible and in need of special education. Decisions regarding eligibility determination are made with reference to criteria that are established by individual states. Such decisions usually require the use of norm-referenced instruments that generate scaled scores that can be used to compare the student's functioning to that of a norm group and that can be used to compare the student's performance with age or grade expectancies. National or local norms are used as per state regulations, and state-determined program eligibility criteria define what constitutes a significant discrepancy in performance and expectancy.

The second purpose for conducting adaptive behavior assessment is "to provide information useful in the development of individualized educational intervention and programming" (Allen-Meares & Lane 1983, p. 298). After having established the student's eligibility for special education there is a need for more precise information regarding specifically what skills or competencies the student needs to be taught and what services need to be provided. Criterion-referenced instruments are typically used for this purpose. This type of instrument measures the student's performance in comparison to specific performance standards, resulting in data that can distinguish between those skills or competencies that have been acquired and those requiring instruction or intervention. Assessment data gathered for this purpose are most relevant to the case management process as they lead directly to decisions regarding what services are needed.

It is important to emphasize that no one instrument will accommodate both purposes for conducting the assessment. Best practice would support the use of multiple measures, and the use of other assessment methods and procedures such as direct observation and interviews, to address both purposes adequately. There are numerous norm-referenced and criterion-referenced adaptive behavior assessment instruments available, for example, the AAMD Adaptive Behavior Scale—School Edition (Lambert 1981), the Adaptive Behavior Inventory for Children (Mercer & Lewis 1978), the Vineland Adaptive Behavior Scales (Sparrow, Balla, & Cicchetti 1984), and the Comprehensive Test of Adaptive Behavior (Adams 1984).

The Keystone Adaptive Behavior Profile (Gallagher, Moore, & Wells 1983) is of particular relevance to school social work assessment as it devotes considerable attention to social functioning. The instrument is designed to assess adaptive behavior with respect to school, home, community, peers, and self and is organized into a school scale that is completed by the classroom teacher and a home scale that is completed by the student's parents. The school scale includes subtests that gather data regarding social skills, emotional development, self-care skills, etc. The home scale includes similar subtests but also gathers data pertaining to the student's functioning in the family and community. This broad-based assessment procedure is consistent with the school social work focus on the student's social functioning in school, family, and community systems and provides information regarding the needs of the student that can be used for planning in the case management process.

Social Skill Assessment

The concept of social skill is a specific component of the broader construct of adaptive behavior and the broad adaptive behavior domain of social functioning. Social skill can be defined as the specific, directly observable social behavior of students. Social skill assessment is an area of behavioral assessment in which school social workers are commonly involved. These assessment data are useful in identifying interventions and services that are needed to improve the social competence of students and that may need to be a component of the services included in the case management plan for some students. The decision to use either adaptive behavior assessment or social skill assessment, or both, is a professional judgment based on the particular circumstances of the student and the purpose of the assessment (eligibility or programming).

Assessment of social skills in school social work practice in addition to assessment of adaptive behavior is important because as Gresham points out, "Children and youth who are deficient in social skills and/or who are poorly accepted by peers have a high incidence of school maladjustment, school suspensions, expulsions, dropping out, delinquency, childhood psychopathology, and adult mental health difficulties" (1985, p. 181). For handicapped students effective social skills are especially needed to ensure successful efforts at mainstreaming.

Social skill assessment procedures typically conceptualize social skill deficits into two general types, *skill deficits* and *performance deficits*. Students with social skill deficits "either do not have the necessary skills in their repertoire to interact appropriately with peers or they do not know a critical step in the performance of a given social skill" (ibid., p. 183). Students with social performance deficits have the necessary social skills in their behavioral repertoire but do not perform them at acceptable levels.

Stephens (1978) has organized social skills into four major categories:

1. environmental behaviors such as dealing with emergencies or caring for the environment
2. interpersonal behaviors such as greeting others, coping with conflict, or accepting authority
3. self-related behaviors such as accepting consequences or expressing feelings
4. task-related behaviors such as asking and answering questions, following directions, and performing independent work.

This organizational scheme provides a structure for comprehensive social skill assessment and intervention in the school environment. The Social Behavior Assessment (Stephens 1981) is an assessment tool that formalizes this approach to social skill assessment and provides useful information to consider in the case management planning process by using teacher ratings to identify target social skills that may require intervention.

Another structured procedure used frequently in social skill assessment is the Structured Learning Skill Checklist developed by Goldstein, Sprafkin, Gershaw, and Klein (1980). The checklist requires teachers, or others, to rate the student's relative proficiency in performing various social skills. The ratings then can be used to target specific skills for training. This instrument also can be a useful tool in identifying what interventions, e.g., social skill training, might need to become a part of the case management plan for a particular student.

Family Assessment

As educators have come to acknowledge increasingly the impact of family factors on the child's educational performance, the assessment of the domain of family functioning has become increasingly refined. The school social worker has typically been that member of the educational team charged with the responsibility of assessing the impact of family factors on a child's academic performance, potential, and behavior in school. Given the family-school-community focus of school social work, details of the child's functioning in the family setting have always been part of the information collected by school social workers. Because of the value of direct observation of the child and family in their own environment, home visits have been one of the strategies employed by school social workers, a strategy that is receiving renewed emphasis as educators attempt to devise more effective means of serving at-risk students and establishing cooperative relationships with their parents.

Viewing assessment in a case management framework that emphasizes it as the basis for future planning places further importance on the process of family assessment.

The growing emphasis on parent participation in education also broadens the context within which assessment should occur. Further, as knowledge of family dynamics and family-focused interventions has expanded, more sophisticated techniques of family assessment have been developed. The assessment of the particular features of the family system that may be functional or dysfunctional provides important information to be utilized in identifying needed services and interventions. For the student who comes to the attention of school personnel because of behavior problems, assessment data regarding family functioning can be critical to developing a clear and comprehensive understanding of the child's experience outside school and specifically how his/her experience in the family system might be contributing to the development or maintenance of the problem in the school environment. Typically, the student who exhibits behavior problems at school is also presenting some kind of problematic behavior at home.

Data gathered in the family assessment can be used to identify services or interventions that need to be directed at the family and thus need to be a part of the case management plan. The school social worker may provide these services directly or may facilitate the family's referral to other community agencies, family service agencies, mental health centers, or other specialized agencies. Ensuring that families make effective connections with such agencies and receive the services they require is another aspect of the social worker's skill in case management. As part of the assessment process identifying the services needed by families is critical because as Brown and Hays point out, "Even the best of special programs at school can fail if the family is dysfunctional and in need of support" (1986, p. 72).

Recognition of the value of family assessment and the need for schools and other service providers to approach services to children with disabilities in a family-centered manner has been underscored by the requirement of IFSPs in Part H of P.L. 99-457, which was discussed earlier. Assessment in this context is directed at identifying child and family needs and family strengths related to meeting these needs. Needs and strengths of the infant or toddler and the family are used as a basis for developing the ISFP and for empowering families themselves to become more capable of identifying and accessing services and supports that are needed.

A number of assessment instruments have been developed for assessing family strengths and needs. Dunst, Trivette, and Deal (1988) have proposed the use of a family systems assessment and intervention model and have developed a number of structured assessment scales to aid in assessing various aspects of family strengths and needs. Instruments such as the Family Resource Scale, the Family Needs Scale, the Family Support Scale, and the Family Functioning Style Scale help to guide the assessment of families of infants and toddlers and to maintain a focus on the identification of needs and strengths that are to be referenced in the development of the IFSP, and that in turn become the focus of the case management process in early intervention programs. The use of such scales should, however, always be used as an adjunct to and not a substitute for the establishment of a client-centered, service-oriented relationship between social worker and parent.

The Assessing Successful Interactions
Problem-Solving Assessment and Intervention System

The ASI is a newly developed instrument, which is designed to measure the domain of social functioning in a broad sense. The ASI (Bryce, Piechowski, & Wilson 1990) is a norm-referenced instrument developed by school social workers that assesses the social functioning of students using an ecological-systems theory orientation. A unique feature of the instrument is the inclusion of an intervention planning module that assists the practitioner in using assessment data to formulate interventions. Consistent with the home-school-community focus of school social work practice, the instrument examines the social interactions of students in these systems. Thus, the scale is organized into four principle factors: (1) school, (2) home, (3) community, and (4) interpersonal skills.

The school factor includes ratings of the student's interactions with school personnel such as teachers, principals, tutors, and playground supervisors. The home factor examines the interactions of the student with parents, siblings, extended family members, and neighbors. The community factor examines the social participation of the student and the family in the community, the family's economic support, and transportation. The interpersonal skills factor includes ratings of the student's interactions with peers along with a checklist of critical social skills. Composite ratings of the student's functioning on each factor are summarized by use of a percentile rank profile, which enables the school social worker to compare the student's functioning to that of the norm group, which is composed of identified behaviorally disordered students. While this type of data may be useful in decisions related to determining program eligibility, the instrument's authors urge school social workers to supplement percentile rank scores with additional objective data and the use of professional judgment.

In addition to the four principal factors, four additional factors are included in the instrument: (1) academic performance, (2) self-help skills, (3) self concept, and (4) mood. Norms are not available for ratings of the student's functioning on these factors but valuable descriptive information is obtained regarding these areas of functioning.

The authors suggest that the ASI rating scale has a variety of uses such as identification of students who are eligible for special education programs, identification of students who are at risk, intervention planning, pre- and postmeasurement of intervention effects, and parent conferences and consultation. Given the scope of the data that are gathered in the process of rating the student's functioning on the eight principal factors, the instrument also provides valuable assessment data for developing a case management plan. The emphasis on assessment that examines the student's interactions across home, school, and community systems generates data that are helpful in identifying the student's current strengths and needs as well as identifying features of these systems that might be contributing to the presenting problem. These data also assist in identifying and prioritizing goals and objectives, identifying resources that may be needed, monitoring progress, and evaluating outcomes, all essential elements of a case management plan.

Conclusions

As is evident from the preceding discussion, a variety of assessment procedures are used by school social workers in assessing various domains. These procedures are selected carefully to match the purpose for conducting the assessment and to individualize the assessment process as much as possible. The broad-based nature of the school social work assessment generates a rich database that is used to develop the case management plan.

Weil, Karls, and Associates (1985) point out that each of the major case management functions requires specific knowledge and skills. In school social work practice, effective case management assessment requires clinical assessment skills including skills in matching assessment procedures to assessment purpose, skills in integrating assessment data from multiple sources, skills related to empowering families, and knowledge of community and school resources. School social workers and other professionals working with children with disabilities should always manifest sensitivity to the emotional reactions of parents who are constantly seeking to come to grips with the frustrations, disappointments, and grief over having a handicapped child, as well as awareness of the family's strengths and coping capacities. The high level of knowledge and skills required for carrying out the assessment function, as well as those required to carry out other case management functions, supports the need for a graduate level of professional training for school social workers whose practice includes case management.

Another issue typically raised in discussions concerning case management is who will assume the role of case manager? Although school social workers do not have exclusive claim to the role of case manager in educational settings, it can be argued that the theoretical perspective (ecological-systems) and the focus (home-school-community) of school social work practice places school social workers in an ideal position to provide case management services. Indeed much of what currently and historically has constituted school social work practice has included case management functions.

The unique contribution of school social work case management to education is to ensure outcomes that are attainable only through the efficient and effective coordination of multiple services in a manner that is person/client centered. There is a great need to document specific student outcomes when case management services are provided and to substantiate claims of improved effectiveness or efficiency of services through outcome data. This represents a major challenge for the future practice of school social work case management and needs to become a central focus of practice-based research efforts. This need will intensify as school social work programs expand and as school social work case management services are utilized in student at risk programs, special education programs, and infant and toddler programs.

Note

1.   While the term "handicapped children" was used in the original law, the 1990 reauthorization of the Education of the Handicapped Act (of which P.L. 94-142 is Part B) has amended this terminology to "children with disabilities." The reauthorized act, P.L. 101-476, has been renamed the Individuals with Disabilities Education Act (IDEA) of 1990.

References

Adams, G. 1984. *Comprehensive Test of Adaptive Behavior*. San Antonio, TX: Psychological Corporation.

Allen-Meares, P. 1987. "Behavioral Disorders: An Empirical Approach for Social Workers in Schools." In *School Social Work Interventions with Behaviorally Disordered Children: Practical Applications of Theory*, J.G. McCullagh, and C.A. McCullagh, editors. Des Moines: Iowa Department of Education.

Allen-Meares, P. and B.A. Lane. 1983. "Assessing the Adaptive Behavior of Children and Youths." *Social Work* 28(4):297–301.

Allen-Meares, P., R.O. Washington, and B.L. Welsh. 1986. *Social Work Services in Schools*. Engelwood Cliffs, NJ: Prentice-Hall.

Anonymous. n.d. *Stay in School Partnership*. New York: Fordham University.

Bailey, D.B. 1989. "Case Management in Early Intervention." *Journal of Early Intervention* 13(2):120–134.

Bishop, K. 1990. "P.L. 99-457: Analysis and Implications for Social Workers." In *School Social Work: Research and Practice Perspectives*, 2nd ed., R. Constable, editor. Chicago: Lyceum.

Brown, C. and S. Hays. 1986. "Family Assessments: A School Social Worker's Tool for Evaluation." *Iowa Journal of School Social Work* 1(1):69–75.

Bryce, M., P. Piechowski, and L. Wilson. 1990. *The Assessing Successful Interactions. Problem-Solving Assessment and Intervention System*. Des Moines: Iowa Department of Education.

Byrne, J., I. Hare, et al. 1977. "The Role of a Social History in Special Education Evaluation." In *School Social Work and P.L. 94-142: The Education for All Handicapped Children Act*, R.J. Anderson, M. Freeman, and R.L. Edwards, editors. Silver Spring, MD: National Association of Social Workers.

Clark, J. 1989. "Iowa Interagency Coordinating Council Training Committee: Social Work Roles and Competencies for Working with Infants and Toddlers." Unpublished manuscript.

Dane E. 1990. *Painful Passages: Working with Children with Learning Disabilities*. Silver Spring, MD: National Association of Social Workers.

Dunst, C., C. Trivette, and A. Deal. 1988. *Enabling and Empowering Families: Principles and Guidelines for Practice*. Cambridge, MA: Brookline Books.

Fiene, J.I. and P. Taylor. 1989. *"Serving Rural Families of Developmentally Disabled Children: A Case Management Model."* Paper presented at the National

Association of Social Workers Meeting of the Profession, San Francisco, CA: October.

Florida Association of Visiting Teachers/School Social Workers. 1988. *The Social History: Best Practice Guidelines for School Social Work Assessments*. Bradenton: Florida Association of Visiting Teachers/School Social Workers.

Gallagher, R., S. Moore, and P. Wells. 1983. *Keystone Adaptive Behavior Profile Manual*. Elkader, IA: Keystone Area Education Agency.

Garland, C., G. Woodruff, and D.M. Buck. June, 1988. *Division for Early Childhood White Paper: Case Management*. Reston, VA: Council For Exceptional Children.

Goldstein, A.P., R.P. Sprafkin, N.J. Gershaw, and P. Klein. 1980. *Skillstreaming the Adolescent: A Structured Approach to Teaching Prosocial Skills*. Champaign, IL: Research Press.

Gresham, F.M. 1985. "Best Practices in Social Skill Training." In *Best Practices in School Psychology*, J. Grimes and A. Thomas, editors. Kent, OH: National Association of School Psychologists.

Grossman, H.J., 1983. *Classification in Mental Retardation*. Washington, D.C.: American Association on Mental Deficiency.

Illinois State Board of Education. 1983. *Pupil Personnel Services Recommended Practices and Procedures Manual: School Social Work*. Springfield, IL: Illinois State Board of Educators.

Lambert, N. 1981. *Diagnostic and Technical Manual: AAMD Adaptive Behavior Scale*, school edition. Monterey, CA: Publishers Test Service.

McDermott, E.E., ed. 1975. *Self Determination in Social Work: A Collection of Essays*. London and Boston: Routledge and Kegan Paul.

Mercer, J. and J. Lewis. 1978. *Adaptive Behavior Inventory for Children*. San Antonio, TX: Psychological Corporation.

Moxley, D.P. 1989. *The Practice of Case Management*. Newbury Park, CA: Sage.

National Association of Social Workers. 1984. *The Social Assessment of the Educationally Handicapped Student*. Silver Spring, MD: NASW.

National Council of State Consultants for School Social Work Services. 1981. "The School Social Work Assessment." *School Social Work Journal* 6(1):51–54.

Reschly, D.J. 1987. *Measurement and Use of Adaptive Behavior*. Tallahassee: Florida Department of Education.

Richmond, M. 1922. *What Is Social Casework?* New York: Russell Sage Foundation.

Roberts-DeGennaro, M. 1987. "Developing Case Management as a Practice Model." *Social Casework* 8(3):466–70.

Smalley, R. 1967. *Theory for Social Work Practice*. New York and London: Columbia University Press.

Smith, A.J. and J.J. Stowitschek. 1989. *C-STARS Interprofessional Case Management Project Resource Directory*. Seattle: University of Washington Center for the Study and Teaching of At-Risk Students.

Sparrow, S.A., D.A. Balla, and D.V. Cicchetti. 1984. *Vineland Adaptive Behavior Scales*. Circle Pines, MN: American Guidance Service.

Stephens, T.M. 1978. *Social Skills in the Classroom*. Columbus, OH: Cedars Press.

————. 1981. *Technical Information: Social Behavior Assessment*. Columbus, OH: Cedars Press.

Weil, M. 1985. "Key Components in Providing Efficient and Effective Services." In *Case Management in Human Service Practice*, M. Weil, J.M. Karls, and Associates, editors. San Francisco: Jossey-Bass.

Weil, M., J.M. Karls, and Associates 1985. *Case Management in Human Service Practice*. San Francisco: Jossey-Bass.

Zipper, I.N., J.K. Nash, et al. 1990. *Proceedings of the Working Conference on Case Management and P.L. 99-457*. Draft. Chapel Hill: University of North Carolina, Frank Porter Graham Child Development Center.

Chapter 6

Care Planning for Children with HIV/AIDS: A Family Perspective

Marcy Kaplan

As human beings begin the second decade of what many have perceived to be the most significant public-health problems of this generation—the human immunodeficiency virus (HIV) and acquired immune deficiency syndrome (AIDS)—social workers must consider the multiple factors that delineate this epidemic from any other. Although HIV has most severely impacted homosexual men and individuals with histories of intravenous (IV) drug use, epidemiologists predict that the numbers of women, infants, children, and adolescents infected will increase dramatically in the 1990s. Thus, the child infected with HIV or diagnosed with AIDS must be seen in the context of the family unit.

Nationwide, 2315 children under 13 years of age have been diagnosed with AIDS (Centers for Disease Control [CDC], personal communication, May 1990). This number does not reflect the large number of children who do not meet the CDC criteria for an AIDS diagnosis. On a national level, the concern about increasing numbers in these groups has provided the following philosophy: It is critical to be proactive in developing services and securing funds rather than reactive to crisis after problems have occurred. In New York State, for example, few support services were in place to address the needs of the large numbers of hospitalized children who could not be discharged because they had no one able or willing to care for them. Other states and communities have learned from the experiences of cities such as New York that early planning for medical care, mental health services, and community services is essential.

Pediatric AIDS primarily affects the impoverished segment of the population. Affected families are poor members of minority groups who have weak support systems and poor coping capacities (Rogers et al. 1987). The majority of these families are unemployed, have relied heavily on public assistance programs for survival, and are likely to have utilized multiple social service agencies before a family member was diagnosed with HIV (Weiner & Septimus 1991). The full magnitude of this disease on individual families will become evident as the number of cases increases among women and children, and fewer are individuals with HIV and AIDS resulting from blood transfusions. Between one-third and one-half of infants born to seropositive mothers will develop AIDS (Oleske 1988).

In a rapidly growing number of adult cases, HIV must be viewed as synonymous with drug use. Pediatric HIV and AIDS is most commonly linked to IV drug use by the mother or her sexual partner (Seibert et al. 1989). HIV infection in the family system often exacerbates preexisting social disorganization. The family's limited capability to survive may shatter completely. The stigma associated with even the possibility of an HIV diagnosis places the family in a world clouded with secrecy and fear. Although in some situations the focus of care may be the child, all services must be family focused. An ultimate societal goal may be to consider HIV infection a "routine" chronic disease; however, this viewpoint currently is not held by society.

With the growing numbers of children and adolescents infected with AIDS, social workers are addressing concerns that have never been encountered before with other health issues. These concerns are empha-sized by a broad range of legal and ethical issues and their interplay with culturally diverse populations. Some of these issues involve confidential-ity, amnesty, and pregnancy of HIV-infected individuals (Lockhart & Wodarsky 1989). Social workers have been considered "pioneers" in the HIV/AIDS health crisis as planners, educators, and therapists. Social workers have initiated efforts to promote and advocate for outreach activities to IV drug users and to promote safer sex for homosexual and bisexual men. In many instances, social workers have served as unpaid volunteers while other health care professionals were fearful of casual transmission (Shernoff 1990).

The growing numbers of individuals infected with HIV and AIDS clearly will demand a broad range of services. A continuum of care must be established to meet the social, health care, and economic needs of all these individuals. Many health care professionals, including social workers, believe strongly that resources developed for persons with HIV should focus on skilled nursing and other care options to avoid excessive hospitalizations. However, children with HIV and their par-ents need resources that will enable them to live with HIV and AIDS in the context of their own families.

The National Association of Social Workers (NASW) has recognized case management as the preferred model of care planning and coordination for individuals infected with AIDS and as encompassing both resource management and a variety of psychosocial treatment modalities (NASW 1987). Ideally, case management should provide a comprehensive coordinated approach to care beginning at the time of intake into a program until the time services are no longer needed, which occurs most often upon the death of a patient. Although endorsed originally for homosexual men and other adults diagnosed with HIV, the model can be applied to the family system, with certain modifications. Case management for chronically ill adults and children requires a broad range of services encompassing financial, health care, housing, and emotional support needs. Any health care system addressing the specialized medical, developmental, and psychosocial needs of families must be comprehensive and integrated (Secretary's Work Group 1988).

An AIDS Health Care Demonstration Project

The need for a comprehensive system of care for children with HIV and their families has been recognized also by legislators. In spring 1988, the U.S. Congress appropriated four million dollars through P.L. 100-202 to be administered under the Maternal and Child Health Bureau (MCHB) of the Health and Human Resource Service Administration. The funding has been allocated in the form of pediatric AIDS health care demonstration projects to 18 regions nationally. The Office of Maternal and Child Health is a Title V program that provides health care for chronically ill children. The rationale for the demonstration projects is to broaden the service delivery for patients and families in outpatient and community-based settings and to reduce hospitalizations. Collaboration between the public, private, and voluntary sectors and grass roots community organizations is stressed. The intention of demonstration projects is to provide new and innovative approaches in the provision of services for children with HIV, approaches that can be duplicated or adapted for use in other areas of the United States.

One MCHB pediatric AIDS health care demonstration project in Los Angeles County, California, was begun in August 1988 under the auspices of California Children Services (CCS), a state-supported county-administered program that provides services for children and adolescents ages birth to 21 years with chronic and catastrophic conditions, including those diagnosed with HIV and AIDS. At the time the idea for the project was conceptualized by the medical director (Dale C. Garell, M.D.) of the Los Angeles County CCS, there were 28 reported cases of pediatric AIDS in the county, 839 nationally (telephone communication, USCDC, February 1988), and an estimated 175 others between the ages of birth and 13 years being treated for HIV in Los Angeles County. An infrastructure of services to care for children and families needed to be established before an expected four- to sixfold increase in the number of infants and children with HIV over the next five years. Before the development of the proposal resulting in the Los Angeles County demonstration project and what currently is referred to as the Los Angeles Pediatric AIDS Network (LAPAN), children diagnosed with HIV infection received medical treatment at seven hospitals in Los Angeles County, including three public county hospitals, one public state institution, and three private, nonprofit institutions. In addition, a small number of community-based organizations providing other support services and a pediatric/perinatal task force (under the auspices of the Department of Health Services) had brought local health care providers together to discuss current needs and begin the development of a long-range plan.

However, within the demonstration project, specialized services that were developed through a case management system for mothers, infants, children, and adolescents utilize a family-centered community-based coordinated approach. The demonstration project includes the following components:

- *case management* to provide an individualized family service plan (IFSP) and to track demographic information encompassing the entire spectrum of needs for the family, using an automated case management system (ACMS)
- *service coordination* to share services between maternal and pediatric centers and community-based agencies
- *community education* to determine education and training needs of service providers in Los Angeles County
- *a resource bank* created and regularly updated for community-based services.

The demonstration project encompasses a wide range of goals and objectives. Some components of the project deal specifically with case management and care planning for children with HIV infection and their families. Other project activities support the case management aspects of the project.

To carry out the objectives of the demonstration project, it is necessary to provide community-based, family-centered, and multidisciplinary services, services that were recommended at the 1987 Surgeon General's Workshop and again stressed at the follow-up workshop in 1989 (U.S. Department of Health & Human Services 1987, 1989). Before the beginning of LAPAN, only one and one-half full-time equivalent social work positions specifically dedicated to providing services to children with HIV infection existed in Los Angeles County. Although children received medical treatment at five centers, only two centers had a complete interdisciplinary team in place, including a physician, nurse, and social worker. The development of the LAPAN project served as a vehicle to provide a clinical social worker with a master of social work degree to each treatment center. The responsibilities of the social worker are to provide therapeutic intervention and case management to the families receiving HIV-related treatment at the center and to track each case on the ACMS.

Headquarters for the project and ACMS system are at Childrens Hospital Los Angeles, which is centrally located among all of the pediatric HIV treatment centers. Social work staff, employed by the project, are housed at each hospital site. Social work case managers are designated to each treatment center on a full-time, part-time, or consultant basis if the center meets the specific criteria for number of patients established in the initial year of the project. These include formulation of an interdisciplinary team, establishment of California Children Services Immunology–Infectious Disease Center, appropriate office space and telephone, and patients consolidated on a scheduled clinic day(s). Each treatment center must have certain program elements in place before the social work case manager is placed. Difficulty completing case management functions or an unsatisfactory work experience may result if the hospital HIV and AIDS program has not yet established an interdisciplinary team to work with families.

Care Planning for Children with HIV

Case management for families with HIV infection necessitates multisystem care planning. Social work intervention has always been an important component of care for children with special medical and developmental needs. The focus of care planning for a child diagnosed with HIV is on the knowledge that an entire family may be at risk for the disease. The social work role in helping families affected by the AIDS crisis is broad and complex. Although social workers have been providing services to AIDS patients for the past ten years, the importance of case management, program development, policymaking, and community outreach has only been recognized slowly (Wiener & Siegel 1990).

Social work philosophy has stressed the involvement and empowerment of the client in all decision-making pertaining to the client's care. Although critically important, such involvement and empowerment can be very difficult when dealing with several individuals in one family who may be infected. The majority of families diagnosed with HIV infection functioned marginally before the diagnosis, barely able to manage as a result of poverty, isolation, and hopelessness, which are further complicated by racial and cultural factors. Involving the client in his or her care can seem an insurmountable task for the case manager, but its importance cannot be overstated.

Of the hospital-based programs that compose LAPAN, the initial visit to the treatment center is critical to the beginning stage of care planning. The child at risk for HIV infection may have been referred to a treatment center for evaluation for several reasons: an HIV or AIDS diagnosis in one or both parents, blood transfusions before 1985, symptoms of HIV disease, parental history (most commonly drug use or multiple sexual partners), or sexual abuse. A psychosocial assessment and early intervention by the team social worker are critical components to family care planning. Families may need education to clarify common misinformation. Conveying hope to families early in care planning is necessary. With support provided early on in the diagnostic process, a family will be better able to move from the crisis of diagnosis to acceptance and realistic expectations.

Through the psychosocial assessment, the social work case manager identifies each family's strengths and weaknesses and assesses their coping capacity. The database generated provides information necessary to develop a complete treatment plan for the child. Assessing the psychological capabilities of parents and other caretakers often will dictate the medical regime prescribed for the child. Although the entire psychosocial assessment is important, social work case managers should pay particular attention to available financial support and medical insurance, health status of other family members, religious and cultural factors that may affect treatment decisions, and who is aware of the HIV diagnosis.

Following the psychosocial assessment, the IFSP is created. The IFSP, generated from the Education of the Handicapped Act of 1986, calls for a "(1) multidisciplinary assessment of unique needs and the services appropriate to meet the needs and (2) a written IFSP developed by the interdisciplinary team, involving the parent or guardian" (National Maternal and Child Health Resource Center 1987). The IFSP should address needs perceived by the family to be most important, including concrete services such as finances and housing. Often the social worker needs to emphasize the family's own priorities to the other health care team members, who may be focused on their own roles. LAPAN staff have reported particular difficulty in their attempts to emphasize to their colleagues that concrete needs are most important for many families. Before moving on to illness-related issues, these concrete needs must be met. These areas must be addressed when the child is being considered for enrollment in a medical research protocol. Because of the complex nature of HIV issues, the IFSP may need to be developed over several visits.

Families impacted by HIV or AIDS frequently express many illness-related concerns. These concerns often are dealt with in crisis and may focus on problems related to the significance of positive HIV test results, the fear that multiple family members may be ill, and the fear that a parent may die, leaving no one to care for the child. Following the diagnosis of one or more family members, parents are faced with making immediate caretaking decisions for both their infected and noninfected children. LAPAN social work staff and other social workers who have worked with parents of children diagnosed with HIV have found it difficult to address delicate topics pertaining to a parent's mortality. Parents usually are reluctant to participate actively in planning for the care of their children in anticipation of their own deteriorating health.

Although the direct impact of HIV on a family is of concern, the majority of issues usually reflect the family's dysfunctional life-style. Accordingly, it becomes the role of the social work case manager to organize these issues for possible intervention, eliciting input from both the family and interdisciplinary team. Generally, families at risk for HIV infection have used the health care system in a sporadic manner. Returning to the same treatment center on a regular basis to attend to their child's medical care is often a new concept. Particularly with children of indeterminate status, when a child appears to be healthy, parents and other caretakers may not understand the importance of ongoing evaluation and monitoring.

Parents also may deny that a life-threatening disease exists. Thus, planning is essential for child custody arrangements and ongoing medical treatment (Chachkes 1987). Often these topics are not discussed until the parents become symptomatic or display neuropsychiatric manifestations. Finding an alternative caretaker for a child (extended family or foster care) is particularly difficult when a child is diagnosed with an HIV-related illness. Therefore, this component of care planning should begin early. Parental involvement in child custody arrangements is especially important and must be initiated when parents are capable of decision-making. The child welfare system should be integrated into care planning early if extended-family members are unavailable.

In addition, the social work case manager must be able to establish an ongoing stable therapeutic relationship with family members to increase the likelihood that compliance with medical appointments will be ensured. During the initial visits to the treatment center, the ongoing IFSP can be used as a tool to involve the family in care planning.

An HIV diagnosis in the family also may result in the discovery of a partner's sexual practices or intravenous drug use. Care planning for the infant or child may be further complicated by the need to balance the parent's responsibility to follow through with his or her child's and his or her own medical care, and the parent's need to begin an alcohol or drug treatment program. Feelings of guilt and anger are commonly experienced by parents following their child's HIV diagnosis, regardless of the mode of transmission. Guilt may be particularly stressful for a mother who has engaged in high-risk behavior and transmitted the virus to her child. Anger may be directed toward the partner suspected of transmitting HIV or toward the hospital where their child received infected blood products through transfusion. These feelings may resurface at different times during the illness, particularly when the child is doing poorly and the parent feels particularly vulnerable and helpless. Clearly, families functioning with great difficulty before an HIV diagnosis are destined to have their lives further ravaged by the consequences of this new tragedy. A key role for the case manager is to assist the family in prioritizing these important tasks.

All aspects of care planning for families with HIV and AIDS must incorporate a racially, religiously, and culturally sensitive approach. Following the diagnosis of one child with HIV infection, it is not uncommon for a parent to face a decision regarding a current pregnancy. Consideration of a termination of pregnancy has significant cultural implications. The social work case manager and other medical professionals may be called upon to assist a family with these issues as well as to incorporate the family's own individual concerns without personal bias. In short, it is important that social workers empower families to make their own choices (Seibert et al. 1989). The social worker should outline options available, provide counseling as warranted, and provide the family with the facts necessary to make their own decisions. The family's only means of control of this devastating situation may be participation in decision-making and care planning (Lewert 1988).

Of paramount importance in care planning for HIV families is their desire to keep the diagnosis confidential. The overwhelming stress and energy that many parents invest in keeping the diagnosis a secret can be counterproductive and may result in disruption of daily living. The majority of families, understandably, are fearful of stigma and ostracism from extended-family members and friends who are told of the diagnosis. This fear can compound an already stressful situation and result in further isolation and depression for the family. At times, it is only when the parents become ill and the family is particularly vulnerable that the family risks rejection by disclosing the diagnosis (Wiener & Septimus 1991). Throughout the course of HIV infection, case managers should counsel family members to anticipate the reaction of others such as friends, extended-family members, and community agencies. This can be a critical component of care planning and may dictate how appropriate support services are provided.

LAPAN social work staff have attempted to support parents in maintaining their day-to-day activities through discussions with parents during the child's clinic appointments. Parents are encouraged to continue family outings and other activities that took place before the diagnosis. As community organizations become involved in providing respite care and homemaker services, social work case managers should be reminded that a parent or other family member may come to expect these services indefinitely.

Over the past several years, a source of contention in terms of care planning has been school attendance for children with HIV. However, this issue seems to have been addressed—more than 86 percent of public school districts have developed their own policies regarding HIV-infected pupils (National Maternal and Child Health Resource Center 1990). The primary concern for these children is the potential for increased susceptibility to infection as a result of immune system deterioration. Care planning must ensure that every child is provided with an education suited to his or her individual needs and must consider the family choice to disclose or withhold HIV status. Families who reveal their children's diagnosis may require a great deal of support to get them through the bureaucratic process and the added stress associated with the risk of public disclosure and to help them educate administrators, teachers, and students about HIV. As a child's medical condition deteriorates, special education classes and home tutoring may be considered appropriate options, particularly when a child has symptoms stemming from HIV encephalopathy. Care planning must allow for changes in the child's or other family member's medical condition.

Some parents have found support groups to be a safe place to discuss the many complex and sensitive issues involved in living with a child infected with HIV. Although support groups may have had questionable success with this population, they may prove to be an effective treatment modality for some parents and family members.

Involvement of the Child in Care Planning

The development of new treatments will permit HIV-infected children to live longer. This means that the interdisciplinary health care team will need to involve children in their own care planning as much as possible. Most parents are fearful of informing their child of the HIV diagnosis.

Parents base their decision on a variety of factors, including the effect that disclosure might have on siblings, concerns about the loss of employment or housing, and worries that the child will not be able to keep this information confidential (Olson et al. 1989). Other factors include parental fear that the child will be unable to cope, curiosity about how the child contracted the disease, and belief that the child is "better off" not knowing the name of the diagnosis (Kaplan 1990).

The social work case manager ensures that the child's emotional and developmental needs are incorporated into care planning. For anyone, the unknown is always more frightening than reality, and a child's imagination is often worse than the truth in terms of HIV disease. Honest answers appropriate to the child's age and level of understanding will help avoid future problems. The case manager should continually reassess the child's developmental status to determine the child's capability to participate in his or her own care. Although some parents prefer to tell the child that he or she has a more socially acceptable medical condition, such as leukemia or a blood disorder, this approach further perpetuates a cycle of half-truths and may be a cause of mistrust.

Discussion with parents about the child's knowledge of his or her own HIV status must begin early in the diagnostic process to pave the way for ongoing communication as the child grows older. For example, parents should be told that although it is inappropriate to discuss the specifics of the virus with a three-year-old child, it is important to begin open discussions with the child about his or her general medical condition.

For most parents of school-aged children (ages six to nine) key concerns are terms such as *HIV*, *AIDS*, *AZT* (azidothymidine), or *immune deficiency*. Many parents will allow the medical team to discuss the actual specifics of the virus, omitting the name of the disease. For example, the following case illustrates an explanation provided by a mother to her seven-year-old child who has begun to question the reason for her clinic visits.

> *Tanisha*: Why do I have to get stuck with needles when I go to the hospital?
> *Mother*: I know you wonder why you have to go to the hospital and have your blood drawn all the time. You have your blood drawn because there is something wrong with your blood that makes it hard for your body to fight off certain kinds of sickness like flues, chicken pox, or measles.
> *Tanisha*: Why do I have to take all those medicines?
> *Mother*: The virus makes it easier for you to catch certain infections, so these medicines will help you stay healthy.

Tanisha's mother may or may not choose to integrate the term *HIV* or *AIDS* into the conversation. However, using specific terms is not critical for an honest, age-appropriate explanation of HIV for a school-aged child. The social work case manager may guide the family members through this process and help them convey adequate, honest, and age-appropriate information to their child. Prolonged secrecy increases the likelihood that a child will discover his or her diagnosis in some other way. Clearly, if Tanisha is told the name of her illness at age nine, it will be less frightening for her if she has been receiving truthful information from her parents and health care providers.

Involvement of Siblings in Care Planning

Case managers and other allied health professionals often neglect to include the siblings of a chronically ill child in care planning. Thus they are often the "forgotten group" (Brett 1988). In addition, many families choose not to share information about the illness of a child or other family members with all of the siblings. Thus, the uninformed sibling may harbor feelings of hostility, resentment, and jealousy. Although both the infected child and siblings may suspect HIV or AIDS, they may sense that this topic is taboo and not open for discussion.

Siblings also may resent the sick child because of the special attention he or she receives, particularly from parents. Sibling stress may result in excessive school problems, acting-out behavior, and potentially severe psychopathology. Individual and family counseling may be warranted as part of the care plan to deal with these problems early.

Involvement of Community Organization in Care Planning

As additional care options become available for children and as HIV-related diseases become viewed as routine chronic medical problems, community-based organizations will be needed to provide assorted services. However, families overwhelmed by the ramifications of an HIV diagnosis may fail to act on referrals. The case manager needs to evaluate a family's ability to follow through on service referrals, particularly if the referrals are in different geographic locations. Children with AIDS and their families need multiple services, including special education, protective services, public assistance, and those services provided by community-based agencies. Care planning, therefore, must include outreach to these services to determine their capability and willingness to provide services to children diagnosed with HIV. Generally, though, it is easier for a case manager to begin a relationship with a new family by helping them meet concrete needs such as applying for Medicaid or locating a food bank. The family may perceive such assistance to be less intrusive than an immediate referral for mental health services. Regardless, care planning should be updated regularly to ensure that the family's physical and emotional needs are addressed.

It has been argued that case management should be community-based rather than hospital-based. Although community-based agencies that provide adult AIDS services can meet some needs of the pediatric population, families often feel most comfortable using services that historically have been geared toward the needs of chronically ill children and their families (Kaplan 1990). Families do not always follow through when referred to community-based organizations. In addition, in many areas of the country, parents have expressed a much higher comfort level with the health care team than with community-based service providers. Thus hospital-based networks such as LAPAN were developed to provide services to HIV patients and their families. Currently, two hospitals in LAPAN provide medical care to infants, children, and mothers in the same setting. Although this is considered by many to be a preferred model of care, it is unrealistic that all treatment centers will be able to adopt this model. Therefore, developing ties with adult AIDS treatment centers to provide collaborative case management is important and will be a focus of LAPAN in the final year of the project ending in July 1991.

In addition to the services provided by the two hospitals in LAPAN, LAPAN provides a consortium of services to meet the many complex needs of children with HIV and their families. Since the beginning of the project in August 1988, direct-service providers in both hospital and community settings have met monthly to discuss hands-on issues in working with HIV patients and to plan for future needs. A community-wide needs assessment was performed collaboratively with LAPAN, the United Way, and the Los Angeles County AIDS Program Office. LAPAN headquarters is viewed as a clearinghouse for information and referral for women, children, and adolescents at risk for the disease in Los Angeles County. Extensive program coordination exists between the National Institutes of Health, National Institute of Allergy & Infectious Diseases clinical trials group, and the CDC-funded Pediatric AIDS Surveillance Study. All of the grants and projects work collaboratively with LAPAN-hospital-based programs.

Meeting the HIV/AIDS Challenge

Children with HIV and their families require multisystem care planning and case management. Although HIV infection encompasses many needs typical of families with other special children, needs exist that are specific to the HIV family. Because of the social stigma and ostracism that may result when HIV status is revealed, and the possibility of parents becoming critically ill, the approaches in care planning must be modified. A general system of care for HIV families must be developed before the numbers of HIV-infected women and children reach the projections of the mid-1990s. The philosophy of family-centered care recognizes the importance of the family unit in the child's life. The integration of social work skills and values is an essential component of the IFSP. The social work case manager must involve the family unit in its own care planning. Although reducing obstacles for clients and avoiding duplications and gaps in services are important objectives, the family should be as involved in the care planning as possible, with the social worker acting primarily as an advocate. Unfortunately, the majority of families impacted by HIV are dysfunctional and do not take an active role in this process. Therefore, thorough psychosocial assessment and intervention are critical in maximizing a family's ability to help itself.

Although placement of a child in a foster home or transitional care facility is sometimes warranted, children should remain with their parents whenever possible. Therefore, services must be developed to permit families to remain intact. Some social workers have perceived the case management role as professionally ungratifying because the focus is often on concrete needs rather than therapeutic intervention. This focus, however, provides the case manager with an essential framework for building therapeutic relationships with families that can be used to address emotionally painful issues and provide needed emotional support. Case management is of critical importance in the overall management of HIV-infected children and their families, and it must be provided by professionals who understand and can help with both concrete and emotional needs.

Social work involvement with AIDS patients will grow in importance as the AIDS epidemic continues. Education and training in graduate schools must prepare social work students to provide intervention to these clients. As the "second wave" of AIDS strikes children and their families in the 1990s, social workers must be willing to learn the basic facts about HIV disease and must be prepared to meet the challenges of HIV and AIDS on individual, community, and policy levels.

References

Brett, K.M. 1988. "Sibling Response to Chronic Childhood Disorders: Research Perspectives and Practice Implications." *Issues in Contemporary Pediatric Nursing* 11:43–53.

Chachkes, E. 1987. "Women and Children with AIDS." Pp. 51–64 in *Responding to AIDS: Psychosocial initiatives,* C.G. Leukfield and M. Fibres M., editors. Silver Spring, MD: National Association of Social Workers.

Kaplan, M.E. 1990. "Psychosocial Issues of Children and Families with HIV/AIDS." Pp. 139–49 in *Productive Living Strategies for People with AIDS,* Binghamton, NY: Haworth Press.

Lewert, G. 1988. "Children and AIDS." *Journal of Contemporary Social Work,* 348–51.

Lockhart, L.L. and J.S. Wodarski. 1989. "Facing the Unknown: Children and Adolescents with AIDS." *Social Work* 34:215–21.

NASW. 1987. *Social Work Policy Statement.* Silver Spring, MD: National Association of Social Workers.

National Maternal and Child Health Resource Center. 1987. *Case Management for Mothers and Children.* Iowa City: University of Iowa.

———. *HIV Positive Children in School: Legal Issues.* Iowa City, IA: University of Iowa, 1990.

Oleske, J. 1988. "Clinical Lessons from the New Jersey Experience." Pp. 232–35 in *AIDS in Children, Adolescents and Heterosexual Adults,* R. Schinazi and A.J. Nahmias, editors. New York: Elsevier.

Olson, R.A., H.C. Huszti, P.J. Mason, and J.M. Seibert. 1989. "Pediatric AIDS/HIV Infection: An Emerging Challenge to Pediatric Psychology." *Journal of Pediatric Psychology* 14(1):1–21.

Rogers, M.P., P.A. Thomas, E.T. Starcher, M.C. Noa, T.J. Bush, and H.W. Jaffe. 1987. "Acquired Immune Deficiency in Children: Report of the Centers for Disease Control National Surveillance, 1982–1985." *Pediatrics* 79:1008–14.

Secretary's Work Group. 1988. "Pediatric HIV Infection and Disease." In *Core Issues and Recommendations,* Vol. 27. Washington, D.C.: Department of Health and Human Services, U.S. Government Printing Office.

Seibert, J.M., A. Garcia, M. Kaplan, and A. Septimus. 1989. "Three Model Pediatric AIDS Programs: Meeting the Needs of Children, Families, and Communities." Pp. 25–60 in *Children, Adolescents and AIDS,* J.M. Seibert and R.A. Olson, editors. Omaha: University of Nebraska Press.

Shernoff, M. 1990. "Why Every Social Worker Should Be Challenged by AIDS." *Social Work* 35:5–8.

U.S. Department of Health and Human Services, Public Health Service. 1987. *Surgeon General's Workshop Proceedings.* Washington, D.C.: U.S. Government Printing Office.

———. 1989. *Surgeon General's Follow-up Workshop Proceedings.* Washington, D.C.: USGPO.

Wiener, L. and A. Septimus. 1991. "Psychosocial Considerations and Support for the Child and Family." Pp. 577–94 in *Pediatric AIDS: The Challenge of HIV Infection in Infants, Children, and Adolescents,* P.A. Pizzo and C. Wilfert, editors. Baltimore, MD: Williams & Wilkins.

Wiener, L.S. and K. Siegel. 1990. "Social Workers Comment on Providing Services to AIDS Patients." *Social Work* 35:18–25.

Chapter 7

Linking the Developmentally Disabled Client to Needed Resources: Adult Protective Services Case Management

Kenneth Kaplan

As case manager for the developmentally disabled adult, a particularly needy segment of the population, the adult protective services (APS) worker in a public social services agency performs several roles. For example, the APS worker acts as investigator, advocate, researcher, protector, and placement coordinator on behalf of the client. An important function of the case manager involves linking the client to needed community resources. This function, as it applies to work with developmentally disabled adults in Maryland, is explored in this chapter.

Developmentally Disabled Population in Maryland

A *developmentally disabled* individual is a person having "one of a group of disabilities, which occurs in childhood, and relates directly to abnormal brain structure, maturation, and functioning, and leads to abnormal development of the child" (O'Hara 1980, p. 3). These disabilities include cerebral palsy, mental retardation, epilepsy, autism, learning disabilities, and other neurological conditions that interfere with normal childhood development.

Although these conditions generally mean that adults who are developmentally disabled and suffering from suspected abuse, neglect, self-neglect, or exploitation fall under the purview of APS in Maryland, this is not always the case. Not all developmentally disabled adults can be considered vulnerable adults, defined by Maryland law as those adults "who lack the physical or mental capacity to provide for the adult's daily needs" (Sec. 14-101(Q) Family Law Article, 1985 Maryland Code). Many developmentally disabled adults, such as those considered "mildly retarded," are able to perform their activities of daily living. Moreover, according to the Maryland Health General Law (Sec. 7-1005(B), 1982), cases of alleged abuse, neglect, exploitation, or self-neglect occurring in a state-licensed facility (such as a licensed domiciliary home) in which any developmentally disabled adult resides will be investigated and managed by staff from the state Developmental Disabilities Administration and the local police if appropriate. Thus, for APS workers to intervene on behalf of a developmentally disabled adult in Maryland, that adult must be considered "vulnerable" and must reside in a facility not licensed by the state, such as the adult's own home in the community.

Mission of Adult Protective Services in Maryland

The Adult Services Program of the Maryland Department of Human Resources, Social Services Administration, is responsible for investigating reports of alleged abuse, neglect, exploitation, or self-neglect of vulnerable adults aged 18 years or older, who reside in a non-state-licensed facility. Such reports are referred to staff of local departments of social services and are investigated by a staff social worker. If the investigation results confirm a particular report, then the social worker develops a service plan to minimize the client's risks and endangerment. The plan includes "an assessment of the kind of services needed, a description of the services to be provided by the local department of social services or other sources, the goal of the services, and the estimated time for achievement of the goal" (secs. 01–14 of the Maryland Code, 1980).

The services provided by the local department of social services or other sources in the community typically include health services, mental health counseling, home care and chore services, transportation, emergency food and shelter, and legal assistance, as well as other services, depending on their availability in a particular community. These services may be used alone or may be combined. It is these services that are vital to APS workers in linking their clients to the resources necessary to eliminate risk and improve well-being. To negotiate the linking function successfully, these services must be in place and must be immediately available to the APS worker.

Linking the Developmentally Disabled Adult
to Community Resources

Community resources in Anne Arundel County, Maryland, as in other jurisdictions, are vital to the APS case manager in providing self-enhancement and eliminating risk to the developmentally disabled client. Typically, community resources needed by these and other APS clients are many and varied. The case manager's primary linking function within the roles of investigating and responding to suspected abuse, neglect, self-neglect, or exploitation is to use community resources to eliminate risk to the client and to prevent a recurrence of the crisis situation. To this end, the APS worker must know as much as possible about every community resource that may assist the client. For example, because an emergency report of abuse or neglect of a developmentally disabled adult may occur at any time, the APS worker must know beforehand the function of every potential resource, the hours of availability of that resource, the location of the resource, and the extent to which the resource can help, as well as any information about the resource that may aid the client. The APS worker, then, must keep a current and easily accessible file of community resource information.

Often, APS workers or their agencies must create their own resources for their clients because of a scarcity or lack of community resources. For example, to meet emergency needs, APS workers in Anne Arundel County have developed agency food closets and have recruited adult foster home providers who are trained to care for a population such as the developmentally disabled and who can offer emergency beds. Other important resources often used include food pantries or home-delivered meals, temporary group shelters, medical services, adult day-care centers, and job training, typically provided by the local department of vocational rehabilitation. With developmentally disabled adults, as with other APS clients, one or a combination of these resources is called on by the APS worker to assist the client.

In addition to knowledge and creation of resources, APS workers often advocate for new resources for all of their clients. In a public agency, such advocacy follows the chain of command, with supervisors informing top administration of the need and assisting administrators in the exploration and development of needed resources.

Related to these other linking skills is an important skill APS workers must possess: the ability to determine when clients are no longer in need of the resource to which they are linked. The APS case manager must determine a client's strengths and weaknesses and carefully monitor the use of resources to which the client has been linked. Remembering the goal of enabling the client to obtain maximum self-sufficiency, the case manager must work with the client to use a resource as little as possible. This process of growth for the client often involves "weaning" the client from use of the resource, with the case manager and client determining a set time for reduction in or elimination of resource use. At the end of the set time, the APS worker and client decide together whether the client has progressed to the point where he or she can reduce the use of the resource, or eliminate its use entirely.

Consider the developmentally disabled or other APS client who lives alone and is in need of an in-home aide, provided by the department of social services. Typically, the aide will assist and instruct the client in cleaning, shopping, and money management, with the goal of enabling the client to obtain the skills to perform these tasks alone or with as little assistance as possible. In this situation, the APS worker, with the client and the aide, will determine a realistic period for this growth to occur and will monitor the client's progress during that time. At the end of the period, the APS worker will measure the client's growth and both the client and APS worker will decide to discontinue use of the aide or extend use of the aide for another set period. In many cases, the client is able to accomplish one goal during the period and is ready, with the assistance of the aide, to move on to another goal. For instance, in a six-month period the client may have achieved his or her "maximum" in ability to clean the home and is then ready to learn to shop. During this process, the APS worker must have knowledge of such factors as the client's ability to perform tasks, the client's attitude toward change, and the amount of time the aide has to work with the client to reduce or "unlink" the client from use of the in-home aide.

Adult Foster Care: A Vital Resource

Although many of the resources described are vital to meeting the needs of developmentally disabled clients, perhaps the most important resource to which the developmentally disabled adult in Anne Arundel County is linked is adult foster care.

The Adult Foster Care Program began in Anne Arundel County in 1979 as a resource for homeless adults in the county. Given the shortage of available housing and the need of many developmentally disabled adults for the type of setting offered by the adult foster care home, this resource has proven to be invaluable to APS workers. Under the program, adults in the community open their homes to adults who do not meet criteria for institutional placement, but for some reason cannot live on their own. Clients are placed in the home of the caregiver, who provides room, board, and a family atmosphere, and who is paid from the client's income and a monthly supplement from county funds for the client's care. In addition, each client placed in a home receives a set amount from this funding combination each month for personal expenses. Caregivers can accept up to three clients in their homes and must meet safety requirements of the local health and fire departments to receive certification. In addition, caregivers can decide which clients they will accept for placement in their homes, such as males or females, smokers or nonsmokers, clients from a particular age group, and clients with a certain disability. Often caregivers are provided specialized training in working with the type of clients they will accept.

The Adult Foster Care Program is vital to the APS case manager who needs to place, often on an emergency basis, a developmentally disabled client who is inappropriate for institutional placement. Many clients who have suffered abuse or neglect have been placed in foster care over the years in Anne Arundel County and have thrived in their new living situation. To ensure a successful link to this resource, the APS worker must regularly confer with adult foster care staff to gain knowledge of and maintain a listing of current vacancies, such as those for the placement of a developmentally disabled client in a home that is wheelchair accessible. In addition, it is suggested that the APS worker visit the caregivers with a vacancy to discuss with the caregiver the APS program and the linking function with adult foster care in an attempt to assess the caregiver's strengths and weaknesses further. Information that the APS worker is able to obtain about the home where the client will potentially be placed is vital in ensuring a successful "match" of client and caregiver when the APS worker must make use of this resource. To be successful then, the APS worker must maintain not only a current list of adult foster care vacancies, but also obtain as much information about the home and caregiver as possible.

Once the developmentally disabled client is placed in an adult foster home, the APS worker must carefully monitor the client's progress in the new living situation. To accomplish this most successfully, the APS worker should meet regularly with caregiver and client, with frequent visits to the home in the period immediately following placement. At the initial visit after placement, the client, caregiver, and APS worker should discuss the rules of the home, the client's and caregiver's expectations of each other during placement, and short- and long-term goals that the APS worker and caregiver will assist the client in achieving. To this end, APS workers in Anne Arundel County have been successful in using a written service agreement called the *Three-way agreement*. This device outlines agreed-on information concerning the client's placement in the adult foster home and is signed by the client, caregiver, and APS worker. It has proven to be beneficial in assessing the client's adjustment to and progress made during placement, and should be renegotiated and signed by all concerned on a six-month basis. However, the agreement may be altered at any time during the period, if unforeseen circumstances arise and if caregiver, client, and APS worker agree to the revision. For example, if a developmentally disabled client is placed in adult foster care and later develops an illness for which he or she must take medication, then the agreement may be amended to include the caregiver tasks of monitoring the medication schedule, informing the client when it is time for the medication to be taken, and, if necessary, assisting the client with taking the medication.

At times, the linking of a developmentally disabled client to a particular adult foster home may prove unsuccessful because of client or caregiver dissatisfaction with one issue or more about the placement. After determining that the issue or issues cannot be resolved, the APS worker may place the client in another home. Again, at the time of placement or shortly thereafter, a new three-way agreement is negotiated and the APS worker may need to develop strategies to prevent a recurrence of the problems that made placement in the previous foster home unsuccessful.

Successful Linking: Case Examples

The following cases describe situations in which county APS workers successfully linked vulnerable developmentally disabled clients to community resources. Through these examples, the reader should gain a further understanding of the linking process as it pertains to this population and of the methods and resources used by APS workers to protect their clients from risk.

Linking under Emergency Circumstances

Paul, age 20, came to the attention of APS when a neighbor of the family telephoned to report suspected neglect of Paul by his father, George. The neighbor stated that Paul was severely retarded and lived alone with his father, who regularly abused alcohol. In addition, Paul's father was described as having been "extremely intoxicated" for the past two days, and he had been heard screaming at Paul on several occasions during that period. The neighbor further stated that the family had moved to Anne Arundel County approximately six months ago, that Paul was an only child, and that Paul's mother had moved out of the home about three weeks ago to live with her sister in the area. The neighbor described the home as "filthy" and indicated that Paul was not attending any school or day program.

Based on the information reported, the case was assigned to be investigated because Paul fit the description of a vulnerable adult under Maryland law and the situation described indicated possible neglect. When the APS worker visited the home the same day on which the call was received, she could smell alcohol on George's breath, but George did not appear to be overly intoxicated. The home was extremely run-down, with no running water (George explained that a pipe was broken) and the front yard was strewn with old tires, rusted metal, and newspapers. The inside of the home was filled with piles of boxes and papers throughout, and appeared never to have been cleaned. Paul was dressed in tattered clothing and sat on a chair nearby, saying nothing during the interview, but occasionally showing the APS worker a broken pencil. Whenever the APS worker acknowledged the pencil, Paul would put it down and then repeat the process after a short period.

George explained to the APS worker that the family had moved to the county from St. Louis six months ago and that he and Paul's mother had recently separated. He further stated that he could not and did not want to care for Paul and that he wanted to move back to St. Louis to live with his brother. He requested that the APS worker take Paul out of the home, and gave the worker the address and telephone number of Paul's mother, stating, "Maybe she will take care of him."

The APS worker was able to contact Paul's mother at her sister's home and explain the situation. The mother informed the APS worker that Paul could stay with her and Paul's aunt for a few days, but after that she could no longer care for him. She stated that Paul had been diagnosed as moderately retarded, needed assistance with dressing and bathing, and could not cook for himself. Although Paul's mother expressed concern for his well-being, she felt that he was too much for her to care for full-time. She stated that she and Paul's father were going to be divorced and that she needed most of her time to "find a good job and make a life of my own."

In this situation, the APS worker determined that she needed to link Paul to several resources, and determined her "linking priorities." First, she was able to link her client to the most important resource, a place to live, albeit for only a few days. This first action removed the immediate risk of neglect of her client, especially after the APS worker transported Paul to his aunt's home, which was relatively new and clean throughout. Also, this link to Paul's mother and aunt placed him with two people familiar to Paul, lessening the impact of separation from his father and his home. Because his mother had expressed concern for her son, the APS worker was able to enlist her assistance in making additional links with other resources for Paul.

At the time of the report concerning Paul, the APS worker's list of adult foster care homes indicated that a vacancy existed for a caregiver willing to work with a retarded client. After verifying the vacancy and alerting adult foster care staff that she would need the placement, she telephoned the caregiver and discussed Paul's case. When the caregiver indicated that she would like Paul to be placed with her, the APS worker arranged for a visit the following day with Paul, his mother, the caregiver, and the APS worker at the caregiver's home. All went well at the visit, and Paul was placed in the home the following day.

For approximately the first month after placement, the APS worker telephoned the caregiver three times weekly to check on Paul's progress. In addition, she visited the home bimonthly, as did Paul's mother, although not simultaneously. Because the caregiver did not report any significant problems and Paul was adjusting well to and thriving in placement, the APS worker initiated links to additional resources. First, she arranged for Paul to receive a complete physical and psychological examination to assess current level of functioning. The examination showed that Paul was well physically and was indeed functioning in the "moderate retardation" range, but close to the "severe" range. Additionally, Paul visited and began regular attendance at an adult day center, specializing in assisting the retarded client. There, he learned skills that enabled him to make products sold by the center.

Paul continues to do well in placement. The APS worker visits him once a month and his mother visits regularly, although his father has not attempted contact. Paul enjoys and looks forward to attending the adult day center and, in addition, has learned to dress himself with the caregiver's guidance. Also, he assists the caregiver with light house-cleaning and accompanies her on shopping trips.

This case exemplifies the need for APS workers to be aware of appropriate resources for use during emergency situations. In this case, the worker was presented with a vulnerable adult who suffered from neglect and possible homelessness. However, she was able to link her client to necessary resources in the short and long term. The final link for Paul will be when he is reunited with his mother in her new home, a goal for which she is striving. At that time, APS can close this case and consider it as a successful case of linking the client to needed resources.

Linking to Provide Self-Sufficiency, and "Unlinking"

Betty came to the attention of APS when her next-door neighbor telephoned and reported that Betty, age 55 and mild to moderately retarded, had confided to the neighbor problems Betty was having in her home. According to the neighbor, the previous evening Betty had informed her that Grace, the woman with whom Betty lived, treated her harshly, was "always yelling" at her, and had threatened to hit her on several recent occasions. Betty asked the neighbor to "help me move as soon as possible" and stated that she was afraid of Grace. The neighbor further reported that Betty had diabetes and could give herself insulin, that Betty had an adult son who visited occasionally, and that she had heard what sounded like loud arguments between Betty and Grace on several recent occasions. She described Grace as approximately age 50, who abused alcohol on a regular basis, but who assisted Betty with medication-taking, cooking, some transportation, and household chores.

Based on the information received, Betty seemed to fit the definition of vulnerable adult, although the neighbor stated that Betty could probably complete most activities of daily living with minimal assistance. APS accepted the case for investigation, and an APS worker visited the home later on the day that the neighbor telephoned.

The APS worker met with Betty alone and then with both Betty and Grace. She learned that Betty and Grace had lived together for three years in the home belonging to Grace, who was a long-time friend of Betty's son. Betty complained that Grace had "picked on her" recently for not cleaning her room and for staying too late at her boyfriend's house nearby. She further stated that she and Grace never really got along well and that, at times, Grace "drinks too much." She asked the APS worker to help her move to her own apartment. Grace denied abusing alcohol and further stated that she let Betty live with her as a favor to her son. However, Grace informed the APS worker that she and Betty had fought off and on for the three years that Betty had lived with her, and that she wanted Betty to move out as soon as possible "before she drives me crazy." She denied ever slapping Betty, but admitted, "If she stays here she may drive me to it." The APS worker felt that Betty was in no immediate danger, and after gathering further information about Betty, left the home, promising to assist Betty on a continuing basis.

The primary issue facing the APS worker in this case was the possibility that mediation could help settle the rift between Betty and Grace, with the two remaining together in Grace's home after the worker linked the two women to community resources, such as ongoing counseling for either or both, personal care, transportation, or whatever might be necessary to assist them. On the other hand, however, both women requested assistance with helping Betty leave the home. Thus, in this instance, as with many other APS nonemergency situations, the APS worker needed to gather important information to assess the focus or goal of her linking efforts.

Over the following two weeks, the APS worker spoke with Betty's son and Betty's physician and visited Betty and Grace's home several times. Her conclusion after assessing all information was that Betty should move, as requested. But was she capable of managing in her own apartment as she asked, or should Betty realistically be linked to a group home or adult foster care? To help answer this question, the APS worker arranged for Betty to have a psychological examination; Betty was extremely cooperative because she felt that this was one step in the direction of moving out. The examination revealed that Betty was "moderately retarded," slightly above the range of "mild retardation." Betty's physician and the examining psychologist believed that Betty was capable of maintaining her own apartment with some supports in place to assist her with cleaning and cooking, as well as with ensuring that she took her needed insulin daily and that she made regularly scheduled visits to her physician.

With this information, the APS worker was ready to link Betty to her own apartment, but could do so only if the recommended supports were in place. The worker was able to ascertain from Betty's son that Betty had been placed by him on a waiting list for one of the county housing authority's apartments for elderly or disabled people. This setting would be ideal for Betty because the units included some but not all of the recommended supports, and the worker felt that if Betty could be placed there, she could be linked to all of the community supports that she needed.

Since her initial visit, the APS worker noted that Betty was getting more insistent on moving each day and was threatening to "go to another state" if an apartment was not found for her soon. In addition, Grace began threatening to "put Betty out on the street" if she were not relocated in the near future. After discussing Betty's case with housing authority staff, the worker learned that any client on the apartment waiting list who was homeless or in imminent danger of becoming homeless was given priority on the list. The housing authority staff felt that Betty met the criteria for priority status and determined that Betty could move into an apartment that another tenant would be vacating in ten days.

This plan enabled the APS worker to line up and put into place the needed resources for Betty. Both Betty and Grace were thrilled with the relocation plan, and Betty's son recruited some friends to assist her on moving day. The worker arranged for a housing authority worker to look in on her daily immediately after the move, and less often after that if Betty was doing well. In addition, she linked Betty to Department of Social Services' staff of in-home aides to assist her with cooking, housecleaning, and shopping. She also arranged for Betty to attend an adult day center three days a week, where a full-time nurse was on duty to monitor Betty's health and assist with the insulin-taking, if necessary. Finally, the APS worker determined when Betty needed to check in with her physician and scheduled in aide to transport Betty.

Currently, Betty has been in her apartment for more than one year. She is doing well, and all of her supports are in place, although her in-home aide has decreased her visits from weekly to bimonthly because Betty has learned to cook and clean her apartment, but still needs assistance with shopping. Betty's son visits his mother regularly on weekends, as he has done since Betty first moved. Because Betty has been "out of risk" for some time, the APS worker has closed her case, and her case is being managed by a continuing–adult services case manager.

This case illustrates the linking used by APS when a client is at risk of self-neglect or homelessness and possible abuse, but is not in immediate physical danger. The APS worker determined the most appropriate setting for her client, where that client could achieve maximum self-sufficiency and growth, and was able to link her client to that setting. That this was not an emergency situation enabled the worker to line up the supports Betty needed by the time of the move. Betty's case now is reassessed every six months; her continued growth will enable her eventually to be "unlinked" from her in-home aide and possibly some of her other supports.

Linking in a Situation That Shifts from Nonemergency to Emergency

Mary, age 20, came to the attention of APS when her mother Alice telephoned seeking assistance for her daughter, an only child. Alice explained that Mary was epileptic and was not taking her prescribed medication, which resulted in two to three seizures weekly. In addition, Alice stated that Mary lived part-time with her and part-time with her boyfriend, who abused Mary regularly. She added that Mary had one child, which she had given up for adoption two years earlier, and that the father of the child also had abused Mary, but had left the area. Furthermore, she stated that Mary regularly abused alcohol, seemed depressed, and often could not or would not perform her activities of daily living. For example, Alice indicated that Mary stayed "in bed until noon," often not bathing or changing her clothes for days. Mary had a regular doctor whom she was seeing regarding her epilepsy, but would not accept his advice to enter counseling or take her medication regularly. Alice stated that APS was her "last hope," and that if Mary did not change her behavior soon, she would force Mary to leave her home permanently. She added that she was politically active in the community and state, and that several politicians were counting on APS to resolve this situation successfully.

APS decided to accept this case for investigation of self-neglect because the mother's description of Mary seemed to confirm that Mary could be considered a vulnerable adult under the law. When the APS worker visited Mary she noted that Mary indeed seemed depressed, often speaking in monotone and stating that life had nothing to offer. However, Mary also showed a great deal of anger toward her mother, whom she accused of "trying to control my life." She stated that she sometimes forgot to take her medication, but added that the resulting seizures were "not that bad." She informed the APS worker that her boyfriend was good to her most of the time, but had hit her in the past when he had been drinking. "Besides," Mary continued, "after thinking about those times, I probably deserved to be hit." Mary stated that although she enjoyed talking with the APS worker, she felt that no one could help her until her mother could be convinced to "leave me alone." Although reluctantly, she agreed to see the worker again.

After assessing the situation, the APS worker developed a plan for Mary and her mother. She suggested that a great deal of the problem centered around Mary's probable depression and wondered about Mary and Alice's relationship and what effect, if any, the relationship had on Mary's current crisis. After gaining Mary's permission, she consulted with Mary's physician, who felt that Mary was depressed and who informed the worker that if Mary did not take her medication regularly, she would continue to have seizures and could become seriously ill. The worker decided that the first step would be to arrange for a psychological evaluation of Mary. Mary did not agree at first, arguing that her mother was the one who needed a psychological evaluation. However, Mary was seemingly able to trust the APS worker, who informed her that this evaluation was a necessary first step in helping her as well as her mother. The worker also discovered that Mary had been taking her seizure medication regularly since the worker had first visited, which was approximately three weeks before Mary underwent the psychological examination.

It appeared then that after three weeks Mary somewhat trusted the worker, saw her as having the ability to help, and was complying with the worker's suggestions, at least about taking the medication and undergoing the psychological evaluation. Also, both Mary and Alice reported that Mary had seen her boyfriend only occasionally since the worker started visiting, and that there were no incidents of either alcohol or physical abuse.

The APS worker was able to secure funds to reimburse a private psychologist for the psychological evaluation from state APS discretionary funds, an important element in successfully linking Mary and other clients to certain services.

Mary's psychological evaluation revealed that she showed the characteristics of "borderline personality disorder" with "moderate to extreme dependency needs." The evaluation mentioned a dysfunctional relationship between Mary and her mother, in which Alice actually tried to undermine Mary's attempts at independence. The psychologist recommended that Mary begin individual counseling immediately, with Alice brought in later as a part of the counseling. Mary verbalized that she was comfortable with the psychologist and thus agreed to begin therapy with him.

A short time after Mary began therapy, matters between Mary and her mother began to worsen. Mary reported to the APS worker that her mother resisted counseling and was trying to "control my life." She spoke of daily arguments between the two and of Alice's recent threats to put Mary out of her home. These threats became a reality when Mary appeared at Department of Social Services a few days later, stating that she was homeless after Alice told her to leave the home because of an incident at a party that Mary had attended the night before. Mary explained that "everyone was drinking" at the party and that after one of the men there began flirting with her, a friend of her boyfriend got angry, started fighting with the man, and then shot the man in the upper leg. Later, the police came to Alice's home to question Mary about the incident. Alice became furious and told Mary to leave the home.

The APS worker was able to locate emergency funds to place Mary in a local motel for two weeks. In addition, she determined that, despite being displaced from her home, it was important that Mary maintain therapy and that other links were necessary to assist the client. First, the worker contacted the Maryland Epilepsy Foundation, which agreed to provide Mary transportation to and from counseling and to have a representative contact her regularly to educate her about epilepsy and monitor medication. Also, the worker contacted the Department of Vocational Rehabilitation, which agreed to work with Mary on job training and getting her high school general equivalency diploma. Finally, the worker spoke with staff at an adult psychosocial residential center, who agreed to have Mary attend their day center regularly, and placed her name on their waiting list for residential placement. Mary followed through with all of these services.

The APS worker was able to visit both Mary and her mother regularly, and Mary was able to return to her mother's home after one week at the motel, because Alice requested that she return and Mary agreed. Mary informed both her mother and the worker that she and her boyfriend had "broken up" and that he had left the state.

Shortly thereafter, the APS worker was successful in getting together representatives from all of the resources to which Mary had been linked to discuss the care and the role that each played in assisting Mary. It was at this meeting that representatives from the residential center announced that Mary could move into one of their apartments immediately and that one of their counselors would assume case management. Mary moved into the apartment a few days later, and the APS worker then closed her case.

Recently the APS worker received a telephone call from Mary, who thanked the worker for her help. Mary has been living in the residential center now for one year and she has reported that she has been medication compliant, has obtained her diploma, has begun working part time, and is still in therapy, as is her mother. She also informed the worker that she and her mother understand each other better, and that her mother has been working part-time at the residential center. She has become less dependent on her mother and her mother has supported her in her growth.

This case clearly demonstrates that in APS, workers must link their clients to needed resources on an emergency and nonemergency basis. When both emergency and nonemergency resources are needed for a client, the linking pattern in most APS cases is that the need for emergency resources usually is met first (such as removing the client from risk), followed by linking the client to nonemergency resources (such as transportation to physician's appointments). However, in Mary's case, the worker became faced with the need for linking on a nonemergency and then on an emergency basis. APS workers must be attuned to both scenarios and anticipate possible emergency situations, even when the client is not in immediate danger, so that the client can be protected.

Mary's APS worker was prepared for this emergency and was quickly able to secure emergency funds for her placement in a motel. Mary's history of emergencies and her fragile relationship with her mother were factors the worker had considered in preparing for possible emergencies with her client and appropriate resources for her client to be linked to if emergencies occurred. Also, the APS worker in this case decided to involve representatives from each of the resources to which Mary was linked in a group discussion of the case situation. It was during this discussion of Mary's history and progress that the client was determined to be a good candidate for placement at the residential center, with the center staff providing total case management. That Mary has made significant progress with her own needs as well as in her relationship with her mother underlines the successful intervention and linking by her APS worker.

Strategies for Successful Linking

In successfully linking the developmentally disabled and other APS clients to necessary resources, several strategies, as illustrated in the case examples, are useful. The APS worker must possess knowledge of resources, anticipate emergencies, develop resources, coordinate linking resources, and be able to change resources.

Possess Knowledge of Resources. A complete knowledge of available resources and potential resources is vital to successful linking, which may occur on an emergency basis. APS workers should keep an updated file of community resources, including as thorough a record on each individual resource as possible. Also, workers should visit as many resources as possible, to familiarize themselves with staff, and observe the resource firsthand. Moreover, workers should contact each resource periodically to check on possible changes in service provisions.

Anticipate Emergencies. APS workers should be especially aware of resources that are available for emergency situations. Strategies for intervention in specific types of emergencies should be a part of APS worker training, and appropriate community resources for specific emergencies should be discussed by APS units. Also, APS workers need to look at specific cases in their caseloads and "brainstorm" possible emergency situations that may occur based on the client's history of *need* to be linked to emergency resources, whether he or she was actually linked, as well as the current client situation. If the APS worker feels that a case could "blow up," it is especially worthwhile to stay one step ahead of any potential crisis by planning on the resources that will be necessary if a crisis should occur, and even alerting likely resources to be on standby where particularly unstable client situations exist.

Develop Resources. At times APS workers in Anne Arundel County have discovered that needed resources are not always available. This lack of available resources could severely hamper efforts to assist the developmentally disabled and other APS clients, especially during emergency situations. Thus, it is sometimes important for APS units and their agencies to develop their own resources for use exclusively by agency workers for their clients.

Coordinate Linking Resources.   As the primary case manager, the APS worker is responsible for assessment, linking, and monitoring for each client that he or she assists. Often, it is helpful to conduct regular meetings with staff from all of the resources to which the client has been linked when multiple resources are working with the client. At the meeting, roles can be clarified, ideas and information exchanged, and direction discussed. These regularly scheduled meetings are particularly valuable to APS when working with difficult clients in terms of coordination of provision of service.

Change Resources.   At times, after an APS client has been linked to a resource, the APS worker will note that for some reason the client has not progressed. When this happens, the worker needs to examine the reasons why growth has not occurred and take action on behalf of the client to remedy the situation. Reasons for nongrowth could be many and varied, such as the client not relating well to his or her Department of Vocational Rehabilitation counselor, or an agency's being too busy to give the client the attention necessary for positive growth. The APS worker must monitor the client's progress closely after linking occurs, and be prepared to link the client to an alternative resource if necessary. Also, the worker must be attuned to progress made by the client and set time lines for "weaning" or "unlinking" the client from the resource when appropriate.

All of these steps are important for APS workers successfully to link the vulnerable developmentally disabled client, thereby offering that client protection and opportunity for growth.

Acknowledgments

The author wishes to thank John Anguay, Denise Stewart-Denefield, Catherine Smith, and Patricia Wilson, adult services workers with the Anne Arundel County Department of Social Services, Glen Burnie, MD, for their contributions to this chapter.

References

MD. 1985. [FAM. LAW] CODE ANN. §14-101(A).
MD. 1985. [HEALTH—GEN.] CODE ANN. §7-1005(B).
MD. 1980. REGS. CODE tit. 07, subtit. 02, §§01–14.
O'Hara, David M. 1980. *Advocacy and Service Provision to the Developmentally Disabled and Their Families.* Baltimore: John F. Kennedy Institute.

State of Maryland, Department of Human Resources. 1989. *Maryland State Letter of Agreement between the Department of Health and Mental Hygiene, Licensing and Certification Programs Administration, and the Department of Human Resources, Social Services Administration, Relating to At Risk Vulnerable Adults in Legally Licensed or Registered, and Illegally Unlicensed or Unregistered Domiciliary Care Homes.* Baltimore: State of Maryland, Department of Human Resources.

————. 1980. *Policy and Procedural Agreement between the Developmental Disabilities Administration, of the Department of Health and Mental Hygiene, and the Social Services Administration, of the Department of Human Resources, in Matters Related to the Protection of Vulnerable Adults.* Baltimore: State of Maryland, Department of Human Resources.

State of Maryland, Developmental Disabilities Administration. 1989. *Access to Services, User's Guide.* Baltimore: State of Maryland, Developmental Disabilities Administration, Developmental Disabilities Access Unit.

U.S. Department of Health and Human Services, Office of Human Development Services. 1982. *Protective Services for Adults.* Washington, D.C.: U.S. Department of Health and Human Services.

University of Maryland, School of Social Work and Community Planning. 1983. *A Supervisor's Workbook for Task Centered Casework.* Baltimore: University of Maryland, School of Social Work and Community Planning.

Chapter 8

Plan Implementation and Coordination: Clinical Case Management with the Chronically Mentally Ill

John R. Belcher

Case management with the chronically mentally ill (CMI) offers the hope of fulfilling the notion of a comprehensive community-based service system. For the individual client, the case manager's functions of plan implementation and coordination directly address that client's need for access to and help with utilizing multiple and diverse services at any one time. In addition, coordinated care (including from hospital to community) over time recognizes the fluctuating nature of the clinical course of chronic mental illness. However, case management as a component of the service delivery system often has failed to meet these important needs and the CMI client has continued to fall through gaps in care.

Existing case management models for the CMI differ significantly in their goals, staffing, and implementation of basic case management functions, including how to create and maintain an agreed-upon plan of care and to ensure coordinated care over time. An understanding of key issues related to these case management functions depends on a broader examination of an appropriate model of case management for this client group. Such an examination should reveal the case management model that works best with the CMI and the criteria practitioners can use to decide what model of case management to endorse in their own practice with the CMI.

This chapter reviews the differing approaches to case management with the CMI and relevant research findings, outlines clinical guidelines for a clinical case management model and describes the plan implementation and coordination functions within this model, and examines the priorities that must be set in motion, including appropriate training, before appropriate case management can become a reality for the CMI.

Research on Differing Approaches to Case Management

Research on case management in terms of its cost effectiveness reveals that if the goal is to stabilize a variety of CMI clients, then the program may prove to be as expensive as hospital-like services. For example, Franklin and associates (1987) found that case management did not decrease costs. Instead, the case-managed group used twice as many hospital bed days as the non-case-managed group, and quality of life did not statistically differ between the two groups. On the other hand, one study found case management to be effective in reducing costs (Weisbrod, Test, & Stein 1980); another study noted an increased level of functioning, a reduction in psychiatric hospitalization, and an implied cost savings (Witheridge & Dincin 1980); and another study confirmed the use of case management as a means to reduce costs (Bond et al. 1988).

Goering and associates (1988) found mixed results. Six months into the study, the case-managed group had used more services than the non-case-managed group. However, by 24 months, the case-managed group was doing significantly better in terms of functioning. Interestingly, however, the rehospitalization rates for the two groups did not differ. Borland, McRae, and Lycan (1989) used a case management model that they labeled "intensive case management," although it actually was clinically driven. Their model was similar to the one used by Community Connections, a private nonprofit case management agency in Washington, D.C., that uses a clinical case management model. Borland et al. found that hospital bed days were reduced. At the same time, however, increased residential care costs and the costs of other case management services offset the savings from reduced hospital bed days. Functioning for the clients was reported to be stable across the study. The study was noteworthy because it was long-term. Borland et al. concluded

> that the majority of treatment-resistant, thought-disordered chronic patients can be stabilized outside the hospital over an extended period of time. Such an accomplishment requires individualized, persistent, often frustrating efforts employing a variety of strategies and interventions to provide and maintain hospital-like functions in the community. (1989, p. 376)

They further concluded that the cost of this care is no less, but no more than hospital-based care.

Moreover, studies that have found case management to be cheaper than hospital-like services often have less debilitated and severely ill clients in their program. More important, as more disturbed clients are discharged to the community, the cost of care may rise. This assumes that the care provided actually meets the needs of the client. Case management will always be cheaper than hospital-based services if the care approach assumes that clients, for the most part, can look after themselves.

Continuing confusion over what defines appropriate case management for the CMI places the social work practitioner in a unique dilemma. Oftentimes the unstated goal may be cost containment. However, the social work practitioner may be attempting to provide the service that best meets the clients' needs. While other less expensive models of case management may be appropriate for less debilitated populations, case management with the CMI is a complex and often expensive undertaking that can provide great promise to persons suffering from chronic mental disorders.

Aside from costs, research also has revealed that the case management services provided should include individualized approaches that are persistent and create a structured and sometimes hospital-like environment. In addition, the staff necessary to provide this level of services should hold a master's degree in a field such as social work, psychology, or another mental health specialty. Appropriate educational training of staff depends upon the sophistication and quality of clinical services desired.

From the clients' point of view, case management can be effective in returning them to a community environment as long as the case management approach provides services that match their needs. Otherwise, the approach may succeed in reducing costs at the expense of lowering the client's quality of life. Thus, a clinical rather than an administrative rationale should determine the appropriateness of case management. Unlike clients who are not as debilitated or ill, the CMI have unique needs that must be met by a case management approach. Some services of a clinical nature are imperative to their survivability. Clinical case management moves beyond simply assessing the clients' basic needs of food, clothing, shelter, medication, and need for social services. It examines the clients' ego functioning and provides necessary supports, such as appropriate role models, that enable clients to better develop sufficient ego strength. However, although clinical case management is a useful means of assisting CMI clients to live in the community and improve their quality of life, the cost of such care can often be as expensive as hospital-based care. Therefore, case management should be approached with caution. Before endorsing it as a viable. means of working with the CMI, the goals need to be clarified. It is important to examine more closely the kinds of clients in terms of diagnosis, severity of illness, and level of functioning that are appropriate for clinical case management, for it is doubtful that clinical case management will benefit or be appropriate for all CMI clients. Careful scrutiny is indicated. Otherwise, case management, like most other mental health initiatives, will be an overly simplistic solution that is quickly abandoned because it fails.

The Clinical Case Management Model

Research on case management often has not highlighted the nature and quality of services. Reasons may involve the continuing debate about the definition and goals of case management and the kinds of services needed to reach those goals. As a result, case management models often have been implemented on the basis of "intuitive assumptions and popular appeal" (Franklin 1988, p. 921). Much of the popular appeal has to do with case management's use as a cost containment strategy and as a focus away from broader system change (Schilling et al. 1988).

One of the greatest barriers to designing case management systems is the lack of definition (Bachrach 1989). Different definitions underlie the different purposes behind case management. For some practitioners and policymakers, the major goal of case management is to reduce costs by reducing the number of hospital admissions. Not surprisingly, approaches that rely on cost reduction as a major goal often fail to provide the clinical services needed by the CMI. Other case management models utilize highly trained staffs, small caseloads, and deliver clinical services in a comprehensive fashion.

Bachrach (1989) observed that there appear to be two general types of case management: (1) "intensive case management," which is used by the Commonwealth of Pennsylvania, and (2) "clinical case management," which is used by Community Connections (Harris & Bergman 1988). The Pennsylvania model is basically an administrative means of attempting to "assist" eligible persons in gaining access to appropriate resources. Lamb (1980) has referred to this process as "brokering." Although brokering may work well for clients who, for the most part, are responsible for themselves, the CMI often need more comprehensive services than a brokering function can provide. The Pennsylvania model uses similar language to the Community Connections model; however, the reality of services is qualitatively different.

Perhaps the most glaring difference is in the staffing patterns. The Pennsylvania model indicates that the most qualified personnel should be used to work with the CMI. However, in reality, case managers may be anyone with a bachelor's degree in the social sciences. Although case managers are supervised by a mental health professional, the clinical quality of the case management in the brokering model is questionable. In contrast, Community Connections only uses master's- or doctoral-level professionals. As a result, costs for the Pennsylvania model are far less than for the Community Connections model. More important, however, the Pennsylvania model offers the CMI client very little in the way of appropriate clinical services. Research on case management has shown that the most effective case management model uses trained master's-level or more advanced professionals. One important reason for the use of professionals with such advanced training is that they have the skills needed both to understand the complexities of chronic mental illness and to have the knowledge to know when and how to intervene to prevent decompensation. Admittedly, employing such professionals may raise the costs of service. However, in some cases, cost containment results in poor practice because the service delivered is of such inferior quality that it cannot begin to provide effective care for and effectively manage a severely ill client.

The case management approach that appears to be most effective in creating an environment for sustaining a reasonable quality of life for a CMI client is one that is clinically based. As Kanter (1987) noted, clinical case management is highly specialized and is more than simply an administrative system for coordinating services. In a clinical model, all case management functions, from client outreach to plan implementation and coordination, are embedded in a highly skilled helping relationship between client and case manager. To sustain such a relationship, the case manager must have the clinical skills to engage emotionally hard-to-reach individuals; empathize and understand people temporarily experiencing disordered thinking; and provide needed support, structure, and practical assistance that is at the same time sensitive to each client's need for self-determination and personal growth.

Certain functions are required of a clinical case manager: "engagement, assessment, planning, linking with community resources, consulting with families, maintaining and expanding social networks, and collaboration with physicians" (Kanter 1989, p. 362). These functions are based on the assumption that caseloads are related to the severity of illness and the availability of resources both in the community and the hospital (Stein & Test 1980). The assumption that CMI clients are homogeneous in severity of illness and eventual outcome often is made by administrators within the community mental health system. They may assume that case management is a fairly simple process of engagement in which case managers do not have to be particularly specialized. Although some literature has highlighted the difficulties in working with clients whose ego strengths and ability to control external stimuli are weak (Borland et al. 1989; Kanter 1989), other literature has portrayed the case management process as relatively easy (Billig & Levinson 1989).

Student Interns as Case Managers

In the Billig and Levinson (1989) model, first-year graduate-level social work students function as case managers. This approach jeopardizes any continuity of care and also overlooks the fluid nature of CMI and the need to view case management from a long-term perspective. It is well documented that the course of chronic mental disorders, such as schizophrenia, is often unpredictable and can change rapidly (Liberman 1988; Liberman & Kane 1986). Sudden changes in the course of an illness, particularly of a psychotic nature, can create great difficulty for clients as they attempt to integrate "conflicting signals coming from the environment into a coherent picture of what is demanded so they can adequately respond to those demands" (Gruenberg & Archer 1983, p. 35).

The use of student interns as case managers reflects a prevalent misunderstanding in service delivery of the potential conflict that can arise when CMI clients are exposed to the multiple stresses of the community. These clients are attempting to integrate the multiple demands of the community into an often fragmented and psychotic worldview. Many CMI have lost interest in social relationships, and their opportunities to learn from others becomes limited. Bellack and Mueser (1986) noted that the pervasive and limiting skill deficits of many persons with CMI are a result of inexperience and lack of social practice. Any added inconsistency, such as when student interns are utilized, increases the difficulty of the CMI client's task of integration. An effective case management approach must recognize that these individuals are not only chronically ill, but that their illness manifests itself in cognitive fragmentation, disorganization, and confusion.

Persistent instability and chronic inconsistency in the lives of many CMI means that is important for the case manager to model stable and consistent interactions with the client. Perhaps the greatest failure of psychosocial programs is that often there is no one staff member with a stable sense of the client. More important, the client may not be provided with an overall model of healthy functioning so that he or she can develop an appropriate level of social competence. Studies have shown that the level of social competence has been determined to be the best single predictor of community tenure (Glynn & Muser 1986). Thus case management with this client group requires a case manager who is, at the minimum, a 40-hour a week employee not subject to exam pressures, semester breaks, and other stresses that a student undergoes.

Use of a Case Management Team

The case manager must be part of a treatment team that includes housing and entitlement specialists, psychiatrists, physicians, social workers, and psychologists (Anthony et al. 1988). As opposed to other client populations, "Severe deficits in the mentally ill person's capacity for psychological integration and internal structure reflect themselves in their inability to structure and integrate an external environment" (Belcher 1988b, p. 80). CMI clients often lack the strong social skills needed to deal with many facets of everyday life. Together, the inability to integrate psychologically and the limited social coping repertoire create a situation in which the CMI client may be unable to coordinate resources and meet needs. Given the fluid nature of chronic mental illnesses, such as schizophrenia, it is not surprising that many CMI clients enter into a pattern of decompensation-recompensation-decompensation (Ciompi 1980). During periods of decompensation, the CMI client is particularly at risk for increasing withdrawal and loss of residence (Belcher & Toomey 1988).

A case management team guarantees that these clients have appropriate access to a set of services that both match their needs and are continuous. These services need to be provided in an atmosphere in which the client feels comfortable with the level and quality of services provided and believes that the services will be provided. The team does not necessarily have to consist of specialists. However, if, for example, a housing specialist is not a member of a team, another team member can fill this role only if he or she has knowledge of housing alternatives for the CMI so that housing placements are found and utilized.

Reducing Levels of Stress

The case management team, through advanced planning and avoidance of potential problems, can facilitate a habitat for the CMI client that is stress-free enough to enable the client to avoid psychiatric decompensation. Levels of stress tolerance will vary from client to client (Belcher & Rife 1989); thus, the case management team must understand how stress affects each person. Otherwise, the team will be unable to plan properly and advocate effectively for its clients. However, the process of integrating a CMI client into a community-based mental health program requires a long-term perspective (Borland et al. 1989). Models that use short-term, time-limited approaches are destined to fail because they overlook the need for empathetic and enduring relationships.

Many CMI clients, particularly those with schizophrenia, can easily enter an existential vacuum characterized by withdrawal from society (Lantz & Belcher 1987). The clinical approach assumes that medicating clients and then leaving them to fend for themselves creates an environment ripe for decompensation. Many CMI clients make attempts to understand the world around them; however, often these attempts are "chaotic and illogical to people who do not have the basic schizophrenic thought disorder" (Lantz & Belcher 1987, p. 18). Although these experiences could be a sign of decompensation and suggest the need for an adjustment in psychotropic medication, they also could suggest the need for empathy. Distinguishing between instances of decompensation and internal struggles may be difficult, but knowledge of the client's baseline functioning and a past record of stressors that are known to affect a client negatively can enable a case manager to talk with a client and make changes in the environment that may ease the client's internal struggle. Such interventions must be undertaken with great skill and knowledge of the client. Otherwise, the client may decompensate, desperately need psychotropic medication, and affect his or her recovery from chronic mental illness.

The case manager's attempts to communicate with the client about everyday concerns may raise transference and countertransference issues (Kanter 1985). For example, the case manager may suggest that the client wear a coat because it is cold. However, the client may view this suggestion as inappropriate because his or her parent always engaged in "suggestions" that were orders and took away the client's autonomy. The case manager must attempt to address this concern, negotiate the practical issue, and do both with awareness that many CMI clients have a limited stress threshold (Liberman & Kane 1986). A seemingly simple issue may be a challenging clinical task.

Providing Individualized Training

A concern for the profession is to link key components of social work practice with realistic outcome expectations. Herein lies a major obstacle that social work practitioners must overcome. A key component of social work practice is client self-determination, yet many case management models are designed so that, because of cost containment goals, the time spent between client and practitioner is minimal at best. Unvarying routines are a problem existing in many psychosocial programs: clients' specific social deficits and needs are not being addressed. Instead, there is a tendency to assume that clients are the same, and that lockstep classes in cooking, sewing, woodworking, and secretarial services can facilitate a client's process of change. It is expensive to provide individualized training. Reimbursement provided by the state to psychosocial programs is set at such a low rate that individualized training is impossible. If one of the stated goals of the client's care plan is to improve the client's ability to keep appointments and to develop basic life skills, such as riding a bus, but the goals of cost containment prevent meaningful interaction between client and case manager, then the goal of improved client performance will most likely not be accomplished. The clinical case manager is more than simply a travel agent; he or she is also a therapist, resource manager, and client advocate.

Kane (1988) has argued that global budget allocations for a group of clients is a realistic and social work value–congruent approach. Although, on one hand, the social work practitioner must work within the framework of the agency, the social work practitioner also is obligated to advocate for his or her client. Given the limited ego strength of many CMI clients, advocacy means that the practitioner should question the budget allocations that policymakers determine appropriate to meet the needs of the CMI. These budget allocations are not facts that are beyond question, as Kane suggests. Instead, they are determined by a process of decision-making that can and should be influenced by case managers. If case management accepts allocated resources for a particular population as given, then client self-determination becomes less likely because the case manager models compliant behavior without questioning how others impose their agendas on those less able to advocate for themselves, such as the CMI. Social work practitioners must determine the goal of the case management model in which they practice and balance their own concerns about client self-determination with the goals of the agency to manage limited resources and foster compliance in their clients.

If the case manager is unable to take the time to listen to the client because of fiscal constraints, and the client does not meet his or her goals, then one must question whether this failure results from social work practice ineffectiveness or outcome expectations that conflict with and inhibit competent social work practice. This dilemma involves the case manager's ability to listen to the client, identify weaknesses in the client, and model appropriate behaviors that can enable the client to overcome these weaknesses.

Yet individualized training and the use of case managers to support clients in learning and integrating new skills can be effective (Test, Knoedler, & Allness 1985). Primarily the case manager can provide an environment where the client feels comfortable in trying new experiences and is reinforced when successful and shown alternative options when unsuccessful. Research has shown this approach to be effective in helping clients enhance their lives. However, it may not reduce costs. Instead, it may increase the costs of care, particularly in the short run.

Assisting Clients with Internalization

One of the frequently neglected aspects of clinical case management is internalization (Harris & Bergman 1987). Functions performed by others that the client defines as significant are internalized by the client (Freud 1940). Many CMI lack sufficient ego strength; consequently, CMI clients may use case management as an auxiliary ego as they attempt to negotiate their external environment (Pepper, Ryglewicz, & Kirshner 1982), resulting in some dependency on the part of the client. However, a skilled clinician can model appropriate and necessary behaviors as well as know when to begin the process of helping the client seek autonomy. This process also helps the client to develop a cohesive sense of self, which is particularly important in the current era of fragmentation of services (Belcher 1988a).

Assisting clients with internalization requires a highly skilled clinician working within a model of case management that provides the practitioner with enough flexibility to respond adequately to a variety of skill deficits. Although the clinician is implementing different components of the care plan, he or she also is attempting to help the client grow and reach the client's goals.

Supporting Rehospitalization

One of the greatest failures of deinstitutionalization that case management may correct is the need for rehospitalization (Belcher & Blank 1989). Case management is not a guarantee that a CMI client will remain in the community. If rehospitalization occurs, it is not a failure. Instead, it generally means that the client's illness is changing and requires a different form of intervention. Interestingly, much of the research concerning success of the deinstitutionalization model has focused on client recidivism to the state hospital (Belcher & Toomey 1988). This approach to evaluating successful community tenure leads many practitioners to continue to view hospitalization as somehow negative. Bachrach commented that "there are cases where patients would indeed show improved functioning outside the hospital under certain conditions, but would be better inside the hospital if these conditions cannot be met" (1980, p. 99). Case management scholars have as yet failed to appreciate that "never in the hospital" is not a productive context in which to view treatment for the CMI. This view places particular pressure on social work practitioners, who frequently have direct contact with the client and experience the difficulties involved in treating a CMI client (Belcher 1988c).

CMI clients respond differently to stress. Some CMI clients do better with lower levels of support because their tolerance for stimulation is less (Gunderson et al. 1984). However, the case manager cannot easily predict the amount and degree of stress that will lead a CMI client to decompensate. Certainly targeting symptom change and responding appropriately may prevent some hospitalizations. However, some clients will continue to need hospitalization. It is at this juncture that the case management relationship may change. Kanter noted that

> conflicts inevitably occur when patients, case managers, and other caregivers disagree in their evaluation of what patients are able or willing to do. Even though most case managers explicitly support the principle of client self-determination, these tensions occur and should be consciously acknowledged. (1989, p. 362)

Perhaps one of the areas with the most potential for disagreement is the need for hospitalization. Some scholars seem to believe that a well-funded community system will dispense with the need for a state hospital system (Okin 1985). However, other scholars point out that, because of the fluid nature of the CMI clients' illness and their tendency to be unemployed, the need for a state hospital will continue (Belcher & Blank 1989). If the client does not want to be hospitalized, but the case manager believes that hospitalization is necessary, an important function of the case manager is to arrange for the involuntary hospitalization of the client. At this point and during the hospitalization, the case manager must attempt to rebuild aspects of the relationship that have been damaged as the result of the involuntary hospitalization. However, the client may have to be assigned to another case manager. In this case, a process of planned disengagement from the original case manager and transition to a new case manager is important.

Hospitalization is a key component of truly coordinated care. Clinical case management creates a loop whereby the client can freely move between the hospital and community without having to decompensate to a dangerously low level of functioning. This is facilitated by the case manager who knows the client well enough to determine when crisis intervention and, perhaps, hospitalization is necessary.

If case management will not always prevent re-hospitalization, and if it is often as expensive as hospital-based services, then why not simply maintain the CMI in hospitals? The case management model described in this section is expensive, yet beneficial to CMI clients because it provides them with opportunity for a quality of life in which self-determination is a realistic outcome. However, this model is not used often. Should social work practitioners settle for a model that focuses mainly on cost containment and overlooks clinical issues surrounding the CMI client's insufficient ego strength and tendency to decompensate in stressful situations? Social work practitioners, to answer this question, must review the goals of their practice setting to determine if they agree with their own model of practice. In addition, the profession must determine its priorities in serving the CMI.

Setting Priorities

Linking Practice and Policy

The primary benefit of case management for the CMI is that it may enhance their quality of life. The model of case management needed to accomplish this goal, however, may prove to be as expensive as hospital-based services. This reality tests the commitment behind the philosophy of deinstitutionalization. If the goal of deinstitutionalization is to provide improved quality of life outside a hospital setting, then case management is probably the way to accomplish that goal. On the other hand, if the goal of deinstitutionalization is to reduce costs, then case management of a clinical nature is inappropriate. The social work profession must resolve the conflict about its desire to gain status by helping to contain costs, which compromises the client-centered nature of social work practice. The profession must set its priorities.

Some social work scholars have suggested that "rationing" is one of the strengths of case management (Wimberly 1988); others have considered it a weakness (Schilling et al. 1988). In terms of the CMI, social work as a profession must choose whether to support case management of any variety or only case management that utilizes a clinical approach.

One priority of the profession is that it must link practice with policy on both the federal and state levels. Unlike other groups, such as clients with third-party health insurance, the CMI depend on some level of government for their care. Since 1980, the factor of state control over mental health initiatives has increased dramatically (Elpers 1989). The Reagan administration shifted more of the cost of mental health care to state governments. Some states, such as Maryland, have engaged in a process whereby cost shifting, as opposed to delivery of services, continues to be a priority (Belcher & Blank 1989). As a result of changes made during the Reagan administration, the CMI increasingly must depend on state as opposed to federal support. Lynn, however, has observed that

> elected state officials have on the whole a greater sense of responsibility toward economy and efficiency in governmental operations than they do toward the effectiveness of human services. . . . In short, fiscal discipline must be a primary objective of governors and legislators. (1980, p. 18)

Given the fiscal conservativeness of state governments, it seems doubtful that clinical case management with its higher costs will receive endorsement. Instead, the more likely scenario is that a brokering model, such as the one utilized by Pennsylvania, will become the norm. The notion of endorsing a model of case management that is unlikely to meet the needs of clients contradicts a professional stance in which advocacy is considered an important function of work with clients. If, however, social work refuses to endorse the brokering model of case management, then other professionals will be brought in to fill the void. Although the consequences of this action are clear, the consequences of engaging in practice that is potentially harmful to the client are just as alarming.

Today's mental health community is fraught with problems resulting from the poorly conceived and haphazardly implemented reforms of the 1960s. For example, community mental health staff in the United States spend a great deal of time collecting monies from a variety of sources, thus increasing the overhead costs. A 1986 study estimated that in the United States up to 22 percent of the health care cost is spent on overhead (Himmelstein & Woolhander 1986), compared with 6 percent in Canada. Continuing pressure to reduce costs has derailed more recent initiatives, such as the Mental Health Systems Act, from correcting the problem (Foley & Sharfstein 1983). Experience suggests that it is problematic to support legislation or initiatives that are conceptually flawed and/or of dubious merit. Instead, a more fruitful tactic is to advocate for an approach that is designed to meet the needs of specific clients.

Reducing Costs

The all-or-nothing approach, in which clinical case management is presented as superior to brokering or supportive case management, needs to be upheld, using innovative alternatives to reduce the cost of mental health care. One way to lower the cost of case management is to reduce the time case managers or other supportive staff spend in collecting reimbursement for clients. This task could be accomplished through a consolidated revenue system in which an arm of the government pays for the cost of care and community mental health centers do not have to spend a significant portion of their time in seeking reimbursement for clients (Bigelow & McFarland 1989).

Practitioners also could play a role in resolving this dilemma by engaging in practice-based research that documents the time they spend on indirect services, such as collecting reimbursement for services. They can use these data to support additional research on streamlining reimbursement. This path of inquiry advocates for the client and also endorses cost containment, but shifts responsibility away from clients, to evaluating the ratio of administrative costs to direct-care costs.

Another innovation is to have the federal government provide all the funds for mental health services (Belcher & DiBlasio 1990). A study of California's mental health system showed that the state had consistently undercut mental health expenditures, which, in turn, had pressured local communities (Elpers 1989). Inadequate funding for mental health services directly translates into increased time and money spent for case management activities. On the other hand, consistent and adequate funding, such as could be provided by the federal government, would lower the cost of case management by reducing stress on the client and freeing case managers to concentrate their efforts on more clients.

Efforts to control mental health costs are a necessary priority; however, the means by which fiscal constraint is accomplished should not negatively affect clients. Unlike the position advocated by some scholars, for example, Wimberly (1988), it is important to maintain the clinical integrity of case management and not sacrifice it in an effort to control costs. On the other hand, efforts to reduce costs by reducing overhead are an effective means of achieving this goal without providing inferior services to clients.

Training Clinical Case Managers

Assuming that the purpose of case management is to enhance quality of life and not to reduce costs, then before it can be implemented on a nationwide basis, it is necessary to train professionals adequately to assume case management positions. Clinical case management requires skill and competence beyond that of a paraprofessional; it also goes beyond brokering and supportive care.

The clinical model of case management assumes that the training for clinical case managers occurs at the graduate level. It is at this point in the educational continuum that specialized clinical skills are taught (Johnson & Rubin 1983). Insistence on this level of training supports a model of case management that is highly skilled and provides appropriate resources for the CMI client group. Certain issues should be addressed in the training. First, students should be given a complete understanding of the illnesses that comprise the category of chronic mental illness. Second, they should learn about the resources necessary for CMI clients. Third, students should be trained with a variety of clinical skills. Fourth, students need to be provided relevant internships. Finally, professional training needs to occur in an interdisciplinary mode.

In addition to this training, these professionals should work under the supervision of a senior clinical case manager for two years before they are certified as clinical case managers. This training will be expensive and time-consuming, which means that clinical case managers must be paid a salary commensurate with their education and experience. Otherwise, the notion of a professional is severely undermined and the CMI quickly fall victim to poor-quality care.

Conclusion

For those clients for whom clinical case management is indicated, care planning and coordination functions need to be understood and carried out within the framework of a skilled helping relationship. Training to meet the requirements of these and other case management functions adequately must foster high-level clinical skills and a comprehensive understanding of the needs of CMI clients. The social work profession needs to decide where its priorities for case management lie and, in the case of the CMI population, vigorously advocate for appropriate case management models and the necessary public policy to support them.

References

Anthony, W.A., M. Cohen, M. Farkas, et al. 1988. "Case Management: More Than a Response to a Dysfunctional System." *Community Mental Health Journal* 24:219–28.

Bachrach, Leona L. 1980. "Is the Least Restrictive Environment Always the Best?" *Hospital and Community Psychiatry* 31:99.

————. 1989. "Case Management: Toward a Shared Definition." *Hospital and Community Psychiatry* 40(9):883–84.

Belcher, J.R. 1988a. "The Future Role of State Hospitals." *Psychiatric Hospital* 19(2):79–83.

————. 1988b. "Are Jails Replacing the Mental Health System for the Homeless Mentally Ill?" *Community Mental Health Journal* 24:185–95.

————. 1988c. "Rights vs. Needs of Homeless Mentally Ill Persons." *Social Work* 33:398–402.

Belcher, J.R. and H. Blank. 1989. "Protecting the Right to Involuntary Treatment." *Journal of Applied Social Sciences* 14:74–88.

Belcher, J.R. and F.A. DiBlasio. 1990. *Helping the Homeless: Where Do We Go from Here?* Boston: Lexington Books.

Belcher, J.R. and J.C. Rife. 1989. "Social Breakdown Syndrome in Schizophrenia: Treatment Implications." *Social Casework* 70:611–16.

Belcher, J.R. and B.G. Toomey. 1988. "The Relationship between the Deinstitutionalization Model, Psychiatric Disability, and Homelessness." *Health and Social Work* 13:145–53.

Bellack, A.S. and K.T. Mueser. 1986. "A Comprehensive Treatment Program for Schizophrenia and Chronic Mental Illness," *Community Mental Health Journal* 22:1465–78.

Bigelow, D.A. and B.H. McFarland. 1989. "Comparative Costs and Impacts of Canadian and American Payment Systems for Mental Health Services." *Hospital and Community Psychiatry* 40:805–8.

Billig, N.S. and C. Levinson. 1989. "Social Work Students as Case Managers: A Model of Service Delivery and Training." *Hospital and Community Psychiatry* 40:411–13.

Bond, G.R., L.D. Miller, R.D. Krumwied, et al. 1988. "Assertive Case Management in Three CMHCs: A Controlled Study." *Hospital and Community Psychiatry* 39:411–18.

Borland, A., J. MacRae, and C. Lycan. 1989. "Outcomes of Five Years of Continuous Intensive Case Management." *Hospital and Community Psychiatry* 40(4):369–76.

Ciompi, L. 1980. "Three Lectures on Schizophrenia: The Natural History of Schizophrenia in the Long Term." *British Journal of Psychiatry* 136:413–20.

Elpers, J.R. 1989. "Public Mental Health Funding in California, 1959–1989." *Hospital and Community Psychiatry* 40:799–804.

Foley, H.A. and S.S. Sharfstein. 1983. *Madness and Government: Who Cares for the Mentally Ill?* Washington, D.C.: American Psychiatric Press.

Franklin, J.L. 1988. "Case Management: A Dissenting View." *Hospital and Community Psychiatry* 39:921.

Franklin, J., B. Solovitz, M. Mason, et al. 1987. "An Evaluation of Case Management." *American Journal of Public Health* 77:674–78.

Freud, S. 1940. *An Outline of Psychoanalysis.* London: Hogarth.

Glynn, S. and K.T. Mueser. 1986. "Social Learning and Chronic Mental Patients." *Schizophrenia Bulletin* 4:648–68.

Goering P., D. Wasylaki, M. Farkas et al. 1988. "What Difference Does Case Management Make?" *Hospital and Community Psychiatry* 39:272–76.

Gruenberg, E. and J. Archer. 1983. "Preserving Chronic Patients' Assets for Self Care." Pp. 29–48 in *The Chronic Psychiatric Patient in the Community*, edited by I. Barofsky and R. Budson. New York: SP Medical and Scientific Books.

Gunderson, J.G., A.F. Frank, H.M. Katz, et al. 1984. "Effects of Psychotherapy in Schizophrenia, II: Comparative Outcome of Two Forms of Treatment." *Schizophrenia Bulletin* 10:565–84.

Harris, M. and H.C. Bergman. 1987. "Case Management with the Chronically Mentally Ill: A Clinical Perspective." *American Journal of Orthopsychiatry* 57:296–302.

———. 1988. "Capitation Financing for the Chronic Mentally Ill: A Case Management Approach." *Hospital and Community Psychiatry* 39:68–72.

Himmelstein, D.U. and S. Woolhandler. 1986. "Cost without Benefit: Administrative Waste in U.S. Health Care." *New England Journal of Medicine* 314:441–45.

Johnson, P. and A. Rubin. 1983. "Case Management in Mental Health: A Social Work Domain." *Social Work* 28:49–55.

Kane, R.A. 1988. "Case Management: Ethical Pitfalls on the Road to High-Quality Managed Care." *QRB* 14:161–66.

Kanter, J.S. 1985. "Case Management of the Young Adult Chronic Patient: A Clinical Perspective." *New Directions for Mental Health Services* 27:77–92.

———. 1987. "Mental Health Care Management: A Professional Domain?" *Social Work* 32:461–62.

———. 1989. "Clinical Case Management: Definition, Principles, Components." *Hospital and Community Psychiatry* 40:361–68.

Lamb, H.R. 1980. "Therapist-Care Managers: More Than Brokers of Services." *Hospital and Community Psychiatry* 31:762–64.

Lantz, J. and J. Belcher. 1987. "Schizophrenia and the Existential Vacuum." *International Forum for Logotherapy* 10:17–21.

Liberman, R.P. 1988. *Psychiatric Rehabilitation of Chronic Mental Patients*. Washington, D.C.: American Psychiatric Press.

Liberman, J.A. and J.M. Kane. 1986. *Predictors of relapse in Schizophrenia*. Washington, D.C.: American Psychiatric Press.

Lynn, L.E., Jr. 1980. *The State of Human Services*. Cambridge, MA: MIT Press.

Okin, R.L. 1985. "Expand the Community Care System: Deinstitutionalization Can Work." *Hospital and Community Psychiatry* 36:742–45.

Pepper, B., H. Ryglewicz, and M. Kirshner. 1982. "The Uninstitutionalized Generation: A New Breed of Psychiatric Patient." *New Directions for Mental Health Services* 14:3–13.

Schilling, R.F., S.P. Schinke, and R.A. Weatherly. 1988. "Service Trends in a Conservative Era: Social Workers Rediscover the Past." *Social Work* 33:5–10.

Stein, L.I. and M.A. Test. 1980. "An Alternative to Mental Hospital Treatment, I: Conceptual Model, Treatment Program, and Clinical Evaluation." *Archives of General Psychiatry* 37:392–97.

Test, M.A., W.H. Knoedler, and D.J. Allness. 1985. "The Long-Term Treatment of Young Schizophrenics in a Community Support Program." *New Directions for Mental Health Services* 26:17–27.

Weisbrod, B., M. Test, and L. Stein. 1980. "Alternative to Mental Hospital Treatment, II: Economic Benefit-Cost Analysis." *Archives of General Psychiatry* 37:400–5.

Wimberly, E.T. 1988. "Using Productivity Measures to Avoid Reductions in Force." *Social Work* 33(1):60–61.

Witheridge, T. and J. Dincin. 1980. "The Bridge: An Assertive Outreach Program in an Urban Setting." *New Directions for Mental Health Services* (26):65–76.

Chapter 9

Plan Implementation and Coordination: Case Management in an Employee Assistance Program

Naomi Miller

The business world in which an employee assistance program (EAP) operates can be conceptualized as a microcosm of the larger, "real" world in which the usual need for and activities of case management occur. As outlined by Greene in Chapter 2, certain principles underlie case management as a service delivery approach across a range of settings. These include recognition of the need for a menu and continuum of services, delegated or assumed responsibility for linking and coordinating different elements of a service system, and a goal of comprehensive services to meet individuals' designated needs.

In the environment of the workplace, problems in individual functioning as they affect job performance and productivity become the focus of concern. Just as in the larger world, improvements in, or maintenance of, functioning in the workplace often require more than motivation, effort, and insight on the part of the person with the problem. Such improvements may depend upon new or different resources being added or built into the environment and brought to bear on the situation, efforts to ensure that things that are supposed to happen do happen, and a range of approaches to problem-solving that can address the multiple sources that influence problem growth, maintenance, resolution, and eradication. In short, case management's programmatic (as well as case by case) simultaneous concern with individual need and "community" services and responsiveness is as useful in the workplace as it is in many other settings.

At the same time, there is a substantial *but* that needs to be considered in drawing comparisons: whereas the usual case management (in the larger world) involves helping professionals throughout the service delivery system who see the individual they are working with *as a client/patient to whom they have a responsibility or offer a service*, the persons who have a role/relationship (apart from the EAP professional) to the employee/EAP client in the workplace usually are more focused on *the organizational need for productivity from that employee*. This is not hard and fast, of course, for supervisors and organizations do leave room for changes in response to employee needs, but that is not their major focus.

Other salient features of an EAP that may also characterize case management in other settings, but perhaps with a more compelling emphasis and different consequences in the workplace, include the voluntary and confidential nature of the program. No one can be required to utilize the service. Although supervisors may recommend its usage to an employee who is having difficulties on the job, that employee need not follow the recommendation. Or, if he or she does, the fact of attendance may not be reported to the supervisor without the client's consent. In fact, no information about the attendance, content, or disposition of a participating employee's case may be communicated to anyone without that employee's written consent. The only exceptions would be in the case of imminent danger (to person or place) or in response to a court order.

These three contractual conditions—voluntary, confidential, and management focus—substantially determine and direct the role of the EAP counselor. The other operating determinant of the counselor's role, which would hold strongly and similarly in any setting, is how that counselor defines his or her role and the arenas for intervention. Although there are contractual limitations to any position, options always are available to the professional that are dependent upon and relate to that individual's vision, initiative, and skill. This chapter illustrates the opportunities and utility for the EAP social worker of case management's dual-intervention focus on person (client) and environment (community or, in this instance, the workplace), and examines with what variation boundaries may be defined as the scope of the case manager's activities. The skill elements and activities of the case management function of service plan implementation and coordination are presented through a case analysis.

Program and Role Definitions in an EAP

In EAPs, and the industries and employers who utilize them, several views of the nature of the service are currently in use.

Corporation-as-Client View.   The EAP counselor defines the client as the company and therefore the counselor's role as company agent. This view results from the rationale that the company contract with an EAP essentially asks that help be given to the employee to resolve his or her problem *in order that* the problem not interfere with job performance and the company's mission. The counselor's work is focused on helping the employee function appropriately in the workplace. This may or may not include dealing with problems off the job.

Employee-as-Client View. In this case the counselor defines and limits the role to that of the employee's caseworker. Holding this view, the counselor typically confines his or her activities to assessment and referral (if indicated), possibly including short-term casework related to the employee's thinking, behavior, and stress related to the presenting problem. However, EAPs do not provide long-term casework.

Dual-Client View. The EAP counselor defines his or her role to include education, advocacy, and organizational development. This broadens the arenas of possible attention and intervention. When this definition becomes operative, it calls forth case management skills that rely heavily on understanding systems and how to negotiate them; organizing and prioritizing abilities, relationship-building, and persuasive powers; and (deliberate or sometimes intuitive or accidental) good timing.

This last way of defining one's role reflects the basic social work paradigm of person-in-situation, and case management's operationalization of that paradigm in actual responsibility to both the individual and the community or service delivery system. For the EAP, this view combines the best of both the corporation-as-client and employee-as-client views. The counselor provides service not only to the individual employee and the organization, but has the potential of intervening to improve the role and access of an entire class of workers as is illustrated in the case that follows.

A Case in Point

Ned, a 38-year-old employee, never married, and living with his mother, referred himself to the EAP because of the distress he was experiencing on his job, distress that he coped with by frequent absences from work, vituperative shouting matches with his supervisors, and twice walking peremptorily off the job. He was employed as an animal caretaker on a research unit and was equally responsible to three supervisors, each of whom wanted him to perform his particular tasks in a somewhat different way, a frustration in itself. His shift was constant whereas the three supervisors alternated shifts, accounting for Ned's responsibility to each of them at the point that a supervisor's shift coincided with his. In addition, although performing simple and menial tasks, Ned had college level (beyond a bachelor's degree) training in the general area of animal research. All of his supervisors had considerable experience in doing the work, but no formal education for it.

When a problem with the animals would arise, Ned would research information about it through library resources and sometimes go so far as to write or call authors and outside researchers to determine the best way to handle a given problem. Then he would bring that "solution" to his (non–academically oriented) supervisors. It is not difficult to imagine the ensuing scenario arising from this type of confrontation.

After several such confrontations and subsequent nonacceptance by any of his supervisors of his research activity and solutions, Ned came to feel that the supervisors were neither interested in nor cared about the health and conditions of the animals he loved. He felt, as well, that they were personally antagonistic toward him, and that they demonstrated this antagonism by not allowing him the freedom of movement and control in his area that workers on his same level of employment were permitted in theirs. On their part, one of the supervisors proceeded to file a disciplinary action (for insubordination) against Ned with the company's personnel department.

Ned first sought out the unit head, to whom the supervisors reported, complaining of personal ill treatment, as well as poor treatment of the animals. Encountering the same unwillingness to accept his proposals concerning the care of the animals from the unit head as from the supervisors, he then contacted the director of the department, jumping several levels above the unit head. Ned felt that the director was sympathetic to his points, but saw no change ensuing as a result of their discussion. He became more distressed and sought help from the EAP at that point. He was considering doing two things simultaneously: filing a discrimination complaint with the EEO (Equal Employment Opportunity) office, alleging that he was being treated differently than the other employees of his unit, and contacting his union representative for possible breach of contract action related to his job description not being followed appropriately.

Were the counselor to operate under the corporation-as-client definition of role discussed previously, certain activities would be emphasized. The counselor might discuss with the employee his absenteeism, argumentativeness and insubordination, and highly inappropriate walking off the job. The resulting likely danger of losing employment altogether would be stressed. The counselor would employ strategies designed to help the employee identify and use better coping skills to deal with stress, assert his views, and deal with anger. The focus would be on how to finesse problem situations at work so as not to cause trouble, not to be so troubled by what transpires, and not to lose his job.

In the employee-as-client role definition, the counselor might proceed somewhat differently, examining with the employee why he has chosen a low-paying, low-status job although academically qualified for more important and better paying positions, and how that choice might be affecting his behavior with his supervisors. Possible difficulties in his personal life and living arrangements might be explored to see if and how these could be factors adding to his distress. Discussion would be client-centered and might proceed to determining his real desires and fears, how to accomplish desired goals, and ways to overcome the obstacles to them. Activities might include a referral for longer-term counseling, or assistance in leaving his present job and locating a new one.

A dual-focus role definition applied to Ned's situation illustrates the counselor as a case manager. In fact, the counselor in this case (referred to as John below) operated under that definition of his role. It should be noted that this role was one that John bestowed upon himself because of his philosophy and because, in his view, there was no other person in the workplace who could or would act in such a capacity. It is also useful to note as a general observation that, when a person assumes and acts out a particular role, others will more often than not respond to that role as factual (unless the person is obnoxious in the process!).

A Case Management Approach

John took Ned's presenting problem and position seriously and at face value, and told him so. At the same time, he recognized additional areas that needed addressing and resolution in the work environment if the same problem were not to be repeated with another employee at a later date. In this respect, John recognized not only the system's contributions to Ned's problem, but the wider system delivery issues that were of concern for an efficient and effective overall operation. These areas included management's difficulties with an erratic employee, employees' problems with inconsistent and unsupportive supervision, and departmental danger from possible court suits.

Within the EAP framework, John needed Ned's agreement (a signed release) to use his personal situation as the entering talking point with others in the workplace, in what was to be an effort to improve not only Ned's work circumstances (and performance), but to address wider "system delivery" issues as well. John presented Ned with his understanding of his role and the variety of issues he felt were involved, including Ned's personal concerns. He explained how he would see attacking the problems. John made clear to Ned that it was Ned's choice whether to proceed into the system more broadly than would be necessary if the counseling was limited to Ned's particular concerns.

In his presentation to Ned, John affirmed the traditional social work values of respect for the worth and dignity of the individual, the right to self-determination on the basis of knowledge of circumstances and possible consequences, and mutual responsibility in carrying out decisions. John's intervention strategy utilized social work knowledge of individual behavior, group behavior, and systems operation. The "service plan" that he was ultimately to execute and coordinate would result from systematic assessments of the various individuals and workplace structures, and skill at building trust in establishing a working relationship with Ned in the first place.

Because Ned felt that John understood and was supportive to his position, and that he genuinely wanted to help resolve it, giving weight to his concerns, Ned gave permission for the counselor to contact Dr. L., the department director (with whom Ned had met previously). The purpose of this meeting was threefold: to learn how Dr. L. understood the situation, where he stood on the issues involved, and to assess with him what movement, if any, might be possible to meet concerns on all sides. Ned also gave permission for John to speak with the personnel department, the EEO officer, and the union representative.

John selected the department director as the first person to meet with in this situation because knowing this man's position would be essential to determining how, where, with whom, and in what order to structure subsequent meetings. John also reasoned that he would have to have the active, explicit support of the director in order to attract the serious ear of the unit head and supervisors who needed to be involved. Beginning with either supervisors or unit head seemed unwise since Ned had already gone over their heads by going to the director. In this instance, any efforts on John's part would likely be interpreted as advocacy for Ned (not a more neutral, problem-solving stance) and would be responded to with hostility by the supervisors. Even if there were no hostility, recommendations stemming from supervisors could be vitiated afterwards by the director. John might first have to help (educate) Dr. L. to a modified or different view and philosophy of the workplace in order for them to develop a joint plan for proceeding that would include utilizing ideas from subordinates.

John wanted to be able to speak with personnel, EEO, and union officials because he expected them to be useful allies in implementing the plan. He had dealt with them before on numerous issues, and had a useful reciprocal relationship with each. John knew that these individuals would be willing to delay action in their areas while a problem was under discussion with EAP. In these departments, official actions could have serious consequences for all levels of employees, including themselves. Thus they were careful, hesitant to act, and pleased when a situation could be resolved on a voluntary and unofficial basis, as through EAP intervention. Plan implementation in this case, just as in so many other settings, requires an ability to identify and work with potential collaborators as well as overcome points of resistance. Skilled negotiation with staff of other departments is frequently a part of this effort.

In all instances there was no requirement that meetings with EAP staff be held or that EAP recommendations be followed. Within the EAP, case management activities necessarily take place without a mandated "treatment plan" or any other official and overarching system of accountability. In this case, the EAP was a contracted-out service that was not integrally bound into the company's policies and procedures on other than a voluntary and recommended basis. In other words, the EAP has no real authority or power base. Therefore, the competence, skill, and integrity of the EAP staff determine the stature of the service within the organization and, consequently, its power to obtain hearings and degrees of acquiescence ("services") from management to carry out recommendations designed to solve individual and collective employee difficulties.

In his meeting with Dr. L., John determined that the director agreed with many of Ned's points but felt frightened of engaging the supervisors. They had been in the company longer, and Dr. L. believed that they had access to his superiors and could bad-mouth him into a difficult position. Dr. L. welcomed suggestions through the EAP channel. Information and facts of such meetings were confidential, following any recommendations was optional, and Dr. L. felt that John understood his situation and wanted to and could be helpful. Over the course of several meetings, John and the director developed a plan that was businesslike and pragmatic, while including consideration of the feelings, attitudes, and opinions of all those involved.

Plan Implementation and Coordination

Steps in the plan developed jointly by John and the director included individual meetings with each member of the unit, followed by selected subgroup meetings, such as one supervisor and several employees, and, finally, an overall meeting of the members of the unit and the department director. The purpose of the individual meetings was to assess the stance and role of that individual and the possibilities for compromise, to develop a trusting relationship, and to engage the participant in developing an expanded and holistic view of the situation that could lead to willingness to develop a plan that would work for as many persons in the unit as possible. John and Dr. L. carefully evaluated with whom each of them would meet and in what order. They used role-playing to give Dr. L. a chance to rehearse how he would handle issues and reactions of concern that might occur. All group meetings were structured to examine common concerns and to search for areas of consensus on needed changes that would address them.

In all, 17 meetings were held to implement the plan. Most, but not all, included John. However, he closely monitored the outcome of each meeting, evaluating the need for modifications in subsequent meetings. The meetings generated a diverse array of activities and tasks. John coordinated communication and information exchange, and did follow-up to keep agreed-upon activities moving. The range and complexity of the case manager's skills in plan implementation and coordination is reflected in the eventual outcomes of "Ned's" case:

- New job descriptions were developed with input from employees, supervisors, and union. Initially, John asked each person to write what he or she felt was an accurate representation of the work each had been hired to do. These became the basis of discussions designed to compare and clarify different expectations. The result-ing job descriptions were based to a large degree on amicable consensus among these individuals, and were posted in each work area for reference in the event of future disagreements. Both the union and the EEO office were satisfied with this resolution. Ned was willing to see if this would result in his three supervisors no longer asking for different ways of performing his work.
- Regular monthly staff meetings with the director were instituted for all staff for the first time. Anyone was able to place an item on the agenda for discussion. Using the concept of "quality circles," introduced by the Japanese and used in many American industries, lent "class" and legitimacy to these meetings. Actually, this is not anything different from the social work concept of people partici-pating in and having some control over the decisions that affect them. John had drawn up a plan and structure for the meetings, provided literature to the director, and sat in on the first two meetings as an observer and commentator.
- Regular monthly individual supervisory meetings were instituted. The thinking was that evaluations should be an ongoing, joint process, with support and training from the supervisory staff for areas in which an employee might be deficient. Prior to this, evaluations had been year-end events, unilaterally written by the supervisor and handed to the supervisee. John's activities included providing informal training in sound supervisory procedures.

- Ned and the supervisor who had filed a disciplinary action against him met three times, twice with John and once with John and an officer from personnel. Participants eventually agreed that the action would be withdrawn from the personnel department, but held in the supervisor's unofficial folder in the event of a recurrence of a job walkoff as Ned had done twice before. John discussed and role-played with Ned other ways to handle his anger and temper at work. John also talked with Ned's supervisor about different approaches with Ned when difficulties arose.
- Ned said he might consider John's recommendation and referral for longer-term therapy, and would talk with his mother about possibly seeing a counselor also. In the meantime, John agreed to see Ned periodically when "things got too tight."
- Dr. L. got an "Outstanding" certificate and cash award for resolving several long-standing problems in his department.
- John felt satisfied that implementation of this plan had contributed to improvement of problems in several ways. Ned's individual needs were addressed along a continuum, with positive effects on his work performance. The system of which he was a part was helped to respond in a coordinated and comprehensive way to both Ned's situation and the problems of all employees represented by Ned's circumstances. System goals and needs, including those of its highest level management, were accommodated.

Conclusion

Case management in the workplace presents an abundance of opportunities to provide managers and employees with more satisfying ways of working together as well as being productive. It humanizes concepts and ideas from organizational development with social work knowledge, insights, and skills. Social workers practicing in EAPs can shape the nature and scope of their case management roles to reflect the skill and perspective that has been presented in this chapter. It is important to recognize that how the case manager defines his or her role is the necessary starting point.

Suggested Reading

Gray, M. and D. Lanier, Jr., 1987. *Employee Assistance Programs: A Guide to Community Resource Development.* Troy, MI: Performance Resource Press.

Hage, J. and M. Aiken, 1970. *Social Change in Complex Organizations*. New York: Random House.

Lanier, D., Jr. and M. Gray, 1987. *Employee Assistance Programs: A Guide for Counselors*. Troy, MI: Performance Resource Press.

Masi, D.A., 1984. *Designing Employee Assistance Programs*. New York: American Management Associations.

Wenzel, L., 1988. "Effective Case Management Systems: Integrating Cost and Service Needs." *Occupational Health and Safety* 61:37–41.

Chapter 10

Monitoring Child Welfare Services

Rebecca L. Hegar

When Abraham Flexner at the 1915 National Conference of Charities and Correction made his famous assessment that social work was not a profession, he observed that the social worker was "not so much an expert . . . as the mediator whose concern is to summon the expert" (Flexner 1915, p. 588). Social workers have contested Flexner's conclusion for 75 years (Austin 1983), and much of the current debate about case management centers around defining the role in professional terms. Although the problem of definition is evident in settings where a major social work function is to coordinate the services of other professionals, such as in hospitals, or other health settings and schools, it also poses challenges in the primary fields of social work practice.

Because child welfare is a field of practice in which social work historically has been the central profession, case managers in child welfare agencies are involved in arranging, coordinating, and monitoring the provision of services by other social workers in public and private agencies, as well as by medical, legal, mental health, residential, and other service providers. This chapter provides an overview and an analysis of the child welfare field as a setting for case management. It also examines different models of case management, explores the place of relationship and interpersonal helping in child welfare case management, and discusses the challenges of monitoring service delivery in the child welfare field.

Child Welfare as a Setting for Case Management

Child welfare is a term whose definitions have ranged from the turn of the twentieth century definition, the broadly construed welfare of all children, to the currently more residual label for services to families at

135

risk for maltreatment of children. Contemporary use sometimes stretches the term to encompass services such as child care for working families, respite care for parents of special-needs children, and school-based services (Costin & Rapp 1984). For example, the literature discusses the case management component of services to families with disabled infants (Aaronson 1989) and Hare and Clark address this special group in Chapter 5 of this book. The focus in this chapter, however, is on the narrower range of services provided to families and children in need of protection: in-home services, out-of-home placement, and related care, including services to return children to their families or to free them for other permanent placement, such as adoption.

The contemporary child welfare field features a blend of public-sector and private nonprofit agencies, with a few areas where proprietary or profit-making organizations also provide services. Before the Social Security Act was passed in 1935, the child welfare field was dominated by the private nonprofit sector, exemplified by sectarian and nonsectarian children's homes and foster care agencies and by humane and anticruelty societies that were given authority by municipalities to intervene on behalf of maltreated children. During this period, the Child Welfare League of America and the American Humane Association emerged as overarching organizations to establish standards, disseminate knowledge, and promote good practice in agencies that provided services to children (McGowan & Meezan 1983).

Federal involvement in the broad field of child welfare dates to the founding in 1912 of the U.S. Children's Bureau, a federal agency initially charged with investigating the condition of children in the nation. Later, partly in response to social work advocates within the U.S. Children's Bureau and elsewhere, the Social Security Act made federal grants-in-aid available to states to provide child welfare services in the rural areas that tended to lack private children's agencies (McGowan & Meezan 1983). Subsequent admendments to the Social Security Act, particularly the 1962 provisions which made federal money available for foster care services for children who are eligible for Aid to Families of Dependent Children (AFDC), dramatically increased public-sector involvement in the child welfare field.

Most child welfare services are funded by federal and matching state monies appropriated for specific purposes, and, until the passage of the Federal Adoption Assistance and Child Welfare Act of 1980 (P.L. 96-272), funds were directed primarily to providing protective services, such as child abuse investigations, and to the care of children in foster homes and similar substitute care placements. P.L. 96-272 mandated and funded efforts to keep children in their families or, if they required temporary placement, to return them to their families as a first priority. Although many child welfare services are provided directly by the state agencies authorized to receive federal funds, others are purchased from private agencies and providers, some of them nonprofit organizations with a history of working with children. Beginning in the mid-1970s, the use of purchase-of-service contracts to provide child welfare services increased as states sought to cut public payrolls, federal funding became more available under Title XX, and state agencies sought effective ways to serve families and children (Rapp & Poertner 1980). The search for the best balance of public and private involvement in an area that historically has included both is the topic of a great deal of lively debate that has implications for the provision of case management as a child welfare service (Abramovitz 1986; Pecora et al. 1990; Rapp & Poertner 1980). For example, Pecora and colleagues (1990) addressed the question of how family preservation services under public and private auspices differ with respect to program design, staffing cost, productivity, effectiveness, and other issues. Family preservation services are discussed later in this chapter because they represent an important emerging area for case management practice.

Child welfare practice is one of the fields of social work that always has included many of the functions that currently are labeled case management. Since the days of the early child protection societies and children's homes, someone has had to assume responsibility for selecting and securing a range of legal help, medical treatment, evaluation and counseling, recreation, education, and other services for children in the care of social agencies. in the case of children in placement, agency social workers fulfilled this management role in addition to other roles that families traditionally provide for their members. It was part of serving *in loco parentis*, or in place of the parents to children. However, as a consciously articulated role with defined functions and boundaries, case management is as relatively recent in child welfare as it is in other settings.

Case Management Models in Child Welfare Practice

Among the earliest child welfare programs described in the literature as employing case management were the well-known Oregon and Alameda permanency planning projects of the mid-1970s (Emlen et al. 1978; Stein, Gambrill & Wiltse 1977; Wells 1985). Permanency planning involves purposeful work, which usually is managed by a state child welfare worker or a person employed under a grant-funded model project, to secure permanent homes for children in substitute care because of abuse or neglect. Permanency planning includes time-limited, goal-directed work with the family to change the conditions blocking the child's return home, and it usually involves a series of conferences with the family at set intervals to monitor progress and update plans for the child.

One of the underpinning philosophies of permanency planning is that children who cannot be safely returned to their families after a period in foster care, perhaps one and one-half to two years, should be freed legally for placement with relatives or in adoption or guardianship (a status available in some states involving permanent custody without adoption). Timely return home or termination of parental rights and another permanent placement involves careful coordination with the juvenile court system to ensure that hearings are scheduled and held, that parties are properly notified, that evidence is gathered and pre-served, and that compelling recommendations are made to the court. Model permanency planning projects have introduced periodic court review of child placement cases to monitor progress toward reunification and make timely decisions concerning return or termination of parental rights. Permanency planning efforts in the 1970s were demon-strably successful in meeting many of their goals (Barth & Berry 1987), and many features of the earlier model projects were incorporated into P.L. 96-272, so that states must comply with their provisions to receive federal funding.

Case management also has been used in the provision of continuing protective services and family treatment in child abuse and neglect situations. The National Demonstration Program in Child Abuse and Neglect involved 11 public and private child abuse treatment programs throughout the United States and Puerto Rico during the late 1970s and early 1980s (Cohn & DeGraaf 1982). It included a research component to assess the factors associated with high-quality case management ser-vices, as well as the impact of services on client outcomes. Using agency records and interviews with case managers, external reviewers rated the management of cases. The study identified both case handling practices, such as use of multidisciplinary team conferences, and workload and training issues that were associated with high-quality services. Case-loads of 20 or fewer, case managers with at least three years of experience working with child abuse, and case managers with profes-sional educations were the factors associated with quality services ($p < .05$) (Cohn & DeGraaf 1982). Although quality of case management services was not found to be related to reduction in the clients' propensity to abuse or neglect, the exploratory nature of the study makes that conclusion very tentative. It also may be unrealistic to expect that time-limited management alone could affect problems as long-term and multicausal as child abuse or child neglect (Hegar & Yungman 1989), an issue considered in this chapter.

In the past decade, priorities within the child welfare field have expanded beyond protective services and foster care, as has the perception of where case management services can be used effectively. Much of the current concern is with the entry of children into state care from families overburdened with the urban problems of the 1990s: homelessness, acquired immune deficiency syndrome (AIDS), crack cocaine and other drugs, unsafe neighborhoods, and isolated, fragmented families (Hegar 1990). With the shift in focus from children drifting in the foster care system to the deluge of children entering care has come a new arena for case management in child welfare—intensive home-based services to families. This broad initiative, which also includes family preservation services, is now in the stage of developing demonstration projects and model programs, much as permanency planning was nearly 20 years ago.

The concept behind intensive home-based services is to make extensive efforts to prevent removal and placement of children by providing concentrated help to families in crisis, whether because of abuse and neglect or because of environmental situations that might culminate in maltreatment if the family does not receive help. Programs try to make available emergency financial assistance, emergency housing, supports such as homemakers and aides for parents, and more hours of professional help than are usually available from overburdened child welfare programs. Pecora and colleagues described family preservation initiatives as follows:

> This service is distinguished from other child welfare services by the fact that workers carry low caseloads of between two and six families and typically work with families for brief periods of time (30–60 days). Therapists meet with clients primarily in the clients' homes and provide a wide variety of counseling and "concrete" services such as transportation, housecleaning, and recreational services in order to improve family functioning and thereby prevent child placement. (1990, p. 289)

Pecora et al. also discussed the merits of locating family preservation programs within public-sector child welfare agencies or using services contracted from private nonprofit agencies. Although that issue is central to the debate over how best to provide the services, there is widespread agreement about the critical role of case management. The recent Child Welfare League of America's *Standards for Services to Strengthen and Preserve Families with Children* specified a major case management role, to include: "engaging the family; assessing needs;

creating the service plan; coordinating and implementing the service plan; periodically reviewing the achievement of service goals; monitoring the service delivery process; and effectively terminating the service" (1989, p. 40).

Some of the innovative program development concerning intensive family preservation services and less intensive family support services is being promoted and underwritten by the Annie E. Casey Foundation as part of its child welfare reform initiative (Center for the Study of Social Policy 1987). Selected localities in Maryland and other states have Casey-funded model delivery systems that make case management a linchpin component of service. Interesting features of the emerging Casey model include a design that cuts across the boundaries of existing agencies and programs, "resulting in a more uniform family service system that pulls together existing responsibilities now performed in the child welfare, juvenile justice, mental health, and developmental disability service systems" (ibid., p. 24). Outside the existing, residual child welfare system, it represents in some ways a return to a broader conception of promoting the well-being of families and children.

Case Management as a Helping Relationship

One of the difficult issues surrounding case management is that it seems to fall naturally into the role of "people-processing" and less readily into the realm of "people-changing" (Hasenfeld 1974). How case management helps people is critical in the child welfare field because the client group is experiencing serious interpersonal problems that unquestionably suggest the need for change. This issue is not as critical in some other settings where case management has been used successfully to coordinate services for clients whose primary needs are physical or environmental, for example, in many medical or nursing care settings.

Some authors do view case management as a helping relationship designed to promote growth and change by the client. For example, in the Casey-funded initiative, case management was conceptualized as a set of functions "performed in the context of a relationship between the worker carrying out these tasks and an individual or family which helps motivate family members and enables them to take responsibility for necessary changes" (Center for the Study of Social Policy 1987, p. 21). Weil and Karls included counselor or therapist among the roles necessarily performed by case managers to provide "support, mental health interventions, and consultation to assist clients in decision making and planning" (1985, p. 21). Roberts-DeGennaro also acknowledged a therapeutic component to case management but stressed short-term, task-centered work. She concluded that case management "focuses on helping clients identify and resolve concrete problems in their everyday lives" (1987, p. 468). However, the type of help people need in making decisions about concrete problems may be insufficient to help them achieve fundamental change in their family relationships and parenting roles. The Cohn and DeGraaf (1982) study in which the quality of case management was found to be unrelated to reduction in the clients' propensity to abuse or neglect is an example of this insufficiency.

The child welfare literature has yet to resolve the issue of whether the case manager also should help with problems that go beyond the need for resources and the coordination of services. For example, should the public agency foster care worker with clear case management responsibilities also function as therapist for children in his or her caseload? Can the worker who is charged by the court with helping families resume caring for their children provide family therapy, if that is needed? These questions highlight concerns about the best ways to deliver services and about what is feasible given the resources and staffing of public agencies. Part of the debate about the desirability of combining roles in child welfare services involves the authoritative nature of the field, particularly public agencies' responsibility to juvenile courts for making recommendations about child custody and placement (Hegar 1982). Wells discusses this issue as it applies to case management:

> The public agency worker also serves as a symbol of authority, helping the family while fulfilling the mandate of the state to protect the child. Some child welfare agencies believe that assigning the helping and authority roles to different workers is better for the client. Another school of thought supports combining these roles in one worker, arguing that the family can accept both authority and aid from the same person. Role strain may be an inescapable part of case management in child welfare. (1985, p. 131)

Regardless of how any agency divides its services among staff, it is important to recognize that the entire field of child welfare is authoritative, not just the roles involving investigation or court work. Whether the child welfare staff who carry out case management are the only helping professionals involved with clients or whether the clients also have other workers from within or outside the agency who help in other ways, the entire system serves the interests of child protection. For example, any employed or contracted staff may be called upon to testify in court, and all must recognize that some service goals, such as to improve child care or change disciplinary practices, are externally imposed by society. Helping clients internalize externally defined goals is an inherent part of all social work involving authority, about which there is an extensive literature (Hutchison 1987; Yelaja 1965). In addition, social work thought relevant to case management concerns the therapeutic impact of taking any help, including assistance with concrete services (Smalley 1970; Taft 1937).

Practical issues of staffing and funding also impinge on the concern about the type of assistance case managers can provide. Certainly, a characteristic of case management is cost containment through better coordination of services, which appeals to policymakers. Social workers interested in case management as a professional role often are alarmed at the assumption that the service can be provided by staff without qualifications in any professional field (Ashley 1988; National Association of Social Workers 1989; Rapp & Poertner 1980). In the child welfare field, the issue of qualifications of case managers is complicated by a 25-year trend toward the declassification of social work positions, opening those positions to workers without professional degrees (Russell 1989). For many years, the standard-setting bodies for the private and public sectors, the Child Welfare League of America and the U.S. Children's Bureau, succeeded in defining the master of social work (MSW) degree as the basic credential for many child welfare jobs. Rapid expansion of services in the 1960s and 1970s, in addition to the growth of bachelor of social work programs, brought more bachelor-level staff into the field. In the 1980s, declassification efforts to remove social work education as required or preferred were advanced as cost-cutting measures and fueled in some places by shortages of MSWs willing to work in the public sector (Russell 1989). In 44 percent of the states participating in one study, entry-level child welfare staff are no longer required to have a college degree of any sort (ibid.).

The result of this trend has been a shift in the required educational qualifications of direct-service staff in public child welfare agencies, although there also is evidence that many states continue to prefer hiring social workers and that the greatest changes still may be ahead if, as better-educated staff retire, new social workers avoid public child welfare settings (Lieberman, Russell & Hornby 1989; Pecora, Briar, & Zlotnik 1989; Russell 1989). The rise of case management at about the same time as these staffing shifts has led some to view the case management role as part of an unsatisfactory trend toward deprofessionalization (Rapp & Poertner 1980). Yet, the educational qualifications of case managers have clear bearing on their ability to integrate that role and each of its component functions into a professional helping relationship. However, regardless of whether case managers also perform therapeutic roles with their clients, high levels of expertise are needed for tasks that are inherent parts of the case management process, including monitoring service delivery.

Monitoring Service Delivery in Child Welfare

Monitoring service delivery is one of the major components of case management that are introduced in Chapter 2 and explicated throughout this book. The remainder of this chapter considers the circumstances that make monitoring a particularly vital aspect of case management in child welfare.

Most child welfare services are delivered under a complex system of legal mandates. Examples include state laws directing agencies to receive and investigate reports of abuse and neglect, federal funding legislation requiring periodic court review of foster care cases, and individual court decrees ordering agencies to supervise placements or oversee the safety of children remaining in their own homes. Many local jurisdictions have been sued in class actions that place their services under the continuing scrutiny of court officials (Stein 1987). Although many social work services are provided under some legal mandate, a high degree of interface with the legislative, administrative, and judicial systems is one of the distinctive features of the child welfare field.

Because the law frequently delineates the obligations of child welfare staff, and because of the serious potential harm to clients if poor decisions are made by staff, liability is a particular concern in the child welfare field. Besharov (1985) cited examples of numerous worker failings that can result in lawsuits against agencies and staff: failure to accept a report for investigation, failure to investigate adequately, unnecessarily intrusive investigations, defamation of parents, failure to place a child in protective custody, wrongful removal of children, returning a child to dangerous parents, placing a child with dangerous foster parents, placing foster children who endanger others, disclosure of confidential information, failure to meet the child's needs for special care, failure to treat patients, failure to arrange a child's adoption, and failure to provide adequate case monitoring. Referring to case monitoring, Besharov (1985) made note of overseeing the care children receive from their own families when they are under the court's jurisdiction; however, each step in the case process requires monitoring, from intake to final case closure. Others who have written about legal vulnerability also see monitoring, review, and assessment of services as ways to prevent malpractice and liability (Holder & Hayes 1984). Because child welfare services are legally mandated and have many lines of accountability, monitoring also may have many meanings, including monitoring by auditors and program reviewers, court officials, citizens involved in case review, and supervisors and administrators in the agency itself. Most of these higher level reviews depend on the monitoring of service delivery done by child welfare staff with case management responsibilities.

Child welfare services are delivered by a network of public and private agencies whose relationships often are delineated by purchase-of-service agreements. However, other services may be obtained for clients because of their own eligibility, without any contracting between agencies or transfer of funds. One child welfare case might involve multiple services. In one case example, the Bennett family was referred for medical and educational neglect while living in housing subsidized by "Section 8" funds, with two children enrolled in public school. A case manager might help the family arrange to obtain medical assistance and Women, Infants, and Children food allowances, refer some family members to the community mental health center for evaluation and possible treatment, and arrange for educational evaluations and the development of individualized educational plans for the children. The case manager also might become involved in getting the children's immunizations through the city or county health department.

In most communities, the services sought and obtained for the Bennetts are available on the basis of income eligibility and other family characteristics, and the case manager has no special control over their accessibility. Case management responsibility for monitoring services in this situation may be no more clearly lodged in the child welfare worker than in the school social worker or the public health nurse. Whoever performs the professional role, the family also has a voice in the services its members use. Child Welfare League of America standards for family services specify that

> the social worker should help the family monitor and evaluate the services it is receiving. Monitoring determines whether the service is being delivered appropriately and according to the contracted provisions, such as the number of hours of service to be provided per week. (1989, p. 41)

In another type of family situation, the responsibilities of the child welfare system to monitor services are much clearer. In a second case example, the nature of the sexual abuse report concerning one child in the Cooper family made an immediate rape exam necessary, and it was obtained at the county hospital. Police arrested the father; however, his release from jail pending trial and his continued involvement with his children made temporary placement necessary for the child he was alleged to have molested. The juvenile court assumed jurisdiction and gave the agency temporary custody of Sally, age nine. She was placed in an agency foster home and began weekly therapy at a sexual abuse program run by a family service agency. She also began attending a support group for abuse victims led by two child welfare workers. The mother was referred to Parents United, a voluntary self-help group for families where there has been sexual abuse, and she was assisted in obtaining a restraining order against her husband. The father was evaluated by a psychologist under contract to the child welfare agency. The other children were seen for medical exams by the agency's contract pediatrician, and two-year-old Timmy was enrolled in a developmental day nursery, paid for by the agency. In the Cooper case, the child welfare agency became the central hub around which other service providers revolved, both because the situation was clearly recognized in the community as a child protection matter and because the agency was in a position to provide or purchase many needed services.

The monitoring responsibilities of the child welfare case manager are different in these two situations. In the Bennett case, "case coordination" might have been the best label for the task of maintaining contact with the Bennetts and with numerous providers to determine whether services were being received as needed and planned. Because it was unclear that this role belonged only to the child welfare case manager, some explicit discussion among staff from different systems was necessary to determine who would take the lead. The more clearly a case is defined by everyone as a child protection matter, the more likely that the monitoring role will be performed by the child welfare agency. Whoever assumed the management role and the monitoring tasks, it was likely that the overseeing of the Bennett case would be performed by the case manager and agency. There was no strong mandate, such as court involvement, for external monitoring of service delivery.

The Cooper family situation was a very different matter. Other community systems including the police, the juvenile court, and perhaps the district attorney's office recognized this as a child protection case. Because of the juvenile court adjudication, the child welfare agency commanded authority with the Cooper family that the medical, mental health, and educational systems lacked, and the child welfare agency ultimately would be held responsible by the community for the management and monitoring of services.

In monitoring services to the Coopers, the child welfare case manager had to ensure that the services were delivered in ways that satisfied the requirements of a range of other systems. For example, regulations tied to federal funding would set into motion a series of review hearings in juvenile court, the agency's permanency planning policy would mandate periodic family team conferences with the Coopers to make and monitor plans for reunification, and the rulings in an earlier foster care lawsuit might have required that an agency worker visit Sally in foster care monthly, or more often, and enabled weekly visitation between mother and daughter. Although the Coopers were entitled to the same role in monitoring service delivery as the Bennetts, the fact that some of the services were imposed involuntarily made the task of engaging family members in this process much more challenging.

Because of the involvement of many different service systems, the lines of accountability linking them to the child welfare agency, and the involuntary relationship with many clients, monitoring service delivery is among the most difficult tasks of the child welfare case manager. It requires strong skills in the engagement of clients under difficult circumstances, good communication and negotiation skills in dealing with other disciplines, highly organized record keeping, the ability to meet deadlines, personal presence and verbal skills when appearing in court, and professional credibility with many different audiences. Whether child welfare case managers work for public-sector agencies or private, whether they hold social work degrees or other degrees, whether they take on other helping roles with their clients, it is clear that they do far more than "summon the expert." Nowhere is this more evident than in monitoring service delivery. Although each step in case management is necessary to support the entire process, monitoring is basic to the provision of child welfare services because it is the platform on which rests the agency's accountability to its clients and the community.

References

Aaronson, M. 1989. "The Case Manager–Home Visitor." *Child Welfare* 68:339–46.

Abramovitz, M. 1986. "The Privatization of the Welfare State: A Review." *Social Work* 31:257–64.

Ashley, A. 1988. "Case Management: The Need to Define Goals." *Hospital and Community Psychiatry* 39:499–500.

Austin, D.M. 1983. "The Flexner Myth and the History of Social Work." *Social Service Review* 57:357–77.

Barth, R.P. and M. Berry. 1987. "Outcomes of Child Welfare Services under Permanency Planning." *Social Service Review* 61:71–90.

Besharov, D.J. 1985. *The Vulnerable Social Worker: Liability for Serving Children and Families*. Silver Spring, MD: National Association of Social Workers.

Center for the Study of Social Policy. 1987. *A Framework for Child Welfare Reform*. Washington, D.C.: Center for the Study of Social Policy.

Child Welfare League of America. 1989. *Standards for Services to Strengthen and Preserve Families with Children*. Washington, D.C.: Child Welfare League of America.

Cohn, A. and B. DeGraaf. 1982. "Assessing Case Management in the Child Abuse Field." *Journal of Social Service Research* 5:29–43.

Costin, L.B. and C.A. Rapp. 1984. *Child Welfare: Policies and Practice*. 3rd ed. New York: McGraw-Hill.

Emlen, A., J. Lahti, G. Downs, A. Mckay, and S. Downs. 1978. *Overcoming Barriers to Planning for Foster Care*. Washington, D.C.: U.S. Government Printing Office.

Flexner, A. 1985. "Is Social Work a Profession?" Pp. 567–90 in *Proceedings of the National Conference of Charities and Correction, 1915*. Chicago: Hildmann.

Hasenfeld, Y. 1974. "People Processing Organizations: An Exchange Approach." Pp. 60–71 in *Human Service Organizations: A Book of Readings*, Y. Hasenfeld and R.A. English, editors. Ann Arbor: University of Michigan Press.

Hegar, R.L. 1982. "The Case for Integration of the Investigator and Helper Roles in Child Protection." *Child Abuse and Neglect* 6:165–70.

———. 1990. "Child Welfare in a Social Context: Challenges for Social Work in the 1990s." *Tulane Studies in Social Welfare* 18:37–45.

Hegar, R.L. and J.J. Yungman. 1989. "Toward a Causal Typology of Child Neglect." *Children and Youth Services Review* 11(3):203–20.

Holder, W. and K. Hayes. 1984. *Malpractice and Liability in Child Protective Services*. Longmont, CO: Bookmakers Guild.

Hutchison, E.D. 1987. "Use of Authority in Direct Social Work Practice with Mandated Clients." *Social Service Review* 61:581–98.

Lieberman, A., M. Russell, and H. Hornby. 1989. *National Survey of Child Welfare Workers: Impact of Education on Attitude and Perceptions*. Portland, ME: National Child Welfare Resource Center for Management and Administration.

McGowan, B.G. and W. Meezan. 1983. *Child Welfare: Current Dilemmas, Future Directions*. Itasca, IL: Peacock.

National Association of Social Workers. 1989. "Case Management in Health, Education, and Human Service Settings." In *Social Work Speaks: NASW Policy Statements*. Silver Spring, MD: National Association of Social Workers.

Pecora, P.J., K.H. Briar, and J.L. Zlotnik. 1989. *Addressing the Program and Personnel Crisis in Child Welfare: A Social Work Response*. Silver Spring, MD: National Association of Social Workers.

Pecora, P.J., J.M. Kinney, L. Mitchell, and G. Tolley. 1990. "Selecting an Agency Auspice for Family Preservation Services." *Social Service Review* 64:288–307.

Rapp, C.A. and J. Poertner. 1980. "Public Child Welfare in the 1980s: The Role of Case Management." Pp. 70–81 in *Perspectives for the Future: Social Work Practice in the '80s*, K. Dea, editor. Washington, D.C.: National Association of Social Workers.

Roberts-DeGennaro, M. 1987. "Developing Case Management as a Practice Model." *Social Casework* 69:466–70.

Russell, M. 1989. *Public Child Welfare Job Requirements*. Portland, ME: National Child Welfare Resource Center for Management and Administration.

Smalley R. 1970. "The Functional Approach to Casework Practice." Pp. 77–128 in *Theories of Social Casework*, R. Roberts and R. Nee, editors. Chicago: University of Chicago Press.

Stein, T.J. 1987. "The Vulnerability of Child Welfare Agencies to Class-Action Suits." *Social Service Review* 61:636–54.

Stein, T.J., E. Gambrill, and K. Wiltse. 1977. "Dividing Case Management in Foster Care Family Cases." *Child Welfare* 56:321–31.

Taft, J. 1937. "The Relation of Function to Process in Social Casework." *Journal of Social Work Process*. 1. Reprinted as pp. 206–26 in *Jessie Taft: Therapist and Social Work Educator*, V.P. Robinson, editor. Philadelphia: University of Pennsylvania Press.

Weil, M. and J.M. Karls. 1985. "Historical Origins and Recent Developments." Pp. 1–28 in *Case Management in Human Service Practice*, M. Weil and J.M. Karls, editors. San Francisco: Jossey-Bass.

Wells, S.J. 1985. "Children and the Child Welfare System." Pp. 119–144 in *Case Management in Human Service Practice*, M. Weil and J.M. Karls, editors. San Francisco: Jossey-Bass.

Yelaja, S.A. 1965. "The Concept of Authority and Its Uses in Child Protective Services." *Child Welfare* 44:514–22.

Chapter 11

Case Manager as Advocate: Family Advocacy in the Military

Robert H. Gemmill, David L. Kennedy, James R. Larison, Willard W. Mollerstrom, and Katherine W. Brubeck

Advocacy is a generic, universally available strategy that cannot be franchised or copyrighted by any one individual or group. It is applicable to virtually all aspects of society, whether to humans, animals, plants, or inanimate objects. However, the application of advocacy skills varies from person to person and from group to group. In addition, some environments are more conducive to advocacy than others. For example, environments that are indifferent or hostile to change are high-priority areas for advocacy. These are the environments in need of advocacy because within them reside the disadvantaged, disenfranchised, poor, oppressed, and exploited—the orphans of empowerment.

Advocacy in the context of case management practice can be a paradoxical phenomenon for several reasons. First, by empowering others to act in their best self-determined interest, the advocate may compromise the established case management treatment plan. It is essential to be "in charge" of a case to accomplish the case management goals, yet to exercise total control or domination of a case in relation to one's clients is ethically questionable. Therefore, the judicious use of power and the mandate to accomplish specific case management plans can be a thorny path to negotiate. Second, the intentional creation of a positive change in a fragile relationship may throw the relationship off balance and place it in a dysfunctional state. Third, the advocate may initiate actions that are extremely beneficial to others and at the same time may place the advocate in emotional or physical jeopardy.

The case management role can be gratifying and can have a significant impact on service delivery, yet the function of advocacy, which is an engine of change, can be a difficult role to play. It is not a glamorous job, because the rewards are few, the work is hard, the hours are long, success is often fleeting, and support can be minimal. This is true for any service delivery system in which the social work case manager practices. However, the military system illustrates the importance as well as the pitfalls of case advocacy in a particularly clear-cut way. As a system, the military makes a contract with its personnel by which a certain amount of autonomy and self-determination (normally available to the average citizen) are renounced in exchange for specific employment and other benefits to self and family. The power structure, status hierarchy, and amount of prescribed behavior (rules and regulations) are more clearly demarcated, formal, and impervious to change by the individual than in many other systems. All of this circumscribes, or at least delimits, individuals' or families' ability and opportunity to "get what they need for themselves." This is a central reality of the case manager in the military family advocacy program.

This chapter emphasizes the pragmatic application of case advocacy, rather than organizational or class advocacy (Sosin & Caulum 1983), and the use of advocacy strategies by the individual case manager. It specifically addresses the skills of the advocacy function, which is one of the eight components of the case management role (Weil & Karls 1985). Although the distinction among role, function, and skills is easy to state, in practice it is difficult to focus exclusively on the skills of advocacy without intruding into the boundaries of the case management role and its other seven functional components. Some of the skills of the advocacy function are similar or identical to the skills of other case management functions. The discussion of case advocacy is based on the authors' experience in the military family advocacy case management programs.

First, this chapter defines the term *advocacy* as it is used here and discusses concepts of advocacy identified in the literature. It then presents a historical background of family advocacy programs in the air force, army, and navy. Finally, the chapter provides three case examples, which are composites of numerous family advocacy cases, to reveal and emphasize the skills of advocacy at work, regardless of outcome, rather than to demonstrate victories or less successful undertakings. One case demonstrates a productive outcome; one, a less than productive outcome; and one, mixed results with a combination of case management functions.

Overview of Advocacy

A common theme in the social work profession is advocating for client rights. A long-standing practice approach designed to help clients obtain specific rights and entitlements, advocacy was originally envisioned as a means of challenging the status quo. With the advent of government-sponsored case management systems, advocacy functions have become legitimized and a standard component in professional social work services (McGowan 1987).

Although routinely used as an intervention strategy for helping clients, a review of the literature reveals that there are at least 30 different definitions of advocacy. Fortunately a common thread exists in these many definitions: McGowan has suggested that case advocacy is a planned, dynamic process that

> can be most accurately defined as partisan intervention on behalf of an individual client or identified client group with one or more secondary institutions to secure or enhance a needed service, resource, or entitlement. (1987, p. 92)

Pinderhughes pointed to the elimination of powerlessness to improve social functioning as the major goal of case advocacy. She maintained that "lack of power or powerlessness and helplessness are the root causes of poor social functioning" (1976, p. 1). The goal of advocacy, according to Brower (1982, p. 141), involves activities that are aimed at the redistribution of power and resources to an individual or group that has a demonstrated need.

Fowler (1989) identified several components of the partisan role: (1) guardian of the patient's rights, (2) preserver of the patient's values, (3) conservator of the patient's best interests, and (4) champion of social justice. While Kohnker (1982) indicated that the advocacy role to inform and to support is carried on at three levels: (1) advocacy for oneself, (2) advocacy for clients, and (3) advocacy for the larger community.

Overcoming a client's sense of powerlessness is the key practice strategy in advocacy (Solomon 1976). Helping a client see him- or herself as having knowledge and skills that can be used to achieve a solution to his or her problem is a major goal. Enlisting the client as a collaborator or partner in the problem-solving process to affect the power structure also is necessary.

The concept of advocacy as power may be somewhat unfamiliar or even uncomfortable to some social workers. That is, although advocacy is a concept embraced by social work that can be traced to the very inception of the profession, the utilization of power strategies may not be embraced by all social workers with the same intensity and reverence. The advocate role is action filled, with risks for both the advocate and the client (Kohnke 1982). In working with bureaucratic organizations, the case manager must possess certain advocacy skills. The case manager must know how to cope with a high degree of frustration within a system, must be sharp mentally, must be able to tolerate ambiguity and obstruction, and must have luck (Brower 1982). In addition, the case-to-cause formulation of advocacy, in which data is collected from a number of individual situations to support a general advocacy stance or position, may place the social worker in a situation where he or she is confronted by conflicting loyalties—loyalty to the client versus loyalty to his or her agency or organization—that must be resolved.

This ambivalence about the use of power is reflected in the nature of the social work direct-practice curriculum. It is an interesting paradox that although the social work direct-practice curriculum often empha-sizes advocacy, the same curriculum is often silent on the strategies of power and of conflict and conflict resolution that often accompany its deliberate use in advocacy. Kohnke (1982) has suggested that in addition to being open-minded about him- or herself, an advocate must have a broad clinical and sociological knowledge base comprising information about systems analysis, social ethics, social laws, politics, and issues related to the medical-industrial complex.

For the purposes of this chapter, advocacy is equated with utilizing a strategy of power to obtain specific services and resources for an identified population that is unable or incapable to secure the services or resources on its own. Case studies will illustrate advocacy as one strategy of power in which the advocate functions as a power broker to secure services and resources for others. If, for example, the case management plan identified the need for three types of services/ resources, which cannot be obtained by the client, then the function of the case manager as advocate is to utilize a strategy of power to secure those services and resources.

Power comes in many forms: power of persuasion, personal power and influence, legal power, and so forth. Regardless of its form, power is used to obtain services and implement treatment plans. Power begets change; powerlessness maintains the status quo.

History of Military Family Advocacy Programs

Impetus for the Department of Defense (DOD) family advocacy program developed in the early 1970s in a climate of growing concern about the adequacy of programs and policies addressing the manage-ment of family violence. A combination of events, both nationally and within the military community, heightened the awareness of family violence in general and focused attention on its negative effects on military force readiness.

In March 1973, Dr. C. Henry Kempe addressed a meeting of the American Academy of Pediatrics on the problems of managing child abuse in the armed services. Inspired by Kempe's remarks, the executive committee of the American Academy of Pediatrics Section on Military Pediatrics proposed a set of recommendations for the assistant secretary of defense for health and environment. Among the recommendations of the committee were the development of specific child abuse policies and programs and ongoing education for medical and ancillary personnel dealing with family violence problems. Also in 1973, following an American Medical Association conference workshop on management guidelines for child abuse, the assistant secretary of defense for health and environment established a triservice (air force, army, and navy) child advocacy working group. This group, which represented both command and medical interests, was charged with monitoring existing child abuse programs in the military services.

The passage of the Child Abuse Prevention and Treatment Act (P.L. 93-247) in July 1974 provided an additional catalyst for the development of military family violence programs. The law established the National Center on Child Abuse and Neglect (NCCAN) and the National Advisory Board on Child Abuse and Neglect. By 1977 each branch of the military services had formulated and published child advocacy program regulations.

The following are brief descriptions of the air force, army, and navy family advocacy programs. Each program comprises ten components:

1. program development
2. prevention of child and spouse abuse
3. early identification
4. early intervention
5. treatment and rehabilitation
6. coordination of a comprehensive program
7. reporting
8. staff education
9. program evaluation or quality assurance procedures
10. cooperation with civilian authorities.

Each program uses a case-managed approach with a designated staff person functioning as case manager to ensure comprehensive, coordinated, and accountable service provision. The term *case manager* is not used widely, however. Depending on the branch of the military, this person may be called the family advocacy officer (FAO) or the family advocacy representative (FAR).

Description of Military Family Advocacy Programs

Air Force Family Advocacy Program

The U.S. Air Force family advocacy program is governed by Air Force Regulation 160-38, Family Advocacy Program. This program is organized and managed through written policies, procedures, and standards. The goal of the program is to enhance the health and well-being of air force families so that military members can fully concentrate on their assigned duties. The regulation assigns specific tasks to the FAO, including identifying, reporting, assessing, and treating families with exceptional medical or educational needs, children who are at risk for injury, and families experiencing maltreatment. The five broad program elements are (1) prevention, (2) direct services, (3) administration, (4) training, and (5) program evaluation.

Primary and secondary prevention services for families are available from many base agencies and are overseen by a member of the FAO's staff: the outreach worker. An outreach worker identifies the needs of air force families and addresses those needs by enhancing family strengths through programs that help families cope with high-stress events, such as separations and reunions. In addition, the outreach worker provides education and supportive services to at-risk families. Direct services to families, however, are provided primarily by staff of the medical facility under the coordination of the FAO, who is a clinical social worker. An FAO is assigned to each of the 122 air force medical treatment facilities.

The air force surgeon general's staff administers the family advocacy program and the Medical Inspection Team ensures compliance with program regulations. Policy guidance, standard setting, and day-to-day operations are managed from Brooks Air Force Base in San Antonio, Texas, by family advocacy program managers who work at the twelve major command headquarters (surgeon general's offices) located throughout the world.

Family advocacy personnel and other base agency staffs are trained in agency training programs, through individual continuing education, and through centralized training sponsored by the surgeon general's staff at Brooks Air Force Base. Family advocacy officers, therapists, outreach workers, lawyers, physicians, and family advocacy data support specialists receive training at least every other year. A few selected professionals are specially trained to be members of the DOD Family Advocacy Command Assistance Team, an interdisciplinary team that responds to multiple child sexual abuse incidents.

The air force has initiated a four-year research program to attempt to determine which maltreatment interventions work, with which people, and under what conditions. The evaluation of the family advocacy program is overseen by the air force surgeon general's staff at Brooks Air Force Base.

Army Family Advocacy Program

Army Regulation 608-18, the Army Family Advocacy Program, establishes the U.S. Department of Army policy on the prevention, identification, reporting, investigation, and treatment of both spouse and child abuse. The army policy is fourfold: (1) to prevent spouse and child abuse, (2) to protect the victims of abuse, (3) to treat families affected by abuse, and (4) to ensure the availability of trained professionals to intervene in child abuse cases.

Objectives of the family advocacy program are to prevent family violence, to encourage reporting of spouse and child abuse, to promote investigation of all allegations, to provide treatment by training professionals for all those affected by family violence, and to restore families to healthy functioning. The family advocacy program is a highly structured program that is empowered to achieve its purpose or mission. The use of power and accomplishing the mission are two subjects well understood in the military.

The regulation specifies who will provide services and describes their function. It identifies administrative procedures, training requirements, key persons and agencies, reporting procedures, and many other activities. The chief of the social work service at each installation is appointed as the family advocacy case management team chairperson. The chief oversees programs that coordinate intervention and clinical treatment in child and spouse abuse cases; provide logistical and administrative support, labor, and funding; provide quality assurance to monitor and evaluate the program; ensure prompt notification of all appropriate people and agencies from initial investigation to case closure; provide case management that includes a treatment plan and quarterly review; and offer annual training to all direct services and supervisory staff.

Navy Family Advocacy Program

The Department of Navy family advocacy program is a multidisciplinary, multifaceted program designed to address the problems of child and spouse abuse. The navy relates family violence to readiness and the secretary of the navy's Instruction 1752.3, Family Advocacy Program, outlines this concept as follows:

> Family violence and neglect can detract from military performance, the efficient functioning of military units, and can diminish the reputation and prestige of the military service in the civilian community. It is incompatible with the high standards of professional and personal discipline required of members of the Naval service.

Program objectives are designed to develop activities that contribute to a healthy family life; ensure interagency cooperation and proper treatment of victims; identify abusers and apply sanctions as appropriate; break the cycle of abuse; encourage voluntary self-referral, ensure confidentiality, and provide family education programs; develop memoranda of agreement with local civilian authorities; establish a central registry for cases.

Responsibility for implementing the family advocacy program is divided between the medical community and the "line," or operational command. In addition to treating medical injuries sustained in abuse incidents, the medical treatment facility, hospital or clinic, is required to appoint a full-time person (a clinical social worker) as the family advocacy representative. The family advocacy representative who implements the treatment/case management aspects of the program receives all reports of abuse, maintains all case records, ensures case presentation at subcommittee meetings, reviews medical records in maltreatment cases, acts as a medical point of contact, and coordinates overall case management including case advocacy. In addition, that person makes clinical assessments, ensures that all families are interviewed as appropriate, corresponds on behalf of the subcommittee, files civilian and military reports as required, screens families for overseas assignments who have been involved in family advocacy, and screens family home care applicants.

The Family Service Center, located on all navy and marine corps installations, has responsibility for prevention programs, and assisting in intervention and treatment of identified abusive families. Each installation commanding officer is required to appoint an FAO (a nonmedical person, and usually the Family Service Center director) to ensure overall coordination among the many parties of the family advocacy program. In addition, the commanding officer must establish a multidisciplinary family advocacy committee to provide recommendations for local policy, coordinate military-civilian interface, encourage a team approach, provide evaluation of the program, recommend resource allocation, and serve as advocate for families and children.

Naval Military Personnel Command reviews all incest cases of active-duty navy (but not marine corps) centrally and makes the final determination regarding the service member's eligibility for the navy treatment option or separation. Marine corps incest cases are handled on the local level.

Advocacy Case Examples

The following are three examples of advocacy at work: a productive child case, a less productive child case, and an equivocal adult case. Much can be learned from less productive cases as well as productive cases, in which the social worker, client, and even the system struggled against resistant forces.

Unanticipated and uncontrolled variables can compromise or constrain the function of advocacy. For example, the emergence of more than one advocate in the same case can result in conflicting interests or opposing advocacy positions. In addition, the often prevailing attitude that right, correct, or noble behaviors will prevail without a dedicated champion can constrain the function of advocacy. Moreover, assigning to the advocacy function the same status given those targeted for service delivery can have a significant negative impact on using and marshalling power for change, because those targeted for advocacy have limited status, position, power, or authority. Finally, the lack of knowledge of the rules, norms, value, and language of the service delivery system or service infrastructure can compromise advocacy.

The first two cases deal with child protection; the third with spouse abuse. Advocacy in these cases focuses on acquiring for any family, including the child at risk, services or interventions that are needed and cannot be obtained by the person on his or her own. Each case is divided into three components: (1) a general case description, (2) case assessment and advocacy strategies, and (3) a summary of the advocacy skills gleaned from the case example.

Case Example 1: Productive Child Case

Case Description. Mary is a 20-year-old, single, active-duty mother with a three-year-old girl who was referred to the hospital for child neglect. Mary had just completed an entry-level medical technician course and was awaiting entry into an advanced laboratory course that was to start in four months. She had joined the military five months ago to "start a new life" and was reported to be estranged from her family and her high school boyfriend who fathered her child. An ex-boyfriend reported to her supervisor that she left her child at home unattended for long periods. When her supervisor asked her about the incident, she said that there had been only one occasion when she had been unexpectedly called up for duty and had been unable to find a sitter, so she had left her child unattended. Her supervisor reported the incident to the family advocacy representative.

Case Assessment and Advocacy Strategies. The family advocacy representative (FAR) contacted the service member and scheduled an interview the same day. During the interview, the advocate explained the purpose of the family advocacy program and that the advocate was required to report the incident to the local child protection services agency. Mary was angry and upset with the allegation but was cooperative when informed that the safety of her child was of prime importance.

During the initial assessment, the soldier admitted that she had left her child unattended for one to two hours on a number of occasions when called to work on short notice. While waiting for an opening at the military hospital child care center, she had patched together a network of friends to care for her child while she was on duty. Because of inadequate income she could not afford civilian child care services. The FAR contacted friends to verify that informal child care arrangements had indeed been made. In addition, a pediatric examination revealed no evidence of abuse or neglect. Mary said that she was experiencing severe stress as a result of her irregular work hours, poor personal relationships, and recent orders to attend a laboratory school at a distant installation. The FAR offered the soldier short-term counseling to help her resolve her problems; Mary accepted the offer.

After a review of the case and reports from the soldier's supervisor and pediatrician, the Family Advocacy Committee determined the case to be "substantiated neglect." The committee recommended that

- the soldier enter a six-month individual treatment program aimed at managing stress, improving child-rearing skills, and enhancing personal relationships;
- the FAR write a letter requesting priority placement for the soldier's three-year-old child in the military child care center;
- the soldier's orders to laboratory school be postponed for six months so she could complete her individual therapy;
- the FAR write a letter to the soldier's supervisor recommending the stabilization of her work schedule during the time the soldier is in treatment; and

- an assignment hold be placed on the soldier for six months to ensure that she would not be reassigned to a new installation before the treatment plan was completed.

In individual therapy, the client successfully explored her feelings of inadequacy as a parent and was helped to identify and develop skills to cope with a variety of stressors. She joined a single-parent's support group, where she gained friends, improved her child-rearing skills, and increased her confidence in dealing with people. Her supervisor stabilized her work hours and her three-year-old child was enrolled in the day-care center. After six months, the committee voted to release the assignment hold and approved a letter requesting that the soldier be enrolled in the next available laboratory course.

Advocacy Skills. The following advocacy skills are illustrated in this case example:

- Champion for service member. The advocate initiated services and resources to include a letter requesting priority placement in the military child care center, postponement of the laboratory course, and then reenrollment back into the course; a letter to the supervisor requesting work hour stabilization, placement of a temporary hold on reassignment, and the provision of individual therapy.
- Judicious use of power. The advocate used just enough power to obtain identified services and resources without destabilizing the problem or creating resistance. For example, the FAR sent a letter to the supervisor soliciting his cooperation in stabilizing Mary's working hours, rather than ordering or demanding work hour changes. The advocate was able to utilize the skill of using the least amount of power to obtain the maximum results.
- Infrastructure knowledge. The advocate possessed the knowledge of Mary's work environment, the working dynamics of the Family Advocacy Committee, and the military system. This knowledge gave direction to the appropriate use of power to obtain identified services and resources. For example, knowing that the child care center would consider an exception to the enrollment policy based on a specifically worded written request guided the advocate to use the appropriate strategy to obtain the child care services. The skill then is not knowing that a service or resource exists, but rather knowing how to access the service or resource with an effective power strategy.
- Case advocacy disengagement. The advocacy function was used to obtain and maintain services and resources, but once it was

determined that Mary had acquired the skills to function independently without assistance, advocacy services were immediately
disengaged.

Case Example 2:   Unproductive Child Case

Case Description.   On Sunday morning, the FAO received a call from
the medical officer on duty informing him that a child care worker at the
child care center had called to report a suspected abuse incident of a
five-year-old boy. She had witnessed the mother slap the child on the
side of his face in front of the day-care center. The medical officer told
the FAO that he was familiar with the family and thought that the
investigation of the incident could wait until the next day.

Case Assessment and Advocacy Strategies.   The next day, the FAO interviewed the child care worker after reviewing her written report. The alleged perpetrator proved to be the wife of a high-ranking commander.
The worker discussed the case with his supervisor, who became concerned about possible political repercussions and questioned the worker
intensely about the procedures to be followed, especially the need to report the allegation to the county child protection services.

The FAO contacted the commander to inform him of the allegation
and the need to interview the entire family. The commander requested
that his own office be used for the meeting; the FAO agreed to this
unusual procedure. During the parents' interview, the commander was
visibly upset, but contained his anger. The commander's wife vehe-
mently denied that she had struck her child on the face. Disregarding
protocol, the FAO interviewed the child in the presence of his parents.
The FAO felt it might be his only opportunity to interview the child,
which proved to be correct. Despite the parents' presence, the child
verified that his mother had slapped him and stated that his face had
"gotten big." The FAO briefed his supervisor on the interview. Following normal procedures, he consulted the family advocacy legal representative and reported the allegation to the soldier's chain of command.

The commander came to the FAO's office to request copies of the case
file, the family advocacy regulation, and other written documents
pertaining to family advocacy. He also filed a complaint with the
inspector general, who initiated a formal inquiry into the family advocacy program and directed the FAO supervisor to explain the reasons for
the suspected child abuse investigation. The commander and his wife
obtained a lawyer and the lawyer and the legal officer requested copies
of all material related to the case and the family advocacy program.

Pressure on the worker escalated when the deputy commander of the
installation initiated his own inquiry. He extensively questioned individ-

ual Family Advocacy Committee members and wanted to know if they had children. It was suggested that one needed to be a parent to evaluate and determine child abuse effectively and to have an understanding of the problems in rearing children. The commander's wife told several female friends that she was being accused of child abuse and being harassed. These friends, in turn, told their husbands, who called the worker to question his conduct. Harassment continued as the military legal officer "chewed out" the worker's supervisor for what the worker was doing to the commander for perceived unfounded reasons. Both the legal officer and the inspector general felt that the Child Advocacy Regulation allowed for some discretion in reporting the allegation to the child protection services. The worker stood his ground, expressing amazement at the suggestion that he should ignore a very clear regulation and state law. No consensus was reached on reporting the allegation.

In the weeks that followed, the worker was required to provide daily updates to his supervisor. He found himself continually supplying information, defending the program and answering telephone calls from persons complaining about his actions. He began to have difficulty sleeping, questioned his own professional judgment, constantly felt on the defensive, and was confronted at social occasions by the commander's friends, who accused him of trying to ruin the commander's career.

At the request of the worker's supervisor, a special family advocacy case management team meeting was convened to review the case. Based on documentation, eyewitness account, and confirmation of the incident by the child, who described soft tissue swelling, the case was determined to be "substantiated abuse." The supervisor became very upset with the finding. Although he agreed the incident took place, he felt it was not abuse. He overruled the team's decision. Within a short time, the commander, his wife, and their child were all transferred to a new military facility. The case ended.

Advocacy Skills. The following advocacy skills are highlighted in this case example:

- Focus on the family advocacy mission. It is essential to use advocacy skill to accomplish the objective, which in this case was child protection and the possible enhancement of family functioning. Instead, performing the advocacy function shifted to performing nonadvocacy functions and skills directed at defending the program and the individual. Simply, the advocacy function and advocacy skills were discontinued and replaced with behaviors unrelated to case management, such as public relations, program defense, self-defense, and the copying of program documents for distribution.

- Effective use of assertive, confrontive, and aggressive behavior. These behaviors can be effective strategies of power. Unfortunately, in this case, the FAO experienced the effect of the strategies rather than employing the strategies. The effectiveness of these skills is well illustrated by the commander, who used them with adroitness to derail the entire family advocacy program objectives and to meet his own needs.
- Reframing. When intervention is perceived as an opportunity by others for help or problem-solving, noncompliance, resistance, denial, and a whole repertoire of defense mechanisms are reduced. In this case, the family advocacy program and the FAO were perceived to be a danger and threat to be eliminated. The FAO was unable to change this perception. Although reframing may not be a primary advocacy skill, advocacy is difficult to practice in a hostile setting. Part of reframing includes education of the staff, supervisors, and community to realize that insulation and isolation of alleged abusers from discovery and treatment is an irresponsible action and denies help for families and protection of children from repeated abuse.
- Risk awareness and tolerance. As demonstrated by this case, the advocate must be aware of and accept risks, stress, ambiguity, frustration, obstructions, confrontation, unfairness, and lack of supervisory support. Low tolerance to these stressors can place the advocate in personal jeopardy and can handicap the advocacy function.

Case Example 3:   Equivocal Adult Case

Case Description.   Diane is a 28-year-old pregnant active-duty sergeant with twelve years in the military. She has been married for four years to Ben, a 38-year-old Viet Nam veteran who is a full-time househusband. He suffers from post–traumatic stress syndrome with current manifestations of agitated depression. The couple have two children, ten-year-old Jimmy, who is Diane's son by her first marriage, and three-year-old Sandra. Diane's 69-year-old mother, who suffers from Alzheimer's disease, lives with the family.

Case Assessment and Advocacy Strategies.   After making several anonymous calls to inquire about emergency shelter, Diane identified herself to the family advocacy social worker as an abused spouse. She was persuaded to go to the emergency room, where bruises about her face and arms were documented. She was treated for a bloody nose. She said Ben had beaten her with a stick when he came home after drinking and found her asleep and perspiring. Ben, who is noncompliant in taking his medications, interpreted the perspiration as evidence she had been sleeping with another man. Diane called the police to receive assistance to stop the abuse, but they told her that they could only assist in removing Ben from the house if she filed charges. She did not wish to file any charges.

Diane resisted going to a shelter because it did not have a day-care facility, it was far from Jimmy's school, and she feared her mother would become more disoriented in her absence. Although Ben was verbally abusive, he had never physically abused the children or Diane's mother. Ben shopped, cooked, and cleaned with efficiency. Diane preferred to risk her personal safety for Ben's live-in care and housekeeping. His presence also provided the required "family plan" by the military if she were ever deployed to the field or called on alert. Her mother's presence in the home probably ensured that Ben did not abuse the children.

When the worker and the community health nurse made a home visit three days after the emergency room visit, Diane had a black eye and she indicated that Ben had a rifle in the house. Because of her imminent delivery, she continued to resist going to the shelter. Her passive solution was to take her children and mother to stay with an aunt during her maternity leave. Because Ben had a history of leaving when she was away from the house for an extended time, she felt that he would "just go away" and not return. She agreed to consider a nursing home placement for her mother.

Because of the high-lethality profile, the worker called an emergency meeting with Diane's commander, first sergeant, legal officer, military psychiatrist, community health nurse, and Diane. The commander arranged a priority neurological evaluation for Diane's mother. The community health nurse arranged for the county adult services to do an in-home evaluation, which was required for admission to a nursing home. A plan was made to get Ben's rifle out of the house. The worker assisted Diane in obtaining Women, Infant, and Children supplements and county child care vouchers, and in being placed on the list for military child care services.

Diane did go to her aunt's home and Ben did leave the house. However, before her maternity leave ended, Diane received orders for an unaccompanied tour (no family members) to Korea, precipitating a new crisis. With concurrence of the case management team, the worker arranged for deletion of Diane's name from the orders. Diane's mother was placed in a nursing home, and the children were placed in day-care, but after a few months, Ben returned home and the beatings began again. Worry about her personal safety, the threat of being sent to Korea, remorse about placing her mother in a nursing home, and job stress resulted in Diane's being admitted for short-term psychiatric hospitalization while Ben cared for the children.

After hospitalization, Diane decided to leave Ben. She and the children moved in with a female friend. With Diane gone, Ben decompensated. He voluntarily entered a civilian psychiatric unit, was discharged in two weeks, and left the state to live with his sister.

The case remains open, with unpredictable problems on the horizon. Ben may return. With military reductions, Diane could be discharged or she may receive new orders for an unaccompanied tour. In either case, Diane would lose child care resources and support from the family advocacy program.

Advocacy Skills. This case is an example of the reality of adult advocacy, where, by definition, adults are empowered to manage their own problems and life. There is often incremental success, combined with unresolved problems and inability to predict how long a treatment plan will fend off existing problems, before another crisis develops. This case does not so much identify advocacy skills as advocacy beliefs and values. It is important to recognize these beliefs and values because they help to place in perspective the limits of advocacy and identify ethical problems. This case reveals the following beliefs and values:

- ability to support an adult client's beliefs and values even if they are perceived to be short-sighted, self-defeating, and unreasonable;
- ability to accept that adults have the right to act in their own perceived best interest;
- ability to accept incremental progress coupled with the reccurrence of long-term career or personal difficulties;
- tolerance of problems without adequate solutions;
- recognition that some clients are maintained by a fragile balance and aggressive intervention can destroy that balance; and
- dedication of extensive time for minimal results that could evaporate at any time, with the belief that the time is well spent.

Conclusion

The three cases presented identified a number of advocacy skills, beliefs, and values targeted at implementing case management goals. The cases reveal that there is no one formula for advocacy that will obtain consistent and predictable results from case to case. The advocate must be able to employ a strategy of power to mobilize services and resources to operationalize identified service delivery goals.

The military system provides a useful context in which to examine and highlight key advocacy issues of power differential, personal risk in confrontation, persistence, and system support and nonsupport. However, these issues are not unique to the military. Social work case managers will need an ability to understand and assess these factors at work and skill in designing strategies that consider those factors, in whatever service delivery system they may work.

Selected References

Brower, H. 1982. "Advocacy: What Is It?" *Journal of Gerontological Nursing* 8(3):141–43.

Fowler, M. 1989. "Ethical Issues in Critical Care." *Heart and Lung: The Journal of Critical Care* 18(1):97–99.

Kohnke, M.F. 1982. *Advocacy: Risk and Reality*. St Louis, MO: C.V. Mosby.

McGowan, B.G. 1987. "Advocacy." Pp. 89–95 in *Encyclopedia of Social Work*, 18th ed., A. Minahan et al., editors. Silver Spring, MD: National Association of Social Workers.

Penderhughes, E.B. 1976. "Power, Powerlessness and Empowerment in Community Mental Health." Paper presented at the Annual Convocation of Commonwealth Fellows. Chestnut Hill, MA, October.

Solomon, B.B. 1976. *Black Empowerment*. New York: Columbia University Press.

Sosin, M. and S. Caulum. 1983. "Advocacy: A Conceptualization for Social Work Practice." *Social Work* 23(1):12–17.

Weil, M., and J.M. Karls, and Associates. 1985. *Case Management in Human Service Practice*. San Francisco: Jossey-Bass.

Chapter 12

Evaluation: Case Managers and Quality Assurance

Monika White and Lynn Goldis

Case management, often described as "good old social work" or "good old discharge planning" or "good old public health nursing" or "good old community work," has become a fundamental method of ensuring that appropriate services are coordinated in response to identified needs of individuals. While the debate about who invented it and how it is similar to, and different from, other professions remains unresolved, the "practice" of case management continues to spread. Not the panacea that many make it out to be (Kane 1988a), it has nevertheless become the method of choice for many private-practice and agency-based professionals working with vulnerable populations (Grisham et al. 1983). And, because it is readily implemented into almost any type of service system with minimal initial disruption, it has been adopted by many disciplines and into many settings (see Kane 1988b).

In the absence of standards, certification, accreditation, or agreed-upon training content, the variation in practice is remarkable. The prospect, then, of controlling or assuring the quality of the service, itself, is extremely challenging. This chapter describes an attempt to meet that challenge in a case management program serving several hundred elderly who reside in the community.

The issues of quality assurance for case management outside the medical arena are just beginning to be addressed in the literature, and are still sparse. Two special volumes on the subject have been recently published (Applebaum 1989; Fisher & Weisman 1988). More frequently, the subject is focused on institutional care or home health (see, for example, Staebler 1990).

Systematic quality assurance in case management programs represents untested ground. This is probably due to the relative newness and continuing evolution of this specialized arena of clinical work and to the inherent difficulty of developing standards of care for process-oriented practice in which outcomes are hard to measure. The fact that case management is offered in virtually every type of human services setting, with great diversity in the way it is provided, adds to the challenge.

For example, case management may be part of a public, nonprofit, or proprietary agency or practice. Its goals can range from cost savings to providing alternatives to institutionalization. Financial support might be through grants, contracts, or fees. Case managers may be social workers, nurses, other professionals, paraprofessionals, or even volunteers. The target populations can be age specific (elders, children), condition specific (persons with AIDS, developmentally disabled), or income specific (low income, able to pay). Further specialization occurs in actual practice within specific domains, for example, medical case management for spinal-injury patients, legal case management for probate or conservatorship cases, industrial case management for employed caregivers, and long-term-care case management for insurance programs.

It is likely that in the next five or ten years some "industry standard" may develop. Several professional organizations have already formulated case management standards, including the National Association of Social Workers (NASW 1984) and the National Council on Aging (NCOA 1988). Others are in the process of developing proposals for standards including national nursing, continuity of care, and private geriatric care management associations. The issue of quality and standards for case management is also of concern to the consumer who is receiving the service, and guidelines for selecting and employing case managers are becoming available (see, for example, Secord 1987).

In the meantime, programs currently in operation appear to be founded on their own unique culture and norms, either by design or default or some combination thereof. Practice standards are derived from the organizational mission in conjunction with funding source requirements and the character of leadership and staff culture within the agency. The professional values reflected in the disciplines of the management structure and the frontline case managers serve as the basis for practice. For this reason, employment of professionally trained staff is an initial step in ensuring some congruence in practice.

Case Management: A Brief Overview

While most program design variables such as purpose, staff, funding, target, caseload size, duration of service, and function of the case manager can differ in case management programs, the process of case management tends to remain fairly intact. Because of this, it is possible to control the quality of the basic case management tasks across programs. Briefly, this process consists of the following functions [based on White (1987)]:

1. Casefinding.   Outreach and intake; identification of appropriate clients according to established criteria; information and referral if not appropriate for program.
2. Assessment.   Comprehensive evaluation of client's current health, psychosocial, and functional status and needs; involvement of or contact with important decision-makers in client's life.
3. Care planning.   Development of written plan to address identified needs incorporating formal and informal systems of care; consideration of payment sources and expectation of duration of planned services.
4. Plan implementation.   Arrangement of service delivery through purchase or referral relationships; family or other support networks where possible and available.
5. Monitoring.   Oversight of quantity and quality of services provided; status of client; problem-solving as needed; implementation of changes as appropriate.
6. Reassessment.   Regular, scheduled reevaluation of client situation and care plan; determination of future status.
7. Case closing or new care plan.   Termination procedures as dictated by agency or services, including transfer to ongoing programs as appropriate, or new care plan and back through implementation, monitoring, and reassessment process.

Case Management and Quality Assurance

As noted by Helen Rehr,

> Many problems beset the process of quality assurance. At what, when, at whom, where, and even how to look are only a few of the questions facing each profession and provider. . . . However, we cannot stop the process because we have not reached the perfect evaluation state. We must proceed with the crude instruments we have, improving and advancing as we go. (1979, p. 151).

Borrowing from program evaluation methodology, quality assurance strategists for case management have made progress, particularly in the area of publicly funded case management programs for the frail elderly. Applebaum and Austin's (1990) recent work, for example, focuses on how the effectiveness of case management can best be monitored and evaluated. These authors apply the classic evaluation framework of structure, process, and outcome to measure the quality of care. Structure refers to the organizational framework in which the program operates. Process is the means and procedures related to the way things get done. Outcome, of course, is the result of the program or service intervention.

It is possible to identify the organizational structure, practice process, and desired outcomes specifically for each component of the case management process. Consensus across team members and congruence with agency or program policies will lead to stated standards of quality.

Casefinding

Structurally, casefinding, which involves client targeting, outreach efforts, and eligibility screening, includes several key tasks. The first is to conduct a needs assessment to determine the types of problems of a given population and the frequency with which the problems occur. The second step involves creating the service, and the third is communicating its availability in an effective manner.

From a process perspective, an effective intake procedure, including staffing, methodology, and documents utilized, needs to be built and maintained. This also involves identification of key referral sources and the relationship-building efforts with them. Factors of the intake process itself that require monitoring to assure quality might include thoroughness, timeliness, risk screening, and interviewing consistency among staff.

Outcome measures for casefinding focus on how well the targeted client group is reached and engaged in the program. Factors such as number of referrals, percentage of the target population served, and appropriateness of referrals received can be tracked.

Assessment

From a structural vantage point, quality assurance of the assessment function involves determining the content or focus of the assessment, determining what the staffing of the function should be, and defining parameters including time frames, instrument to be utilized, amount of information to be garnered, who is to be involved in the process, and how and where the assessment is conducted.

The process of assuring quality of the assessment function can involve activities such as peer and/or supervisory review of documents, training of assessors to ensure consistency among different staff, comparing assessment data from multiple staff for the same client, and live monitoring of assessment interviews by supervisory staff.

The key outcome measure regarding the assessment is accuracy of client-related information. The two ways in which accuracy can be checked are (1) evaluating how well the picture of the client gathered from the assessment process holds up over time and how closely it relates to case management interventions, and (2) getting feedback from the client, client's family, or other involved professionals regarding the accuracy of the assessment conducted.

Care Planning

Structural aspects of the care-planning process include who is involved, what the format is in regard to formalization, team composition if in a team format, documents utilized, and standards for time frames.

Process aspects of care planning include document review, correlation of assessment data with problems identified in the care-planning process and their relationship to interventions planned, and supervisory and/or peer involvement in aiding the practitioner in focusing the care plan (identifying and prioritizing problems).

Beyond review of care plan documentation, the most crucial outcome measures of care planning are that the plan produced is viable, that a full array of possible interventions have been considered and the best options selected, and that client preferences and priorities have been incorporated. It is also important that the plan be individualized to the client and the client's situation to avoid "cookie cutter" care plans (Schneider 1989).

Implementation

In addition to time frames for implementation, structural aspects of this phase involve the role definition and function of the case manager, and the involvement in implementation on the part of the client and the client's informal system. It is the "who," "what," and "how long" of the case management process. It is also congruent with social work values, which supports the position that the client and those in the informal network of the client be encouraged to be as involved in the implementation process as they are capable.

In terms of process, clear and explicit "therapeutic contracting" between the practitioner and the client/client system that delineates the plan and includes the division of labor, expected time frames and frequency of home visits, provides a built-in venue for evaluating how successfully the implementation is proceeding. In addition, monitoring of the implementation process by peer and supervisory staff is an essential component. There is also the opportunity to compare the practice of different clinicians on similar types of cases when such factors can be identified. But, most importantly, implementation of the plan of care should solve identified problems. This is the key outcome measure.

Follow-Up

In regard to structural aspects, the frequency of contact, the method for the contact, and the individuals to be contacted are the key pieces. Minimum standards for frequency of home visits, phone contacts, and parameters around key collaterals to be contacted (physicians, conservators) are generally an established part of case management program design.

In regard to the process aspects of follow-up, peer consultation and individual supervision represent the key ways in which quality can be assured and a clear focus for follow-up (problem-solving) maintained. Since follow-up involves monitoring and evaluation of the direct services arranged as well as client status, reports from vendors and contact with agency personnel are key components of the process.

Another useful monitoring method is client satisfaction surveys. Whether by phone or in writing, they are helpful during the monitoring phase to discern the client's view of the value of case management intervention. If surveys are utilized to assess client satisfaction with case management, it is important that clear distinctions be made between the case management service—such as assessment and service coordination—and any other services—such as personal care or transportation—so that the effectiveness of each can be fairly judged.

In addition to problem resolution, the emergence of new problems over time can stand as a positive outcome measure for the follow-up period. Cases should not often remain static in terms of defined client needs. Crisis resolution and stabilization should ultimately result, at least for a period of time, for the problems addressed in the care plan.

Reassessment

A reassessment or reevaluation step should be built into the case management process at a frequency determined in the care plan. Within formal programs, reassessment is usually mandated at regular periods such as three- or six-month intervals, depending on the program structure. In all cases, a reassessment should be performed prior to discharge from case management.

Often the reassessment format is a repeat of the initial assessment or an abbreviated version of it. It is conducted where the client lives and is presented for team discussion. Reassessment forms undergo peer review for completeness, timeliness, and thoroughness. The primary focus is to track client status and changes that lead to appropriate planning for the next designated period of time. Individual supervision is important to this process and case managers need to be ready to justify their recommendations.

The major outcome desired at this point is a decision for the future of the client's involvement with case management and other service systems. If problems are resolved, then the result will be to close that case, but only if all systems are stable or the client is transferred to another program. If the client situation is not yet in hand, and a determination is made to continue the case management involvement, then the outcome of this step is the development of a new care plan that reflects any changes in client status or needed services.

An important aspect of this decision is to standardize termination policies so that staff, families, and the client are clear as to why and when a case will be closed. Team review of recommendations will assist in this effort. Since the outcome of reassessment, i.e., continuation or termination, impacts both caseload mix and intake capability, constant examination and refinement of this component are essential.

Senior Care Network: A Case Example

Senior Care Network (SCN) is a nationally recognized model for hospital-based program initiatives in community long-term care services for the elderly and their families. The program was designed in late 1984 to promote health and independence, provide easy access to information and services, and enhance the capacity of the community to support the concept of aging well.

A department of Huntington Memorial Hospital, a private, nonprofit, 606-bed, full-service teaching hospital in Pasadena, California, the program was developed and implemented and is now administered by social workers. Initial efforts to frame the need and problems to be addressed by this program were originally conceived by the hospital's social work staff, who were in a prime position to see the consequences of gaps in coordination and continuity of care for the elderly.

The program has focused on ensuring that any person in need of assistance who is referred has equal access to professional help regardless of frailty level or financial status. For instance, diverse funding streams of both public and private sources support multiple case management programs, which enables the organization to provide a comprehensive system of care coordination. Medicaid waiver (2176) and state funds support case management and some purchase of in-home services for eligible groups. Those with means can obtain services on a fee-for-services basis and a combination of hospital charitable funds, foundation grants, and donations subsidize case management for others. This diversification in funding enables a more rapid response time to new referrals with no waiting list at any time because clients can be served somewhere in the system.

The culture of SCN is one that values innovation, creativity, teamwork, professional training, and dedication to the highest quality of client service possible. This approach is manifested in a dynamic environment that encourages inclusion rather than exclusion, in other words, a constant quest for how to say "yes, we can."

Other philosophical bases in the program include an expectation that staff at all levels will not accept the status quo if changes need to be initiated internally or within the external delivery system and that constructive problem-solving efforts are the responsibility of everyone. There is also a recognition that due to individual style, total uniformity in practice may be unrealistic, but enough similarity can be achieved that outcomes can be articulated. These norms or operational rules reflect the character and value base of the program's leaders.

The challenge, then, is to implement quality control and assurance methods that do not disturb the balance between this approach, the diverse organizational and funder demands, and the sincere effort to serve all clients equally. The ability to maintain this balance is one of SCN's major accomplishments. As noted by Applebaum and Austin (1990), the best reason to implement quality assurance methods is to achieve beneficial outcomes consistently regardless of the variations surrounding the service.

Assuring Quality of Service at SCN

SCN utilizes a number of quality assurance strategies incorporated into program structure and process. A major one is centralization of key activities that affect all clinical staff and client care. These facilitate easy access to SCN services, with a process that involves team thinking and decision-making. Strong social work values and practice methods have influenced the case management design, illustrating the adaptability of case management into existing organizational culture.

Centralized Intake

A licensed clinical social worker staffs a centralized telephone intake, consultation, and referral service that channels callers to appropriate community, hospital, and SCN programs. This central access to SCN programs enables logging of calls, disposition, and follow-up while providing an invaluable service to the community with professional assessment and referral. It is conducive to automating data collection of information not only on clients, referral sources, and presenting problems, but also provides a basis for decision and time monitoring since all referrals are given the same multivariate functional and psychosocial risk assessment. The major purpose of the model is to ensure that those considered to be at risk are identified and consultation for intervention is given. To increase the confidence level in the determination of risk, only highly qualified, experienced clinicians perform the "triage" task.

Case Assignment

Another centralized activity is the assignment of cases referred for case management within SCN. This is called "triage rounds" and is performed daily by three or four clinical staff, including the triage worker and either a clinical supervisor or manager from each program. In this way, referrals can be prioritized, decisions can be made about which program is most appropriate, and caseload numbers and mix can be considered in assignments to case managers. The team thus redetermines appropriate eligibility, controls the flow of cases, and monitors caseloads.

This mechanism was instituted to determine the disposition of each case. The meeting involves supervisory, administrative, and line staff from the three case management programs, who review the calls received that day to make trilevel decision:

- Does the case situation require an in-person assessment?
- If assessment is needed, to which program should the case be referred?
- If in-depth evaluation is not indicated, what community-based resources are being utilized and what additional resources or expertise is needed?

This process, taking half an hour of intensive staffing on a daily basis, serves as one of the most far-reaching quality assurance interventions of all those in place within the department.

Document Content and Format

As simplistic as it seems, the forms and instruments utilized in a case management program serve as the minimum standards for clinical practice and content. The assessment tool provides the focus and framework for clinical evaluation. The care-planning document, including the style of problem statements and notation of solutions or possible interventions, serves as the scaffolding of the clinical process.

The assessment summary narrative used by SCN provides a thorough outline of content that each case manager is expected to address. Clearly, this structured format ensures a baseline of expected quality of practice. The same can be said of SCN's intake/assessment and referral form. Its thorough completion in a 15-minute telephone interview conducted by experienced master's-level clinicians also ensures a minimum quality of clinical data, which, taken together, provide a detailed picture of the client situation.

Organizational Structure and Communication

There are two distinct features of the structure of SCN that support quality and consistency of practice. First and foremost, it is designed around a matrix/team model of collaboration rather than a hierarchical structure. Communication flows readily in all directions instead of linearly, and senior management staff participate in planning meetings, staff meetings, and task forces at all levels of the organization. Similarly, line staff are represented on committees and team structures at all but the strategic personnel issues levels of operations.

Second, open communication, including criticism of the organization's status quo and "interesting errors" from which emerge useful lessons for the individual as well as principles for others, is not only welcomed but is expected. "Fireside chats" staffed by the director and associate director are held several times a year to provide an opportunity for all staff to verbalize how things are going and to voice what gets in the way of optimum functioning and ease within the department. There is a demand from the leadership that clinical line staff as well as nonclinical staff not tolerate what does not work organizationally, and all opinions of constructive criticism are openly considered.

Individual Supervision

Because of the very broad scope of clinical and systems issues that case management encompasses with the case manager as principal overseer, problems may emerge in a caseload on a day-to-day basis that are of no small significance. Some of the issues that routinely arise might include crisis intervention around elder abuse, determining the most appropriate residential level of care change, providing supportive counseling to family members with divergent viewpoints, resolving agency problems around gaps in quality service provision, mediating the public benefits system on behalf of a client, or serving as communications conduit between a client and a health care provider.

In fact, all of these events could occur in the same case at the same time and find the case manager as the primary advocate and problem-solving agent. Multiplied by numerous case managers, consultation by the supervisor is necessarily a minute-to-minute, crucial function, which ensures consistency of practice between staff. The traditional, scheduled, one-on-one supervisory times provide a more sedate, focused opportunity to look at larger staff development needs and serve as counterpoint to the day-to-day problem-solving efforts.

Both on-the-spot and scheduled supervision are essential because the influence of the individual case manager cannot be taken lightly and day-to-day practice can unintentionally stray from established norms. One of the ways this occurs is that a staff person at the line or middle-management level will make a practice decision—perhaps around prioritizing types of clients to be served, or number of face-to-face visits versus telephone contacts on a particular case—that can inadvertently affect the larger system in a deleterious way or run counter to the culture and expectations. Monitoring of daily activities is essential to preventing unanticipated field policy setting.

Team Care Planning

Because of the holistic scope of the generalist, and perhaps unlike traditional casework or counseling, the case management practice of the individual clinician is most enhanced by input from peers, either informally or in a team case or care-planning conference. In its purest form, each new case is "care planned" in a formal interdisciplinary team format soon after the initial in-home assessment or routine formal reassessment. This structure provides a built-in peer supervision and consultation methodology, with the clinical supervisor or program director keeping the practice of each individual on the "balance beam" of normative practice.

It is in the collective experience of formal care planning that "types" of cases and expectations around practice behaviors emerge over time. Variables such as length of service, kinds of interventions or services that may be useful with a particular presenting problem, what works or does not work for a given type of client, and what community resources are known by a member or members of the team for a particular client situation are all discussed. Here, anecdotal "outcome measures" can begin to be tracked for the benefit of all.

For example, a clinician's experience with several nursing home placements for severely demented clients or the expertise of a clinician working with clients with a particular type of psychiatric disturbance may benefit the practice of all team members. A collective wisdom develops that raises the baseline of knowledge and practice for each individual and thus for the entire team, whether the team consists of two or ten members.

It is the job of the leader/manager to set the tone for expected practice norms—the culture of the team or program. Team care planning, although expensive in terms of personnel time, is perhaps the most concrete quality assurance mechanism in day-to-day case management practice.

In-Service Training

Due to the breadth of the knowledge base required for effective case management practice, there is an ongoing need for continuing education for the practitioner. Such education helps to ensure a minimum baseline of practice knowledge among program staff. In-service training is a format that allows for such content to be tailored to meet the needs of staff dealing with types of cases specific to the agency or community. For example, a program might have a particular emphasis on working with clients who have specific kinds of problems such as cognitive impairment, physical frailty, or social isolation. In-service training needs should be a combination of basis core content plus topics that emerge from the day-to-day practice experience. Presentations are conducted by both internal staff and outside guest experts.

At SCN, practitioners and administrative staff serve on a committee to formulate content for in-service sessions held at least monthly. Some core content includes chart documentation, psychiatric conditions in the elderly, time management, dealing with dementia, elder abuse, mental status testing, and evaluating risk and degrees of frailty. Additional content has included topics such as the "pack rat" syndrome, psychotropic medications and the elderly, helping families manage caregiver stress, and dealing with death and dying.

Conclusion

In order to apply quality assurance methods to case management practice, it will be necessary to define a number of variables and consider a number of issues as they relate to the structure, the process, and the desired outcomes of the program, among them:

- What is the purpose of the case management service?
- Who is the target of the service?
- Who is the appropriate case manager?
- Who will the program/service be accountable to?
- How long should case management be provided?
- How many cases can be effectively managed by one person?
- How much information should be obtained and retained?

Often these types of questions are answered by a funding source who defines what is to be done, why, to whom, how many, when, where, and for how long. Usually, accountability requirements will necessitate some mechanisms for both qualitative and quantitative data collection and reporting, which will serve as some basis for quality assurance. The nature of case management in these programs and in those that are totally independent of formal regulation requires close attention to development of good evaluative methods. The fact that case management is practiced in so many different settings by such diverse individuals makes it particularly vulnerable to legal, ethical, and moral scrutiny.

Case management quality assurance cannot truly be conducted in isolation. This would fail to address the impact of the environment in which it functions. Since the primary focus of case management is to link clients with needed resources, the systems that provide those resources will act to constrain or facilitate the desired outcome.

In publicly funded programs, case management is conducted within mandates and regulations of the funder and restrictions of available dollars. The presence or absence of formal services within a community and the ability of the case manager to access those services on behalf of the clients are variables as critical to a successful case management process and client outcomes as the presence or absence of family and other informal supports. Furthermore, the case manager has many masters and, therefore, multiple accountability responsibilities. In addition to funder and agency requirements, the case manager must meet expectations and demands of direct-service providers, families, other decision-makers, and the clients themselves. These factors add to the complexity of case management functions and to the importance of good quality assurance mechanisms.

Private-practice, fee-for-services case management has its own set of dilemmas. With no regulation, any quality assurance relies solely on the individual agency or practitioner's values, ethics, and policies. As case management continues to gain a stronger foothold and acceptance into the helping professions, a commitment to quality service is needed, not only to individuals' practice, but systemwide.

References

Applebaum, R., ed. *1989*. *Generations*. Issue on assuring quality of care, winter. American Society on Aging, San Francisco.

Applebaum, R. and C.D. Austin. 1990. *Long-Term Care Case Management: Design and Evaluation*. New York: Springer.

Fisher, K. and E. Weisman, eds. 1988. "Case Management: Guiding Patients through the Health Care Maze." *Quality Review Bulletin*. Joint Commission on Accreditation of Healthcare Organizations.

Grisham, M., M. White, and L. Miller. 1983. "Case Management as a Problem-solving Strategy. *PRIDE Institute Journal of Long-Term Care Home Health Care* 2(4):21–28.

Kane, R.A. 1988a. "Case Management: What Next?" *Generations* (Fall):77–78. American Society on Aging, San Francisco.

Kane, R.A., ed. 1988b. *Generations*. Issue on case management, fall. American Society on Aging, San Francisco.

National Association of Social Workers. 1984. *Standards and Guidelines for Social Work Case Management for the Functionally Impaired*. Silver Springs, MD: NASW.

National Council on the Aging, National Institute on Community-Based Long-Term Care. 1988. *Case Management Standards: Guidelines for Practice*. Washington, D.C.: National Council on the Aging.

Rehr, H., ed. 1979. *Professional Accountability for Social Work Practice: A Search for Concepts and Guidelines*. New York: Neale Watson Academic Publications.

Schneider, B. 1989. "Care Planning in the Aging Network. Pp. 3–25 in *Concepts in Case Management*, R.A. Kane, editor. Papers from the University of Minnesota Long-Term Care DECISIONS Resource Center, Minneapolis.

Secord, L.J. 1987. *Private Case Management for Older Persons and Their Families: Practice, Policy, Potential*. Excelsior, MN: Interstudy Center for Aging and Long-Term Care.

Staebler, R., ed. 1990. *Caring* IX(8, August). Issue on case management and home care.

White, M. 1987. "Case Management." Pp. 93–96 in *Encyclopedia of Aging*, G. Maddox, editor. New York: Springer.

Chapter 13

Mastering the Case Manager Role

Betsy S. Vourlekis and Roberta R. Greene

This book has taken an in-depth look at the case manager in action, as that practitioner works to meet the needs of clients in the context of service and resource systems. The focus has been on the direct-practice role of case manager, analyzed as a progressive, although overlapping, series of functions. These functions constitute the case manager's "work." Each function has been examined and richly illustrated with a variety of clients, presenting problems, and service contexts. Taken together, the role of case manager described in Chapters 3 through 12 demonstrates the impressive array of skills and activities, and range in the professional use of self, that are required of the practitioner in what is frequently described as boundary-spanning work.

Social work case management requires a blending of clinical and interpersonal skills, systems-spanning perspective and activities, and fiscal and program resource management and accountability. Mastery of the role of case manager involves a valuing of this complex use of self, as well as practice to proficiency in the skills that support it. This requirement is both exciting and intimidating: exciting because diversity in role performance can be stimulating and call forth many competencies; intimidating because multiple demands and tasks can overwhelm the time, energy, and spirit available. Therefore, it is not surprising that job descriptions and program designs often oversimplify what is required or expected of a case manager, choosing to emphasize one or two functions, without appreciating the interdependence of each of them. Perhaps it also is not surprising that many practitioners opt for a more restricted practice focus, limited to the worker-client field, and the settings and practice avenues that provide this focus, rather than the inclusive wide-angle lens of case management.

For those who choose or are offered the opportunity for case management practice, or who are designing policies and programs that incorporate case management, this chapter highlights and summarizes the skills and characteristics of the professional use of self that undergird the social work case manager role. Central to overall mastery of the role is a grasp of the dual-practice concern with individual clients' needs and a service delivery system that can in fact meet these needs.

Boundary-Spanning Work

It can be said that the historical social work commitment to address the person-environment interface has been strengthened through the profession's involvement in case management. The boundary-spanning nature of case management has been well described in the social work literature. Drawing upon Gordon Hearn's (1974) discussion of a systems approach to connecting a client to the formal and informal community service network, Seabury (1982) applied the term "boundary work" to describe the case manager role. Boundary-spanning work is done in the context of a supportive client-worker relationship: this is focused on day-to-day coping, and provides the client with one stable relationship across institutional, community, and agency boundaries. The daily demands of implementing the dual concern with client and service system led Moore (1990) to suggest that the case manager must possess the clinical skills of a psychotherapist and the advocacy skills of a community organizer. Johnson and Rubin (1983) made a similar point, discussing the dynamic tension between psychotherapeutic and socio-therapeutic orientations in the practice of case management.

O'Connor (1988) used Bronfenbrenner's (1979) schema of a differentiated environment to conceptualize the boundary-spanning properties of case management's multilevel systems approach. He suggested that the case manager's interventions deal with increasingly encompassing environments: moving from the micro—which deals with an individual's primary relationships, to the meso—referring to the linkages between the client system and community resources, to the exo—dealing with the structures, programs, and resource allocation policies that affect the client's situation; and finally to the macro—the realm of legislation, regulation, community, and social norms and expectations.

To bring this to a practical level, Austin, Low, Roberts, and O'Connor (1985) suggested that case management is an intervention with impact on two levels: the client and the service system. Case management practice simultaneously involves direct-practice activities, which revolve around development and implementation of the case plan, and case management structures, which refer to the administrative arrangements, interagency networks, and informal and formal community resources that are the vehicle for service delivery (O'Connor 1988). The case manager attends to both. Austin (1987, 1988) pointed out that coordination of services and advocacy at the client level requires extensive knowledge of the local delivery system. A care plan made without such knowledge is probably not feasible. At the same time, working for client-level service coordination requires a concern for systems-level effectiveness and equity. This involves the case manager in activities of resource development, service management, cost control, resource distribution, and gatekeeping, and frequently involves the use of the worker's authority.

This boundary-spanning view of social work case management practice has been illustrated in action with each program and client group presented in this book. In what follows, specific skills at each of the two levels—the client-system and service-system—are highlighted for each of the case management functions. It is important to bear in mind that this manner of presentation represents a somewhat artificial distinction and grouping. In reality, case management functions are interwoven, and the same skills may be as useful for one function as another. What is being suggested is that the case manager will call upon all of these skills in practicing case management—some infrequently, some at relatively predictable points in the case management process, and some practically all of the time.

Key Skills

Client Identification and Outreach

In this initial stage of the case management process, consultation with potential consumers provides information on potential barriers and obstacles to service utilization and access. The case manager uses engagement skills to establish helping relationships with clients, based on mutual trust, which promote client dignity and self-determination. The case manager negotiates a partnership role with family members, when appropriate.

At the service system or community level, the case manager provides input into policy and program plans, helping to define the scope and shape of services. Educating, sensitizing, and increasing the awareness of other providers, agencies, and the community at large are required. Interagency relationships are built (formally and informally) to encourage referral of clients, and ensure access to a range of services once clients are engaged.

Individual and Family Assessment and Diagnosis

The case manager uses systematic data-gathering skills to answer critical questions about needed improvements in the fit between the person and family, and the relevant environment. To accomplish this, the worker employs skills in individual and family interviewing and keen observation, as well as knowledgeable use and interpretation of standardized assessment instruments. The case manager assesses the service system resources and deficits at the same time. Conceptual ability and a systematic conceptual framework allow the case manager to organize and integrate in a meaningful way the data and information from a client's complex reality. Writing and communication skills are necessary to inform others of the substance and conclusions of the assessment process.

Planning and Resource Identification

The case manager mobilizes client problem-solving capacity to develop jointly a care plan that is workable. Negotiation—requiring contracting skills—among client, family, and other providers concerning goals and expectations may be necessary before a realistic plan can be determined. Plan and care decisions have practical and emotional implications. The case manager uses counseling skills to help the client and family explore, confront, and resolve painful dilemmas or interpersonal disagreements that impede sound decision-making.

At the service system level, the case manager searches for appropriate resources, including those that are culturally sensitive. Resource gaps are identified as well. Planning frequently involves multidisciplinary teams, or views of different providers. The case manager calls upon collaborative working skills, including his or her own professional self-assurance, to achieve a working consensus.

Linking Clients to Needed Resources

At this point, accessing, acquiring, and even creating needed resources is a central concern. In working with the client, the case manager addresses any of the client's specific concerns or perceived obstacles to using a resource. It may be necessary for the case manager to provide emotional and practical support to the client at this stage. At the same time, the case manager calls upon client competence and self-care to the extent possible, recognizing the need to handle the client's dependency on the case manager and the service system resources in a manner that facilitates growth, change, and increasing independence whenever feasible.

On the system side, resources often are individual providers or program staff who may need education or information to serve a client appropriately or at all. Case managers persuade, persist, and creatively maneuver to circumvent program and policy rigidities that erect barriers (whether of time or substance) to clients receiving needed services. When services are no longer needed, or are not useful or appropriate, the case manager handles "delinking" as well, recognizing elements of an orderly process of termination for both the client and the resource. In instances of unsatisfactory client-resource matching, the case manager must handle the resulting negative feelings of both parties, if the client is going to try again and the resource is to be available for future clients.

Service Implementation and Coordination

With some clients, the case manager must draw upon advanced clinical skills to assist the client throughout the process of using services to reach desired goals. This, it should be noted, is not the same as suggesting that the case manager should or should not provide therapy (as a planned service) to that client *in addition to* serving as case manager. This is an important, but different issue. The point here is that the case manager, *as case manager*, will need to use clinical skills in the service of implementing and coordinating an agreed-upon plan with certain clients. A client may require help with managing stress. Or a client may need an ongoing interpersonal exchange with the case manager that promotes trying new experiences, allows for failures, and reinforces success. A client may need a helping relationship that provides structure and consistency to achieve personal growth. Professional empathy skills allow the case manager to reach for feelings that lie behind negative, hostile, or apathetic behaviors that may interfere with a client's progress and alienate others.

Clients may need practical assistance from the case manager as well. Emergency transportation, assistance with making a move, coffee and danish, and a chance to get outside—these requests might be made of a case manager. This requires a flexible professional use of self that can comfortably accommodate a range of helping activities. On the other hand, the case manager develops a feel for limits, recognizing when requests and activities would be better provided by a different resource or process.

At the service level, the case manager judges the timing and pacing of services—anticipating gaps, lags, and other delivery problems in an effort to achieve some degree of coordination from a fragmented system. Pressure for policy changes may need to be brought to bear when obstacles persist. Systematic communication of needed information among providers must be ensured. This may mean arranging meetings, case conferences, regular telephone consultations, or other forms of reliable information exchange. The case manager frequently has to have emergency or backup plans and procedures in place also, in the event that crises disrupt the routine plan of care.

Monitoring Service Delivery

It is at the case level that the case manager makes sure that the system is accountable to the client, and that the client meets agreed-upon expectations. The case manager works actively to make things go as they should, and reports and intervenes when things go wrong. The case manager uses clarification and confrontation skills to ensure that problems are acknowledged and addressed, and consequences are clear. The case manager may work with clients and families to help them monitor their own services. Organization and writing skills help the case manager keep a clear case record for accountability.

When case management occurs in the context of legally or administratively mandated service delivery systems, monitoring requires the case manager to interface with courts, oversight commissions, and other administrative structures. The case manager must develop skill at reporting and presenting complex circumstances in a clear, timely, and objective manner to those with oversight responsibility. Even when legal parameters are not operative, monitoring requires that the case manager exercise well-honed professional judgment, based on an overall view of the client situation, in notifying or alerting interested (if not responsible) parties of changed circumstances, and emerging problems or needs.

Advocacy to Obtain Services

This function involves the case manager in implementing a planned strategy of power to obtain specific services or resources for a client (case advocacy) or perhaps for the total group of clients (cause advocacy). At the client level, the case manager generally (although not always, as in the case of many child protection advocacy efforts) seeks the client's agreement to act, an agreement based on a careful consideration of risks and benefits. Advocacy strategies can engender conflict and hostility, producing additional stress for a client. The case manager needs to provide emotional support and help with stress management.

The advocacy effort, whether on behalf of an individual or a whole group of clients, is directed at some component of the service system or its policymaking context. The case manager must mobilize power. This may take many forms: expert knowledge, new information, influential allies, legal mandates or precedents, use of the authority vested in the case manager through the program the case manager represents. Whatever the source of influence that is to be brought to bear, the case manager will need skill in persuasive, forceful writing and speaking to make a clear and compelling case. Confrontation skills help the case manager minimize defensiveness and hostility. Skills in negotiation and conflict management and resolution are employed, as a solution that is satisfactory and achievable is sought.

Evaluation

The involvement of the direct-practitioner case manager in evaluating the quality, appropriateness, and effectiveness of the case management services provided takes place on two levels as well. At the level of the individual client, the case manager provides through forms and record keeping the accurate and timely information about each case and the case manager's activities that is the basis of most monitoring and evaluation systems, including the practitioner's own efforts to evaluate the effectiveness of his or her practice. At the delivery system level, achieving needed program improvements or addressing critical gaps and problems in the service delivery system depends on reliable aggregate data from many cases in order to demonstrate needs and document problems.

The case manager participates in peer supervision and consultation. This provides assistance with particularly difficult or complicated client circumstances, and permits a variety of inputs in problem-solving. Effective use of a peer supervision process requires a commitment to scrutiny of one's practice and thinking by others, and openness to feedback and new perceptions and information. Peer supervision and peer review activities also require the case manager to critique and evaluate the work of colleagues, and to find constructive ways to provide honest and helpful feedback. At the system level, team care and case planning with built-in peer supervision and consultation methodology provides a structure for identifying program and system delivery problems, and for developing practice-generated ideas about solutions. Direct-practice case managers are in the best position to see the consequences of the existing program and delivery system for clients. This view carries with it a responsibility for constructive efforts to influence and change.

The "Political" Use of Self in Case Management Practice

Inherent in case management approaches to deal with diverse areas of client need is the recognition of wider system goals of increased effectiveness, efficiency, and equity, in addition to responsive provision of individual client care. Austin calls this "service management," emphasizing the resource control component of the case manager's job (Austin 1987, p. 12). Service management goals may be overt and explicit, as in the instance of a case manager functioning as part of a program with a designated budget with which to purchase needed services for clients. The case manager in this example is fiscally accountable, and the case manager's influence on the distribution of resources is directly monitored. This is a distinguishing feature of what is commonly called managed care. In other programs, the case manager's access to and use of resources is neither ensured nor monitored. However, the case manager necessarily retains the potential to affect delivery systems and to alter the distribution of resources for better or for worse.

Austin (1987) has suggested that although many social workers have not yet become comfortable in the service management aspect of the case manager role, the prevailing trend is toward more managed care. She suggests that this will mean that social workers will have more authority to purchase and terminate services, thereby directly and overtly controlling access to and utilization of services.

Whether service management goals are explicit or implicit, the case manager is a representative of a service system and the services it does and does not deliver, as well as a provider of individualized client care. The case management approach *assumes* that the client needs assistance above and beyond what an individual case manager, no matter how versatile or clinically skilled, can or will offer. The client expects the case manager to be more than a responsive *individual*. The case manager is the client's link to the delivery system as well. Therefore, the case manager is not in a position to concentrate solely on each individual client's coping, adjustment, and social functioning. The mechanisms and resources of service delivery, and the outcomes achieved or not achieved through involvement with the delivery system, must be of concern.

This requires a model of professionalism that includes a "political" self. In its widest meaning, a political professional self is tuned in to and allocates energy for intervention in the broader service delivery system of which one is a part. Without this component of professional identity— valued and consciously owned—the requisite skills and activities to carry out the case manager's boundary-spanning functions will be only partially mastered.

White and Goldis (Chapter 12 in this book) describe this commitment to a political professional self when they write of their case management program, "There is the expectation that staff at all levels will not accept the status quo if changes need to be initiated internally or within the external delivery system, and that constructive problem-solving efforts are the responsibility of everyone." Embedded in the case management process and its functions are opportunities for constructive delivery system problem-solving at each step of the way.

Just the same, case managers will sometimes work in imperfect and less than adequate systems. Ideally, case management involves working to meet client needs within the context of a comprehensive continuum of services. Then, in theory, case management's goals of ensuring appropriate care (not too little or too much), equitable resource allocation (something for all who have need), and coordinated care (working together and not at cross-purposes) are reasonable and achievable. Case management has become popular precisely because society recognizes that fragmentation, lack of coordination, and profit-driven rather than need-based decision-making are often characteristics of service delivery. However, case management (and case managers) cannot, in and of itself, fill in gaps and meet needs when the services and resources simply and fundamentally are not out there. That remains a political agenda for all Americans.

References

Austin, D.D. 1987. "Case Management: Reinventing Social Work?" Paper presented at the National Association of Social Workers Annual Meeting of the Profession, September 9, New Orleans.

———. 1988. "Case Management: Myths and Realities." Paper presented at the National Association of Social Workers Annual Meeting of the Profession, November 11, Philadelphia.

Austin, C.D., J. Low, E.A. Roberts, and K. O'Connor. 1985. *Case Management: A Critical Review*. Seattle: Pacific Northwest Long Term Care Geontology Center, University of Washington.

Bronfenbrenner, U. 1979. *The Ecology of Human Development*. Cambridge, MA: Harvard University Press.

Hearn, G. 1974. "General Systems Theory and Social Work." Pp. 364–66 in *Social Work Treatment*, F. Turner, editor. New York: Free Press.

Johnson, P. and A. Rubin. 1983. "Case Management in Mental Health: A Social Work Domain?" *Social Work* 28:49–55.

Moore, S. 1990. "A Social Work Practice Model of Case Management: The Case Management Grid." *Social Work* 35:444–48.

O'Connor, G. 1988. "Case Management: System and Practice." *Social Casework* 69:97–106.

Seabury, B.A. 1982. "Boundary Work: The Case Manager's Role." Paper presented at the National Association of Social Workers Clinical Conference, November 20, Washington, D.C.

Biographical Sketches of the Contributors

John R. Belcher, Ph.D., is assistant professor, School of Social Work, University of Maryland at Baltimore, Baltimore, MD.

Katherine W. Brubeck, MSW, is a clinical social worker with the Family Advocacy Section at Walter Reed Army Medical Center, Washington, D.C.

James P. Clark, MSW, LSW, is consultant for social work services, Iowa Department of Education, Des Moines, IA.

I. Lorraine Davis, MSSW, is a child advocate in McFarland, Wisconsin.

Robert H. Gemmill, DSW, Lieutenant Colonel, United States Army, Medical Service Corps, is the assistant chief, social work service, and director of education and research and regional social work consultant at Walter Reed Army Medical Center in Washington, D.C.

Lynn Goldis, MSW, LCSW, is assistant director, private program development, Huntington Memorial Hospital Senior Care Network, Pasadena, CA.

Roberta R. Greene is Associate Dean, University of Georgia School of Social Work. She is the author of *Social Work with the Aged and Their Families* (Aldine de Gruyter, 1986), and co-author with Paul H. Ephross, *Human Behavior Theory and Social Work Practice* (Aldine de Gruyter, 1991). Dr. Greene has also authored numerous journal articles dealing with the application of conceptual frameworks to social work practice.

Isadora Hare, ACSW, LCSW, is staff to the National Association of Social Workers Commission on Education, Silver Spring, MD.

Rebecca L. Hegar, DSW, is assistant professor at the School of Social Work, University of Maryland at Baltimore, Baltimore, MD.

Barbara Kane, ACSW, LCSW, is co-director of Aging Network Service, Inc., a national counseling and care management firm Bethesda, MD.

Kenneth Kaplan, MSW, LCSW, is supervisor of adult services, Anne Arundel County Department of Social Services, Glen Burnie, MD.

Marcy Kaplan, LCSW is project manager of the Los Angeles Pediatric Aids Network, Los Angeles, CA.

David L. Kennedy, MSW, Lieutenant Commander, United States Navy, is head of the social work department at the National Naval Medical Center, Bethesda, MA and is the specialty advisor for social work to the Navy Surgeon General.

James Larison, MSW, ACSW, Colonel, United States Air Force, Biomedical Science Corps, is the program manager for the Air Force's programs dealing with child and spousal abuse and handicapped children.

Grace Lebow, ACSW, LCSW, is co-director of Aging Network Service, Inc., a national counseling and care management firm, Bethesda, MD.

Naomi Miller, ACSW is president of Mental Health Resources, Ltd., a firm providing EAP services and consultation to management, Rockville, MD.

Willard W. Mollerstrom, MSW, MPH, Ph.D., Major, United States Air Force, Biomedical Science Corps, is director of research and deputy program manager for the Air Force Family Advocacy Program, Office of the Air Force Surgeon General.

Betsy S. Vourlekis, is assistant professor in the department of social work, University of Maryland, Baltimore County. She joined the faculty there in 1988 after serving for three years as the staff director to the National Association of Social Workers' Health and Mental Health Commission. Her current research focuses on quality assurance of psychosocial care in health and mental health settings. A graduate of Columbia University School of Social Work, she has extensive practice experience with the seriously mentally ill.

Monika White, Ph.D., MSW, is associate director, Huntington Memorial Hospital Senior Care Network, Pasadena, CA and adjunct professor of gerontology, University of Southern California, Andrus Gerontology Center Leonard Davis School, Los Angeles, CA.

Index

AAMD (*See* American Association on Mental Deficiency)
ACMS (*See* Automated case management system)
Acquired immunodeficiency syndrome (AIDS), 4–5, 29 (*See also* Children with HIV/AIDS)
Activities of daily living functioning, 43
Adaptive behavior assessment, 64–66
Adult Foster Care Program, 92–94
Adult protective services (APS)
  and Adult Foster Care Program, 92–94
  case examples of
    under emergency, 94–96
    from nonemergency, to emergency, 99–103
    for self-sufficiency, 96–99
  case manager in, 89
  linking client with needed services, 91–92, 103–104
  Maryland law on, 89–90
  mission of, 90
  strategies for successful, 103–104
Advocacy, 149 (*See also* Military family advocacy programs)
Aging Network Services (ANS)
  assessment function in, 37–39
  assessment process in
    client assessment and diagnosis, 44–48
    family assessment and diagnosis, 41–44
    linking client with needed services, 39–41
    situation assessment, 48–49

AIDS (*See* Acquired immunodeficiency syndrome)
Air Force family advocacy program, 154–155
American Association on Mental Deficiency (AAMD), 64–66
Annie E. Casey Foundation, 140
ANS (*See* Aging Network Services)
APS (*See* Adult protective services)
Army family advocacy program, 155
ASI (*See* Assessing successful interactions)
Assessing successful interactions (ASI), 69–70
Assessment (*See also* Client; Evaluation of services; Family)
  adaptive behavior, 64–66
  problem-solving, 69–70
  social history, 61–64
  social skills, 66–67
Automated case management system (ACMS), 78–79

Background information, 42–43

Care planning
  and case management quality assurance, 171
  and case manager's skills, 184
  for children with HIV/AIDS
    child involvement in, 83–85
    community organization involvement in, 85–86
    focus of, 79–83
    sibling involvement in, 85
  team, 177–178
Case assignment, 175–176

DATE DUE

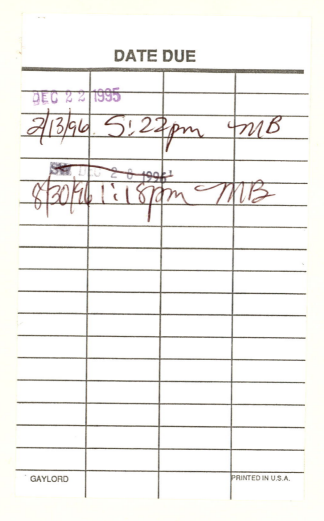

GAYLORD   PRINTED IN U.S.A.